THE TOP 10 MARRIAGE ESSENTIALS

PAUL R. SHAFFER

authorHOUSE®

AuthorHouse™ LLC
1663 Liberty Drive
Bloomington, IN 47403
www.authorhouse.com
Phone: 1-800-839-8640

Published by AuthorHouse 01/06/2014

ISBN: 978-1-4918-3636-1 (sc)
ISBN: 978-1-4918-3634-7 (hc)
ISBN: 978-1-4918-3635-4 (e)

Library of Congress Control Number: 2013921160

Contents

Acknowledgements

Much of the content in this book originated from the couples that I have worked with over the past twenty-some years. Relationships are their own particular universe and I've spent a good deal of my life exploring them, discovering the truths that different parts of that universe have in common. So, it only makes sense that, for those just entering this universe, or those who have been in it for a while but may have lost their way, I be able to share some of the more important principles that make this particular universe function. My thanks to those couples, and fellow professionals, who helped refine my knowledge and understanding of what the essentials are for making a marriage work.

Foreword

When I attend social gatherings and people discover what I do for a living (relationship counseling), they will typically do one of two things: immediately try to find someone else to talk to for fear of being analyzed, or start with the questions. Not questions about me, personally, but questions either looking for free advice or questions such as, "So what's the most common problems couples have?" - which translates into the solution-focused question of, "What do you think it *really* takes to make a relationship work?" This presents a dilemma for me because I hate answers that over-simplify. Easy answers often ignore the depth and complexity that some questions deserve. And relationships are, if anything, complex.

Over the span of time that I'd done couples' work, there were frequently recurring problems that I would see in regards to the basic knowledge, attitudes and expectations that predictably handicapped the relationship from moving forward. While I'd written two books on couples' conflict resolution, I needed something that more broadly addressed the foundational aspects, the essentials, than what I already had available - which is what prompted me to write this book. So, now, for those who ask me, "What do you think it really takes to make a relationship work?", I can simply say, "You know, that's a great question. And I really took some time coming up with an answer for you. Check out my book." ☺

❖   ❖   ❖

As with a relationship, what you get out of a book often depends on the attitude with which you approach it. As with every new couple I see, my initial concern is with *rigidity* and *ego*.

One of the initial hurdles in doing couple's work is that you really can't start doing the in-depth work until everyone has adopted the same language or strategies. You can't jump into resolving conflict until you know the couple has the basic tools with which to go there. If you just waded right in, everything would quickly fall apart because there was no new way to approach the problem. Granted, part of the counselor's role is to lead the way, modeling for the couple how to walk through differences, but, if the couple relied solely on the counselor to do all the work for them, they would become dependent on the counselor to solve their problems – which isn't the goal of couple's counseling.

The couple has to be willing to let go of some of their beliefs about what their relationship is and isn't. Typically, they've formed a diagnosis of their partner already based on how their particular expectations for the relationship have or have not been met. But who's to say that their expectations are realistic, or that their conclusions concerning their partners are formed with a correct interpretation of the evidence?

Say I have a rock collection. In this collection are some very valuable rocks. I know which ones are of greatest value because I'm a rock expert and these are *my* rocks. So now I pull in someone off the street and say, "Hey, take a look at this collection. Pick out the rocks that you think are the most valuable." Now, the likelihood is that this person has, at different points in his life, encountered rocks. He may have had a rock collection of his own and become very familiar with the rocks in his particular collection. He may have even been taught some basic geological information when he was in school. But the odds are that the stones he's going to pick out are not the most valuable ones because he's not an expert. He knows what looks pretty to him, or what he's most familiar with, and that's about it.

When it comes to doing couple's work, the most difficult type of client to work with is the one who thinks he's a relationship expert. He already knows everything you could possibly tell him. He's invulnerable because he's put himself above criticism. And it's typically this same rigidity of "knowing" that is part of what's killing the marriage relationship. He's the kid with the rock collection who insists that he knows as much about those rocks as the rock expert because, by God, he's seen rocks too!

Many times clients have assumed that the issues of the relationship are about their partners' character or personality (things that are unlikely to change), when, in fact, it's actually an issue of lacking the right information, or possessing better skills - both of which are things that can still be learned no matter what the age.

The clients that benefit the most from counseling are the ones that approach it with humility. Going into it they've accepted the fact that they don't have all the answers, and that that's okay. Because they are receptive to help, they get helped.

There are two ways of approaching a book like this: defensive and closed, or humble and open. You have to be willing to question your own conclusions and pre-conceived ideas of what makes a good relationship. You have to be looking for how this information applies to *you*, and where you need to grow.

It's recognizing that, though both you and your partner are in a relationship together, and you may have had prior relationships, *neither* of you is an expert. Ideally, you're both open to learning new things together, or having old knowledge re-affirmed.

❖   ❖   ❖

Regarding attitude, there is another question I'm often asked that I want to briefly address here at the start that, on the surface, sounds like it would be better reserved for a different book.

"What justifies getting a divorce?"

The reason I bring this up here is because it has to do with how people approach *commitment* in a relationship, especially a marriage; the nails that hold the ship together.

It's very common to meet couples who have been married for years and continue to stubbornly hang on to unhappiness. When you ask them, "Why are you still in this thing?" the answer often given is, "I made a commitment – for better, for worse." So, obviously, they're upholding their commitment for worse.

What I am criticizing is the notion that the marriage commitment is just about being committed to *stay*. The couple thinks they're upholding the marriage commitment, but they're not. The actual commitment is supposed to be that you will continue to *love* each other – which is about how you *act*, not solely how you feel. Seldom in those marriages do you find the individuals continuing to be *loving*.

So, the question that needs to be asked, whether it's in regards to divorce or just during difficult times, is, "What is my commitment to continue to show love to this person?" To remain and just co-exist is not really a relationship at all, and it isn't honoring the foundational covenant of the marriage.

This is part of where a healthy definition of love applies. **If the marriage is based on a true commitment to be loving, it means that the couple continues to act in loving ways towards each other, *even when they're not feeling the love*.** It is a dedicated, conscious *action*, not a feeling. By continuing to *act* in a loving fashion, we promote better odds for a loving response and it keeps the door open to continue to *experience* loving feelings. I'm not suggesting that there is no accountability for wrongs, but the focus of the couple remains on who they themselves need to be to make the relationship work, upholding their commitment in the process.

Two side-notes.

In referring to personal pronouns in my books on conflict resolution I used "he" and "his" rather than "he/she" and "his/her". In this book, for sake of balance, I'm choosing to use "she" and "her". So, don't take it personal.

Also, for what it's worth, the specific examples of couples I use in this book aren't any one actual, living breathing couple but a conglomeration of any number of couples I saw with those particular issues. So, if you're a former client, and it sounds like you, it wasn't you. It was any number of people like you.

Chapter 1
Flexible Roles & Realistic Expectations

One of the most common problems encountered by couples during the first year of marriage is adjusting their *expectations* of marriage to fit the *reality* of what it actually means to be married.

This isn't just a problem for the first year together. Couples who've been married twenty or thirty years can often be gravely unhappy with each other because the expectations have never been met, or never adjusted to meet the need. The initial question in such cases is, "How realistic are those expectations?"

When I refer to expectations I'm referring to the "shoulds" ("This is the way it's *supposed* to be.") that we enter a relationship with. There are role expectations around lifestyle, such as the traditional, "The man's the breadwinner and the woman manages the home." And there are role expectations around chores, such as, "The man takes care of the cars, and the woman cooks the meals." There are communication expectations, financial expectations, parenting expectations, and intimacy expectations.

Most people's expectations started back in the dating days with the expectations they had about how a man is supposed to treat a woman, and vice versa. If those expectations had been met, or sufficiently adjusted, and the couple has moved on to marriage, the next hurdle is how those expectations change once the marriage has begun.

A man may have been aggressive during the dating stage, but now his continuing to "take charge" is labeled as dominating, when it wasn't before. A woman may have waited on the man to initiate things when they dated, but now the man is upset because she's continuing to not initiate now that they're married.

For a marriage to work in the long run, the couple needs to have compatible, realistic expectations of the relationship, and the roles need to be flexible enough that they can change as the needs shift over time.

This can be a little confusing during the transition into marriage because we may *think* we're both on the same page, but, when it comes to the day-to-day reality of living together, we find out just how accurate, or inaccurate, our expectations were.

❖　　❖　　❖

One typical unhealthy expectation that is often brought into a marriage is that "We each should already know how to be married". Both partners may already have some overly concrete visions of how it's all supposed to work.

While it's certainly good and even necessary to have *some* idea of how a marriage works, the more rigid and inflexible those ideas are, the less room the relationship is going to have to work with.

If you've never been married before, then *neither* of you is going to be experienced at it. And while you don't *need* to have a lot of experience, you *do* need to be honest with each other that you're both in the same boat – learning how to best meet each other's needs.

Don't get me wrong. There are some expectations that should not be compromised. Infidelity isn't something you just work around. Physical or emotional abuse isn't something you just need to learn to accept. What I'm referring to are the expectations of the *roles* of a relationship that either allow for the positive growth of a relationship uniquely tailored to that particular couple, or negatively choke the life out of freedom and choice.

Often, I will see young couples who have been living by the model of their parents' marriages, rigidly attempting to adhere to roles that may not even have worked for the previous generation. As we talk about how their relationship is unique to them - that what they choose to create with it is only restricted to the limits of their own creativity - suddenly the mental lights go on and you start to see their world expanding. Suddenly, choice and freedom have been introduced into something that had been anything but! They're being given permission to be themselves (within reason) rather than to robotically re-create someone else's vision for their relationship.

The Family Mirror

Bob and Angela were a young couple in their early thirties. They'd been married for about three or four years and had no kids. Surprising to both of them, things were actually getting to the point where conflict stopped just short of becoming physical.

In session, Bob was a quiet guy who talked in a very focused way. He would get upset at times but he'd contain it well. He wouldn't call Angela names or throw judgments. He'd painstakingly try to explain himself but you could tell he was, at times, gritting his teeth.

Angela had no intention of containing her anger at Bob. She had no difficulty throwing judgments at him. She'd question his manhood and dismiss his attempts to try to understand her.

"Bob's just not the guy I thought he'd be," Angela would say, as Bob would sit there with his head down, taking the verbal punches. "When we met we were head over heels about each other. He went out of his way to see me and spend time with me, but now he's tired all the time and he never wants to go out. All there is for me at home is work to do. I need to get out more."

Bob steps in while Angela's catching her breath. "She's right, I am tired. But it's because I'm working a different job now, and it's exhausting me. We're also financially tight right now so we don't have a lot of extra money to do things like go out on dates. My home's my home. I should be able to relax there. Besides, when she goes off on me with her temper, she's the last person I want to do something with."

"If you did more of the housework I wouldn't be such a bitch," Angela jumps in quickly.

"I DO do housework," Bob's quick to reply. "I just don't get credit for what I do, because it's not up to your expectations."

Not to be bested, Angela laughs sarcastically, "Well, forgive me for having standards."

Bob and Angela have what I would call a "passionate relationship". What brought them together was their passion, and what was pushing them apart was the flip side of the same thing. The difficulty with passionate people is they often lack emotional discipline. While they get swept away by the depth of their romantic passion, there are just as few controls for their passionate hostility. Now, Bob had learned how to manage his temper to some degree in the presence of others, but that control didn't last as long in the comfort of his own home where he was just as good at mud-slinging as Angela.

Interestingly, their current behavior was unique to this particular relationship. Neither had a history of volatile behavior in previous romantic relationships, which was part of why they had no idea how to handle it - it was a new experience for both.

Angela's expectations of marriage didn't include a tired husband, financial limitations, and different standards of cleanliness. Bob's expectations didn't include a wife that expected him to clean more than his typical routine, that talked to him with such cruelty, and that wouldn't let him relax in his own home. Since neither side respected each other's "rules of conduct", their own rules were eventually abandoned.

This common decline in behavior over time often has to do with failing boundaries (which we'll get into in Chapter 4). Because we've become distracted from the relationship, or the relationship has become overly familiar or routine, we allow unhealthy patterns to slip into it that weren't there at the beginning. We gravitate back to what's most natural, sometimes what we grew up with, when we're no longer paying attention to the relationship, even if what's most natural is very uncomfortable for us.

When it comes to role expectations, the behavior in the relationship is not always a gradual decline. If the expectations are rigid from the start, and not compatible with the partner, negativity can be present from the beginning.

Bob & Angela's discussion of family history was very informative. I asked Angela to start by describing her mother and father.

"My mother was a doormat. She was very tolerant of my father's work schedule and just suffered in silence, raising me and my brothers and sisters. I knew she wasn't happy but she'd hardly ever show it. My sisters and I, when we became teenagers, would tell her she should get a divorce because my father was so insensitive to her. To him it was all about what he wanted and everyone else was supposed to jump. Nothing was ever good enough for him."

She rattled this off pretty quickly, and almost matter-of-factly. I'd expected a little more emotion from her since she was so emotional about everything else.

"So you don't feel like you're anything like your mother?" I asked.

Angela looked offended. "Not at all. I'm not a doormat."

"What's interesting to me," I put in, "is that how you've described your father is actually how Bob has described you. He feels that nothing is ever good enough for you; that when you get home he's supposed to jump when you say jump. Do you see the similarity?"

Angela was surprised at this. She took a moment to respond. "I guess I didn't think of that before. I don't see myself as being like my father, but I guess I can see how, on the surface of things, we appear similar."

Angela, so overly focused on not wanting to be like her mother, had, instead, become like her father in many ways – even though she didn't much like him. Very unintentional, very unconscious, but, nonetheless, quite evident.

Since people tend to operate in extremes, because the extremes are always the easiest to see, it's not uncommon that people either adopt qualities or rituals similar to those of their parents, or consciously work at being the opposite of them if their experience growing up was a negative one. Because it is an extreme, these styles are often without balance.

Over and over you will see families where one parent grew up in an overly strict home and now, in reaction to that rigid upbringing, the parent has become overly permissive with her own kids. Yet, such a style typically results in kids that feel entitled and show little respect to the parent who lets them do whatever they want.

Even the negative models we grow up with aren't *completely* negative. Angela's father was a very hard worker. Yes, he was lacking the skill of knowing how to be intimate with his own family, but he never physically abused them, never cheated on his wife throughout the marriage, never abused substances. I'm not saying that he was a model husband or somebody worth emulating, but we form these unbalanced pictures early on and carry the same perceptual standard into our marriages.

If we're looking for a partner that's nothing like our negative parent we may end up choosing partners that are in the other extreme, meaning that they're also devoid of that negative parent's unrecognized *positive* qualities. For instance, a person who had an overly-disciplined parent keeps choosing undisciplined partners and struggling with the resulting emotional chaos that that typically brings.

We may be so sensitized to a particular negative quality that our parent possessed that when we see the slightest reflection of it in our spouse we over-react or over-judge them for it.

In our own marriages, it's easy to over-focus on the negatives in our partners to the degree that we can't see any positive anymore. And what positive there is, we come to dismiss as insignificant compared to the negative. **The problem with this is that if we stop seeing the positive in our partner, then, in addition to having lost perspective, we've also lost the ability to positively motivate change. I can't positively motivate my partner to change if all I verbally recognize is what I see wrong.**

So, what about Bob?

Bob takes a little longer to put his thoughts together. "My mother was over-controlling. Personally, I think she was always afraid of us not being able to make it financially. I think her need to control everything was because she lived in fear of just how little really was in her control.

"My father struggled at his job and there were a lot of hard times. He was blue collar and he worked hard, but he never really got to a place where things were easy. I respected my father. He always tried to be there for me, even though he would be working two jobs sometimes. He didn't really yell at my mom when she'd get upset. He just kind of took it because I think he felt like she was partly right - that he should be more successful."

It was interesting that Bob, even though he described his mother negatively ("over-controlling"), rationalized her behavior to the degree that it became "normalized". He did the same thing with his father. Angela's description of her parents had been very black and white – right and wrong. (Mom was bad because she was a doormat. Dad was bad because he was a workaholic.) This was very informative of how each of them saw the world differently. Angela's view of things was very judgmental; things were good or bad, with no middle. Bob's view saw the negatives but attempted to understand them, going beyond the overly simplistic labels. Yet, Bob's more mature view wasn't helping him in terms of the rigidity of the marriage's role expectations.

In regards to the family patterns, Bob now had an over-controlling wife of his own. And Angela was deathly afraid that Bob's parent's relationship was going to become theirs, if it hadn't already.

❖   ❖   ❖

Sometimes the person that we marry becomes someone else after marriage partly due *to* the marriage. Angela wasn't "over-controlling" from day one. It took more than a year for that to develop in their relationship. So, was that the role Angela took for herself, or was it the role Bob moved her into? Or, was that just who Angela was all along and being in-love just masked it for a while?

Let's "normalize" Angela's experience for a moment. If we're having financial difficulties, it is natural to be fearful, to feel insecure. Insecurity is about feeling like we're not in control of something that we very much want to have control over – such as our future. So, one of the problems wasn't that Angela had no reason to be fearful, but rather how Angela was choosing to handle her fear. And, part of the problem was that Angela wasn't really viewing her reaction as a choice.

In reacting, we have given up our ability to choose. We're no longer thinking about options of any sort; options for what our partner might have meant other than how we took it, or options for how we can respond other than to just react. We are going solely by instinct – which is to fight or seek flight. But part of moving past reacting is understanding that it actually leads us *further away* from resolution, not closer to it, and, in the process, we are also giving up the only control we really have – control over ourselves. (We'll get into this further in Chapter 6 on validation.)

The problems of this relationship were not as simple as that it was just about Angela's insecurity. Neither of them knew how to resolve conflict well – neither had had good models of this while growing up. The model their parents set for them was that one person in the relationship dominated, and the other was supposed to just take it. But continuing to re-create those roles in their present marriage was not working for them at all – Angela was attempting to dominate, and Bob was refusing to be a doormat. Even though they didn't see that lifestyle (dominant/submissive) as working for their own parents, they were still instinctively buying into that lifestyle in their own lives.

Bob would say that he wasn't "buying into" it, because he wasn't trying to dominate Angela and neither was he being overly submissive. But by not being more balanced in helping Angela with the household work, Bob was putting Angela in a position where she needed to be more aggressive with him. The further difficulty was that Angela was confusing accountability with domination when trying to get his help.

Some might say that Bob was attempting to dominate Angela as well, but that's not really accurate. Angela was trying to control Bob's choices – making him work when he wanted to play. Bob wasn't trying to control Angela. While he wasn't crazy about her overdoing it with the chores, he was willing to let her continue to do housework if she chose. His struggle was with not being willing to be dominated - a refusal to submit.

It *was* a control struggle. The opposite ends of a control struggle are over-control and under-control. Angela was over-controlling, and Bob was under-controlling. She was taking on too much, and Bob wasn't taking on enough.

So how does a situation like this, where the expectations on both sides are not being met, get better? **The first step is always ownership of the problem**. Angela and Bob needed to own that neither of them was filling their roles in a way that was functional for the relationship. They needed to acknowledge that the models set for them by their own families weren't effective in their own marriage. *They needed to re-start with a better template of what actually worked for them, supporting each other's legitimate needs, and re-exploring better ways of meeting those needs.*

Prescribing a Crisis

I wish that more people had a mid-life crisis much earlier in their lives, and were willing to stay in crisis longer than they often do.

(Perhaps I should insert here that I'm *not* a sadist.)

The term "mid-life crisis" is often applied only to men. "Menopause" is reserved for women, but we tend to view menopause as more of a biological/chemical change. Both can be emotional crises that occur revolving around the acceptance, and inevitability, of aging. Usually, neither of these is seen in a positive light – typically because they both involve a good deal of discomfort.

I remember going to a neurologist at one point who had a very distinctive way of looking at physical pain. He was insistent that any physical pain that I experienced I should consider as something abnormal – which seemed odd to me since I *always* had some degree of aches and pains. I didn't like the idea of feeling like something abnormal was going on with me just because I had some minor degree of discomfort. Also, coming from a mental health perspective, my view of pain was very different.

To me, as a counselor, **pain is useful. It's a guide to a problem**. If I'm hurting, typically, there's a reason for it. If I were hurting and there was *no* reason for it, then I'd have a right to worry. I can choose to ignore pain, but at the risk of something significant going untreated, and, therefore, getting worse.

Emotional pain can be a direct route to accessing someone's heart. When it comes to emotional wounds, which I'll talk about more later, the best time to help heal that wound is when we're in the middle of our suffering. It is then when the emotional walls are the thinnest and we, sometimes, are the most vulnerable. Yet, because we are just as uncomfortable with the pain of others, the opportunity to support or explore it is readily allowed to pass.

Pain can be a great motivator. If I can't stand how I've let my body go, the intensity of that emotional pain can move me to actually do something about it – go to the gym or start going for walks.

When couples first come for counseling, they are often in crisis. They are looking for relief. Yet I have to tell them up front I don't want them to feel too much relief just because they're getting help. *Their discomfort is what will help continue to motivate them to do the work of getting better.* If they feel too good too quickly they will typically drop out of counseling prematurely because "We're doing well again" – which also means they will most likely start to take things for granted again and stop doing the work.

Our focus naturally tends to gravitate to what's next on the "to-do" list. If we've "fixed" the marriage, our attention is naturally going to want to move on.

It's also an illusion that people are doing better just because they're not having as much conflict. Often what's happened is that they've stepped away from the issues and are experiencing relief, but the issues may have not really been resolved; they're just not being focused on. For the couple to have a true sense of progress, they need to experience competence at working *through* issues, not go back to avoiding them.

We have to be willing to hang on to some degree of discomfort about our relationships if we're to keep them healthy. I don't mean so uncomfortable that you're not able to enjoy each other and what you have together, just not so comfortable that the relationship is no longer a conscious priority.

❖   ❖   ❖

A mid-life crisis is supposedly when a man hits the mid-way point of his life and is looking at the remainder of his years. I think that many view it as a panic period where a man goes into denial that he's getting older and desperately tries to recapture his youth. While I agree that that can be part of it, I think there's a more significant piece to it as well.

Many of us live "borrowed" lives. When I was a teen, the plan was that I was supposed to go into business with my father when I got older, ultimately taking over his CPA practice when he was ready to retire. That was my father's dream. When I started to gravitate to psychology during my high school years I knew he was concerned because he didn't see this field as being lucrative or secure, and I'm sure there was a more personal disappointment for him as well – giving up the idea of a father passing on his trade to his son. But, from the start, this career, for me, was all about using some of the time in my own life to make a difference in other people's lives. It provided the degree of variety, challenge and people-contact that fit my personality. It was *my* dream.

We all need to have some orientation to life, some sense of the way things work. If you arrive late for a meeting, the first thing most people want to do is catch up on what they missed. They want to get "the scoop" on what's happening so they can fit into what's already started. For every one of us, life has been going on before we got here. And most of our childhood is about trying to get the scoop on what our role is supposed to be and how we fit in. But, in order to do that, we have to give credibility to what everyone else's opinion is as to what we should be doing and how we fit.

If this weren't the case, if we didn't try to fit in or adapt to that structure, this would be a chaotic world with everyone doing her own thing regardless of rules or consequences. So there is a meaning, a purpose, to learning that pre-existing structure in order for society to continue. But, for many people, that's as far as they take it. They learn the rules and they fit in, but they never mature past that point – until, hopefully, a mid-life crisis comes along.

For many, an emotional crisis is simply reaching a point where things aren't working and we can no longer deny, repress, ignore, or run away from it. We are being forced to deal with something that we'd prefer not to. At the same time, **most relationship crises are necessary.** If I'm in a horrible marriage, I *need* a crisis to help move it to a place of change, where it's either going to get better because we're willing to do whatever it takes to make it happen, or where we finally own that it needs to end because it's not working and it's going to continue to not work.

I am often amazed at the tolerance people have to remain in miserable situations, actively avoiding calling it for what it is when, if they just owned that things had gotten so bad, things could actually have a chance to move forward rather than stay stuck. There's a natural fear people have that if they say it's gotten that bad then they are forcing an end to the relationship, instead of seeing it as an opportunity to end only what was not working for the relationship. The crazy part is that, by *avoiding* the pain of confrontation, they are *prolonging* the pain of remaining in an unhealthy situation.

A person in mid-life crisis is often someone who has lived a borrowed life that has finally gotten to the point where she recognizes that it's really not working for her – it was someone else's dream, or it was hers for a while, but now she's outgrown it. Often, it's a person who, for the first time, is really struggling with meaning and significance because the reality of mortality has hit her in a very conscious way.

Every one of us, at some point in life, needs to go through the painful process of questioning what we believe about life, including the roles that we automatically assume, both in our individual existence and in our relationships. If it's going to be a life that we can buy into, then it needs to be something that retains and enhances our identity, not something that suppresses it. While compromise and sacrifice are part of any relationship, the balance we are trying to achieve is one where both the individual *and* the couple thrives.

Roles versus Type

One of the questions couples often ask themselves is, "How much do I have a right to ask my partner to change? At what point is what I'm asking too much?"

Because the core of a relationship is about acceptance (balanced with accountability), to over-focus on changing our partner gives off the message that they have to be somebody different in order to be accepted by us. In other words, who they are isn't enough.

Part of thinking this through involves separating whether what we're asking for is a change of *core personality* versus changing a *relationship role*.

There is the **type** of person that we are, left to ourselves - when we don't have to answer to anybody, or any role to play. That may be very different from the **role** that we assume in the relationship. Some roles may very much fit our personality, and some may not.

Ideally, there isn't too much room between who we are and the role that we take on as partner, or we may, over time, come to feel like we're losing ourselves to the relationship or resent the amount of sacrifice that we're making to fit the role that we feel is expected of us.

You can be a very different person at the office than you are outside of work. You've taken on a particular role in your workplace in order to succeed or be accepted by those you work with. That doesn't mean that that person is truly who you are, though it may have some reflections of your particular type.

Similarly, we often take on particular roles in our relationships in order to show love or be loved, or to just get along. We take on chores and a degree of discipline when living with someone that we might not normally apply if it was just us living by ourselves. That doesn't mean that we're living a lie or being deceitful with our partner, it's just that we're responsibly trying to accommodate the needs of the relationship by taking on an accommodating relationship role.

Often when we are approached by our partners about change, we tend to take it as a personal criticism, or rejection, because we automatically interpret it as them asking us to be different than who we are, rather than understanding that the criticism, more often than not, is a request to change how we've been filling the *role* of partner. A role adjustment doesn't have to be personal, simply an acknowledgement that how we've been going about things isn't working for "us". Change is still do-able.

Granted, there *are* times when our partners may approach us about change and inappropriately or incorrectly direct their criticisms at our character, rather than how we've taken on the partner role – which is why it's important for people to understand the distinction. If we can't accept our partner's personality or character, then we're not going to be able to have a relationship with them - that's who they are, and we're asking them to be somebody else.

Needs and Preferences

A lot of exploring expectations has to do with looking at the value that you attach to each. Those values typically have to do with whether or not the expectation is connected to a need or a preference.

Preferences are things we typically can live with or without. Some of us have particular preferences about how our food is cooked. However, if our food is not cooked exactly the way we like it, it shouldn't lead to a melt-down. If someone consistently gets upset about preferences, we often label her as being "high maintenance", because, to her, *everything* is a big issue.

Needs are the things we really can't go without for very long or we start to feel emotionally starved. **We all have the same core emotional needs: security, significance, and fun. Core needs are *always* legitimate. The problems arise in how we go about trying to get those core needs met**.

I feel *secure* when I know I can *trust* my partner financially, physically and emotionally. I feel secure when I feel like I have an equal voice in the relationship; that I have some *control* over where things are headed.

If I know my partner *values* my opinion and praises my efforts in the relationship, I feel *significant* - that what I'm doing counts to her. If the words my partner uses with me are consistently *respectful*, I also feel significant, because I feel she sees me as somebody worthy of her respect.

On a larger scale, *both* significance and security have to do with a sense of meaning and purpose in life. If our lives are adrift and we really don't have anything we're steering towards, something that connects us to the world around us, something beyond ourselves, we will often experience a certain sense of futility or anxiety. Why am I here? What am I doing with my life? What's the point? Couples that have a sense of mutual purpose and direction typically feel both more secure and significant.

If I continue to structure my life to allow for *fun*, then I am typically staying in touch with my freedom to choose, rather than getting bogged down in responsibility and obligation – things that typically fall under the label of "work" and "have to's". While security and significance are vital, if I ignore taking any time to enjoy the ride along the way, my quality of life will suffer.

Ultimately, the most healthy state you're trying to achieve with everything this book will discuss is *balance*. **The problems are always in the extremes**. Work needs to be balanced with play. Self balanced with other.

❖   ❖   ❖

Couples will often confuse their needs with their preferences. When it comes to chore expectations, this can often be the case.

Back to Bob and Angela. I asked them about the break-downs they had in relation to the chores.

Bob starts. "When the weekend comes, Angela's got a list of things she wants to get done. And she doesn't want to let up until it's all finished. We've been working all week and I want to take some time to relax and enjoy the free time. The projects that she's got on there sometimes would take up the whole weekend and then it's back to work on Monday and I didn't feel like there was any break."

I address a possible contradiction. "Does your need for fun complicate the financial situation?"

Bob shakes his head. "No, I don't have to go out to relax. I can stay around home, and if I do go out, I'm not doing things that cost much."

So I ask Angela, "If you're wanting to get out more, why isn't that an opportunity for you - the weekend?"

Angela nods, "I know, I know. But the problem is that so much has been left undone during the week that I can't just walk away from it. I

feel guilty for having let it go that long." She looks to Bob. "Bob doesn't want to touch anything that resembles work at home. We both hold down jobs. We both are hard working at them. But the stuff around the house has to get done sometime. Basically, what Bob's telling me with his attitude around the house is that he doesn't care about making my life any easier."

I step in. "So you feel that when Bob doesn't embrace the housework like you do that he's essentially saying you're not important to him."

Angela nods. "Yes, exactly."

Bob is shaking his head. "But that's not it at all. All I'm saying is *the housework* isn't as important to me as taking some time to enjoy our life together. It doesn't have anything to do with how important Angela is to me."

Notice the odd twist to this. Based on what they said earlier, when it's during the week, Bob wants to stay in and Angela wants to get out. When the weekend comes around, Angela's work-focused and Bob's willing to go out. They each keep taking opposite roles that are too extreme to allow for balance. And Angela's definitely sabotaging her own happiness by not allowing herself time to play even when it's available.

So, who's right in this situation?

Often, stalemates occur in these situations because they're *both* right.

Angela's right in that the things around the house need to get done. Bob's right in that they also need to be taking time to have fun. *The problem is that they have yet to find an adequate way to balance the situation.* By Angela pushing her agenda, she invalidates Bob. By Bob pushing his agenda, he invalidates Angela. But both have valid points, which is why it isn't a simple issue. It's not a simple matter of, "He's wrong and she's right, or vice versa."

So, is the housework a need for Angela or a preference?

For Angela, the housework represents *both* security and significance. It's about security because it gives her some sense of control over the condition of their home. And it's about significance, because she measures it in terms of how much Bob values what's important to her. So the housework *is* need-related.

But the housework is *also* about preferences when it comes to *when* and *how* Bob attempts to help her get it done. Angela's being overly rigid if she expects Bob to jump when she says "jump". And she's being unrealistic if she expects him to do things that will consistently meet all of her expectations. Bob needs to attempt a consistent effort at helping out around the house, but he's never going to be an Angela clone because it wouldn't be healthy for the relationship.

An interesting side-note to this is how Angela interprets Bob's behavior. Part of what Angela needs to understand to help balance her conclusions of Bob is that *housework represents a very different thing to her than it does to him*. By Bob putting a priority on the play over the work, especially the work Angela has expectations around, Bob ends up *unintentionally* saying to her that she's not important to him. But the only thing she should accurately conclude is that *housework* isn't as important to Bob as it is to her. Her inaccurate conclusions automatically make it personal for her. (Notice I didn't say that housework isn't important to Bob at all – that would be an exaggeration – it's just that play is *more* important.)

If housework meant the same to Bob as it did to Angela, and he *still* refused to help her, *then* she would have good reason to draw the conclusions that she did.

At the same time, while Angela *does* need to be more careful about how she interprets Bob's behavior, knowing the significance that Angela places on the housework *should* move Bob to alter a little how he himself values it, especially when he understands this is one way she looks for him to show to her that she's loved.

So the solution for Angela's issue is that: 1) Bob needs to be more attentive to the fact that this is a *need* for Angela, and 2) Angela needs to be more flexible with her *preferences* of how Bob goes about meeting that need (the "when" and "how").

So is play a need for Bob or a preference?

Obviously, play is connected to the need for fun. But, in this case, it's also about security. Bob needs to feel that he has some control over what happens in the relationship and, at this point, he's feeling like Angela's trying to take all of his control away. Angela shouldn't attempt to invalidate Bob's need for fun, since 1) it's legitimate, and 2) she needs to have fun too, even if she can't see it yet.

So the solution for Bob's issue is that: 1) Angela needs to be more respectful of Bob's need for fun, and 2) Bob needs to be more balanced in making sure his play doesn't consistently override getting the housework done.

Notice that, for each issue, there were *two* solutions: Bob's part and Angela's part. Since this particular situation involved issues for each, it required a 2-part solution for each issue. We'll get into this later, but it's important to recognize that, **in a relationship, there are usually two sides to any one problem and two parts to each solution**. If the problems are continually viewed as being a *shared* responsibility, something that *each* contributes to, it reduces the "blame factor" and positively underlines the fact that "we're a team". A shared solution for a shared problem.

❖   ❖   ❖

Sometimes it is possible to relieve a surface need by satisfying the core need in a different way. A **surface need** is how we go about satisfying the **core need**.

Let me break it down like this. Angela's *core* need is both security and significance, so it is doubly powerful. Her *surface* need is "getting the chores done". The **preference** is the "when" and "how" those chores get done.

Preference
∧
Surface Need
∧
Core Need

If Bob was really good at satisfying Angela's need for security and significance through other means (praise, intimacy, random acts of kindness, etc.) she may find that the housework was not as big a deal for

18

her. *The value she placed on getting the housework done would be lessened because the core need was still being satisfied.*

The same can be said for preferences. If Bob was able, doing it his way, to still consistently get the housework done, meeting the surface need, Angela might not remain as rigid with her preferences (the "when" and "how").

❖   ❖   ❖

Romantic relationships go through transitions - casual dating becomes exclusive dating, exclusive dating leads to an engagement, being engaged to married. Past the marital line, other transitions occur when jobs change, children are born, moves occur. Even if none of these outside circumstances occur once married, time alone forces transitions as we age and mature.

For each of these transitions, the surface needs and preferences change for the relationship. If the relationship isn't flexible enough to keep up with these shifts, it starts to break down in different ways because it is trying to meet current needs in outdated ways. For those with rigid role expectations, such shifts are resisted and refused because it doesn't compute for them with the way they think things are "supposed" to be.

Many times couples coming for counseling are continuing to try to put energy into meeting needs for each other, only to feel like it isn't making a difference. Usually this is because they are attempting to try to satisfy each other in areas that are no longer as significant; or they're trying to do it their way, versus the way the partner would desire it to be done. So the effort goes unrecognized or without impact.

For many, just to start getting recognition for what they *are* doing, even though it's no longer effective, is a good start. They had stopped feeling motivated to try because what they had been trying wasn't being given any credit or strokes.

To up-date this information (what the couple needs from each other in the present), and re-focus the energy, can often have a major impact for the relationship.

Balanced qualities

Many people looking at Angela and Bob would think, "It sounds like they're too different. It's not going to work." But that's not necessarily so. The reason I said that it wouldn't be healthy for the relationship for Bob to be like Angela comes back to balanced qualities in a relationship.

We typically find ourselves attracted to people that have *complementary* qualities to our own. The introvert likes how her extroverted partner helps bring her out of her shell. The disciplined individual enjoys how his passionate partner helps him be in the moment and not have to always structure things. There is a part this plays early on that really does bring out the best in each other.

For each of these positive qualities, though, there is often a negative flip-side that is more extreme depending on how unbalanced the positive quality is. If the extroverted partner cannot stand sitting at home and has to be out and about all the time, at some point, the introvert will likely become exhausted and start to feel pressured to keep up. Or the extroverted partner may feel like the introvert is becoming a "stick in the mud" because she has to put up with his natural resistance to participating in her constant adventures.

The disciplined partner may come to resent his passionate partner when he comes to see that her passion goes both ways – she's passionate when she's happy and passionate when she's upset. She shows little control, or even desire to control herself, when she gets angry and says the most hurtful things. At the same time, she comes to see his discipline as being impassionate and cold because he doesn't participate in her flare-ups but, instead, controls his reaction by withdrawing or attempts to control her reactivity.

So, **while it's those positive opposite qualities that draw the couple together, it's also, predictably, the *same* qualities that will later force the couple apart**. This doesn't mean that they're doomed from the beginning, especially if they know what to do about it, but it's a good reason why they need to take time during dating to examine *both* sides of the qualities they admire in their potential partner.

For those couples that are already married and have already discovered the flip-sides to what attracted them, they need to be careful not to "throw the baby out with the bathwater". It's too easy to forget that there typically remains a positive side to the quality we are currently having a problem with in our partner.

Bob *needed* Angela to help balance him in order to keep him from going too overboard with play. Angela *needed* Bob to help balance her in order to make sure she didn't turn home into being all about the work. *Their problem was not that they were incompatible, but that they had stopped allowing each other to balance the relationship in necessary ways.*

❖   ❖   ❖

Couples whose marriages have seriously deteriorated no longer make the effort to balance. Things quickly escalate because *both* sides are actively aggressing or withdrawing.

With Bob and Angela, they had become "polarized". They were taking opposite positions, but *in reaction* to their partner's position. By taking up rigid residence in opposite camps, the differences between them became all the more exaggerated. Their focus was on personal rejection, rather than the unbalanced roles.

If we can begin to see that the roles we have assumed are not roles we are bound to, that there is freedom in most relationships to move beyond what we've automatically taken on, then we start to reconnect with our choices and possibilities. We regain a degree of flexibility and a sense of freedom that we might otherwise have assumed was impossible. And a lot of that has to do with 1) identifying any existing overly rigid role expectations, 2) dropping the unhealthy templates we were brought up with, 3) not letting our partner's choices determine our own actions, and 4) finding positive ways to support and inspire necessary change of the relationship roles, accepting that change is part of a relationship's positive growth.

Discussion Questions:

1. **How did your parents relate to each other (both your and your partner's) - can you see any similarities between your parent's**

relationship and yours? Do you have any role expectations for the relationship that don't work for either of you? Have you adjusted roles over the years, or rigidly tried to keep everything the same? Do you feel like the roles, as they are, move your relationship forward, hold it back, or just keep things afloat?

2. **Do you feel like the two of you can negotiate both the good and the bad?** Does the relationship work because you avoid issues, rather than resolve them? On an individual level, how do you handle emotional pain – work through it, avoid it, ignore it?

3. **Do you know the difference between a need and a preference?** Do you feel like some preferences are given too much of a priority in your relationship? Do you feel like the needs are being adequately met? Do the two of you touch base from time to time to explore whether or not the surface needs have changed?

4. **What were the positive qualities in each of you that drew you and your partner together?** Was it a situation of like personalities, or opposites attract? Are the dilemmas you encounter in the marriage an issue of like styles of interacting, or distinctly different? How do the two of you attempt to balance each other with those styles? What do each of you need from the other in order to be able to accept your partner's efforts to balance your own perspective?

Chapter 2
True Intimacy

For some married couples, after the "honeymoon period" fades, there is a re-grouping time that attempts to answer the question "So, what now?" Since we already have some role expectations, most people just move into "role-playing mode". We're supposed to make a living, have kids, get a house, and grow old together. And that's what most people get busy doing – going through the routines that make all of that happen.

Yet, for many, there is a degree of disillusionment that goes along with all of that. They're bringing in the money. They're raising the kids. They have that initial security of a place to live and a committed relationship. But there's also a question that starts to make itself more visible as time goes by. It can be asked in different forms but ultimately what it comes down to is, "Is this it?" Because, for some reason, they feel like "this", the married life, was supposed to be something more.

They can go down the checklist of what they're supposed to be doing, and the majority of things may even be checked off, yet it still feels like something's lacking – like things are falling short. They just don't feel as content or happy as they thought they were supposed to be.

Often, in such situations, *the problem is that at least one person in the relationship has mistaken filling the roles of the relationship as **being** the relationship,* when in reality it's just *part* of a relationship.

No one's cheating. No one's abusing. No one's refusing to work. They may not even be neglecting being present at home, helping with the kids, or helping with the chores. But, despite doing all that's "expected" of them, they are still lacking the one thing that they signed up for in the first place - a truly intimate adult relationship.

Tom and Hannah were in their early 40's. They had the "picture-perfect" marriage – two kids, two great jobs, a beautiful home by the lake. They were both physically fit, balanced the chores at home, and shared the parenting. Yet Hannah was seriously considering divorce.

"My friends think I'm crazy," said Hannah, in session. "They look at my life and say they're envious of what I've got. Tom's a good looking man who obviously cares about me and the kids, yet I've never felt so alone. It all feels somewhat empty to me."

Tom's less distressed-looking than Hannah. He's appearing tolerant and sympathetic. "And I can see that in her," he acknowledges. "But I'm at a loss as to what to do about it. She doesn't need for anything financially. I help out when she asks for it. It just never seems to be enough."

Hannah's shaking her head. "I appreciate all that you do for me. That's not the problem. The problem is that I feel like we live together but we're not a couple."

Tom sits back. "Of course we're a couple; we're married. We do everything that married people do. But I think this thing goes deeper for you. I think you're depressed and we need to talk about the possibility of medication to help get you out of this."

Hannah looks to me. "And that's where this goes. I'm the problem. I'm depressed. I just need medication to get me straight. Does it sound to you like I need meds?"

And the majority of men out there reading this nod and say, "Yes, it certainly does."

In these kinds of situations there *is* always the possibility that part of the problem is that one partner is experiencing depression, and that depression is clouding how they view the relationship. Also, if someone has serious self-esteem issues, then there is the tendency to constantly be looking for signs of rejection, or ways she's not important, and finding them even when they're not there.

But a good diagnosis is not made with a minimum of information. Before it's safe to conclude what Hannah's problem is, the relationship needs to be further explored.

I ignore Hannah's question and ask one of my own. "What makes the relationship feel like the two of you are just roommates?"

Hannah takes a moment to organize her thoughts. "Well, we each have our jobs. We check in with each other at the end of the day. We take care of the chores that need doing. We're polite. But there's no passion. I want to feel excited about doing all this together, but it's all just so much routine."

Tom shrugs. "Marriage is about routine. If we didn't take care of the routines then we'd be in the poorhouse. Besides, we do do things together."

"The majority of the things we do together either involve the kids or other family. We hardly ever do things just the two of us."

Tom responds with, "Well, the kids are still too young to be left completely on their own. We bike together, run together."

Tom is making good points, and Hannah's starting to look more unreasonable. But we're still only scratching the surface.

"So how's the sex life?" I ask.

There's a noticeable pause before either responds, which is what you'd expect when things shift to something so personal.

"Our sex life is fine," says Tom.

Hannah nods without saying anything.

"Has that become routine as well?" I persist.

Tom looks at Hannah. "Well, I think we'd both *like* it to be a little more routine than it is."

"Meaning?"

"We're both so busy with everything that it's become relatively infrequent," admits Tom.

"So how infrequent are we talking?" I ask.

"About once a month or so. Maybe once every other month."

My eyebrows go up.

"Has there been some kind of change in the routine lately? A change in the time demands of the jobs or something that's pushed your physical relationship onto the backburner?" Both of their children were no longer infants, so I knew they couldn't be the reason.

"No," said Tom. "We're both so active that we're often too tired at the end of the day. So it just doesn't happen."

"So, when it does happen," I ask, "is it meaningful for the two of you?"

"I think we both know how to satisfy each other," says Tom. "I don't have any complaints."

I look to Hannah. "So what's your perspective on this, Hannah?"

Hannah looks uncomfortable, but she answers. "Tom's right. It doesn't happen that often and we are very busy. When it does happen, it's good. Tom takes time for me, he's not rushing through it."

"So you'd like to see it happen more often?"

"Of course," she says.

"And, you, Tom?" I ask.

"Sure. I'm certainly not trying to avoid it."

"Hannah," I ask. "When you talk about feeling like roommates, how much does the lack of physical relationship play a part?"

"Well, it certainly plays a part, but I think a physical relationship is just one part of feeling connected. I don't want to oversimplify this and say if we just had sex more often we'd be fine."

And I want to be careful that I don't give that impression either. Sex is just one part of being intimate, but it's a helpful gauge of the presence or absence of passion.

What made the absence so surprising for this couple was that they were both healthy and physically active. Usually that degree of activity, especially if a couple is engaged in it together, creates *more* energy for sexual activity, not less.

You automatically start wondering then if they were getting those intimacy needs met somewhere else.

I was really having to work at bringing the details out in order to get a better picture of what was going on with this couple. It was easy to guess that that was how the problems had continued for as long as they had - they avoided getting into the issues. And, when they did, Hannah's issues had been dismissed as depression so often that she had stopped "complaining". Still, they were trying to get help now, and, like it or not, it was time to really take a look at what was going on.

The Relationship is not just the Work

"So, Tom, what's your ideal of marriage? What does an intimate relationship look like?" I asked.

Tom frowned with concentration. "Well, obviously, more sex than we're having."

"Okay," I said. "And what else?"

"Well, time for each other."

"Okay. And what does time for each other look like?"

"Maybe going out more? Like dates. It's been a while since we saw a movie together, or had dinner out."

"Okay. Any other activities besides movies and dinner?"

"Well, we already exercise together, so I think that pretty much rounds it out."

"Anything the two of you used to do when you were dating that you don't do anymore?"

"We would travel more, weekend trips. We haven't done that in a while."

"And if we did," put in Hannah, "it usually involved our families or the kids."

"Yeah," conceded Tom. "That's pretty true."

"So, Tom, in your mind," I asked, "how should Hannah know that you love her?"

Tom paused. "Well, just the fact that I'm here in counseling should be one way. The fact that I've responsibly handled my job – we're financially secure. I help out at home. I try to do the things she asks of me."

"So, basically, because you've handled your role responsibly?"

"Yes, I guess so."

"Hannah," I asked, "do you agree that Tom has been relatively consistent with those things?"

"Yes," she replied, easily enough. "I think he's been a good provider and tries to do what I ask."

"So what things do you ask of Hannah, Tom?"

Tom thought a moment. "Well, Hannah's usually the one with the lists. I don't think I ask Hannah to do much, but I think that's also because she's already doing it."

"So tell me a little more about the things that Hannah asks you to do."

"The typical things," replies Tom. "Help with the dishes, folding clothes, taking the kids off her hands."

"And, Hannah, you're saying he does a good job with being responsive to your requests?" I ask.

Hannah nods. "I find it frustrating sometimes that I have to ask, but, yes, he's usually pretty respectful of my needs."

"Why do you find it frustrating that you have to ask?" I persist.

"Well, because I don't like to have to be the one to point out those things. I wish he could just see them on his own."

"Things improved, though, when she realized that I'm not a mind-reader," puts in Tom. "When she realized I pay attention to different things than she does, she got it that I wasn't intentionally trying to disregard helping her."

This is a good point to make. Often, couples will bicker over what is important to them when the partner doesn't attach the same value. She can't stand it when he lets his clothes drop on the floor, seemingly leaving it to her to pick them up. He doesn't know why she can't check the oil in the car herself. While some of this *can* be disregard for the partner's time and energy, it can often also be about getting lost in focusing only on what is important to us - the blind spots we have to the things we don't value.

If the spouse understands that the partner really doesn't even see what needs picked up as they go through the house, because they're attending to a totally different spectrum, it's not as hurtful as making the assumption that they *do* see and they're *intentionally* choosing not to pick things up, knowing how it bothers the spouse. The first scenario is about raising *awareness*, while the second is about intentional *neglect* – two very different things.

It *was* important that Hannah made the leap to bring things to Tom's attention. By Tom being able to follow through with her requests, he was able to give her visible evidence that he *did* care about her concerns - once she raised them to his awareness.

Now does that mean that Tom was supposed to jump every time Hannah said jump? Not at all. In the same way that Tom showed respect for Hannah by respecting her requests, Hannah would need to be realistic and respectful that "now" wouldn't necessarily be a good time for Tom, but that she could trust he would get it done if he committed to do it. While that is often an opportunity for the partner to abuse ("I'll get around to it when I get around to it," and getting around to it never happens), it doesn't change the fact that we aren't each other's property to order around, and respect should always be at the center of adult communication.

❖   ❖   ❖

Tom *had* been doing a good job of filling the roles of both husband and father. Many women would be very grateful to have a husband like him. It *is* important that Hannah, in exploring ways to improve their relationship, takes the time to recognize and support the things that Tom has already been doing well; otherwise, she gives the message that nothing he does is good enough for her because she's not recognizing the efforts he's already making.

Remember, the best motivator in a relationship is recognizing the positives in your partner, even the small successes.

Tom brought the fact that he's been a consistent provider in as evidence of his love for Hannah. Thankfully, that wasn't all that he included, but I need to underline his comment.

Even in this day and age there are still many people who use their job as evidence of their love in a marriage – but that's all that they've got to show. They feel that, as long as they're providing for their family, nothing more should be expected of them. They come home and collapse on the couch, and they won't lift a hand to help around the home.

Sometimes, such couples can last a lifetime in relative peace if both are accepting of those roles. There *are* some needs that are being met, to a degree, in this arrangement.

In terms of *security*, financial security is being satisfied for both the breadwinner and the house-parent by the breadwinner holding down a job. However, security is also about feeling that you have some control over your life, and the house-parent may feel that the breadwinner has all the control.

In terms of *significance*, the breadwinner may feel valued because the job is his contribution to the family. The house-parent may feel significant through her role as parent to the children, and/or taking care of the breadwinner.

In terms of *fun*, the breadwinner is getting to relax at the end of the day. For him, there is a clear distinction between work and home. The house-parent has no such clear distinction between the two. Her work *is* her home and so her job has no end *unless she's willing to place limits on how much work she does.* If the breadwinner's not respectful of those limits, then he's essentially trying to force the houseparent to work overtime. Since he's already identified there's no overtime for him when he gets home, it's automatically raising a double standard. This potential imbalance is usually where the point of resentment first starts to take root, especially if the breadwinner's openly placing a higher value on his job rather than on the house-parent's.

What typically plays a big part in this resentment is the extreme transition between the expectations created during the dating experience versus the reality of the marriage experience. Most dating relationships didn't start and thrive through routinely hanging out at home, going through a mundane ritual of eating dinner and watching TV together night after night. Dating relationships usually involve a noticeable degree of activity – whether it's going out together, doing things as a couple with other friends and couples, the intensity of the physical relationship, etc. One thing is for sure, what brings couples together usually isn't their desire to work together, but how they played together; or a common vision or purpose *beyond* the work. So, if such a relationship becomes all about the work, is it any wonder a couple starts to feel that something's missing?

◆ ◆ ◆

It's interesting to me that, when I have couples do a needs list, it's not uncommon for at least one of them to view it as another chores list. "Oh, great, even more things for me to have to do to make her happy."

When couples get to this point it's often clear that the priorities have shifted in a negative direction. Either there has been too much emphasis on getting the chores done as a decider of whether or not someone's happy, or making a partner happy has now become a chore. Either way, it's a problem.

You shouldn't *ever* base your happiness in a relationship *solely* on how many chores your partner has completed, how quickly they were completed, or whether or not they were completed to the standards that you expected. This reeks of a parent-child relationship being forced onto an adult-adult relationship. Whoever is playing the parent is never satisfied because they are trying to force their standards on someone who is never going to be them. And whoever is in the child role will never feel significant because whatever they do for the partner will never be felt to be enough. The underlying message is, "I will only show love to you so long as you do exactly what I want you to do."

Yes, we all play a part in getting the chores done, but even the chores can be given too great an importance in a relationship. This is sometimes about over-generalization, where we will over-focus on one area of the relationship that is not working the way we want it to, and allow that to color how we see everything else about the relationship. Our partners may actually be making great efforts to meet our needs in other areas, but we will allow this one aspect to become the central focus for our unhappiness.

Remember my example from last chapter about how we can mistakenly get confused between what we truly need versus what are simple preferences?

The spouse who sees meeting the partner's needs as a chore has forgotten all about *choice*. You are not trying to make each other happy because you have to. You're trying to do it because *you care*.

If you start putting the focus on the freedom you have to please your partner – the when, the where, and the how – you are moving away from seeing the needs as just one other "to do" list. Hopefully, your partner's happiness is a greater priority than anything that you would attach to just a mundane chore.

The concern becomes that things have shifted too much from how they started. What was once about the joy of surprising each other in thoughtful ways has now become about, "What have you done for me lately?" Our requests have become demands. Our kindnesses have become expectations to the degree that they have lost any lasting impact towards feeling loved.

I don't know if you can see it yet, but a picture is starting to form of why Hannah's feeling emotionally starved, and it *doesn't* have to do with Hannah's being clinically depressed.

The Relationship is not just the Kids

"So, tell me, what happened when kids came into the picture?" I ask. "How did the relationship shift?"

"We'd talked about the 'evils' of daycare," said Hannah. "But, financially, it seemed like the only way to do this was for me to work part-time while the kids did a partial day in daycare."

"So what impact did this have on the marriage?"

"I think it was fine, for the most part. We had the routines down. I'd pick up the kids at the end of my work-day. We'd be at home and ready for Tom when he got home."

"Okay," I said. "So the relationship's rituals were successfully adjusted. But what impact did these new rituals have on the relationship itself?"

"I think I know what you're asking," said Tom, stepping in. "When kids came into the picture, Hannah's attention shifted to them. I understood that this was to be expected, so I was okay with it, for the most part."

"Did you start to feel left out?"

"Not so long as I was willing to feel connected by doing things with her and the kids. But, in terms of just her and me, it was sort of understood that we had kids now and they were supposed to be the focus."

"And has that shifted back since the kids have gotten older?" I asked.

"Well, they're still young," said Hannah. "I don't imagine this will change too much until they're in their teens."

I find this dilemma to be somewhat predictable in the current American culture. The generation of the early 1900's was quite reversed. *The children revolved around the parents. The parents didn't revolve around the kids.* When my father was a child in the 1930's (along with his 12 sibs), another child was regarded as another hand to work on the farm. Children were helpers for the parents – they *contributed* to the family. It wasn't all about what the family could do for them.

I said before how the tendency for people in attempting change is to go from one extreme to the other, because the extremes are the easiest to see. So I'm not suggesting that either "extreme" is desirable, but, rather, a balance between the two. **Children *do* need to be nurtured and focused on, but not to the degree that the marriage relationship becomes neglected, and not to the degree that the child's contribution to the family goes unaddressed.**

We tend to focus our attention on whatever the most *noticeable* demands are, so there's a natural tendency for our lives to become solely structured by our jobs and our children. But part of this comes back to how we measure priorities.

We tend to think of priorities in terms of a 2-dimensional list:

- Family
- Job
- Self
- Social
- Health
- Hobbies
- Spiritual/purpose

Each person's list is going to be ordered differently based on the priority they attach to each of the "categories", but the idea is that, for many, there is always something that is supposed to come first, then second, then third, etc.

I didn't separate "family" from "spouse", "children" and "relatives" in order to make the point that often these are all lumped in together - which is part of the problem. We need to be attaching a separate priority to our partners – separate from the priority we attach to our children and relatives.

But the actual act of maintaining balance with priorities is how good we are at shifting our attention between each of them – *not* always putting one first. In other words, sometimes job comes before family, social comes before health, but hopefully never to the degree that those others are actually neglected.

For some people, because they have difficulty with multi-tasking, balance becomes very difficult to maintain – which is part of why we have a partner who is supposed to be there to help keep us balanced.

One of the purposes of a conscious relationship is to be approaching life making choices as to how we invest our time and energy - and not allowing life to make those choices for us. If, as a couple, we are able to have input on a regular basis as to how things are in or out of balance, and developing strategies to adjust the use of our time in order to be more effective, we are taking a very proactive step in order to keep this from getting out of hand.

There seem to be many couples who, when a baby is born, the mother becomes overly absorbed with the child, and the father retreats into his work. While part of this is due to the natural bonding that takes place between mother and child, hopefully there is also time invested to help the father remain involved with the family experience. For many, the problem is that the father automatically steps out of the dynamic, maybe even thinking he's doing the right thing by sacrificing time with his family, or that it's the wife's role to raise the children, but he ends up creating his own experience of being left out.

While this will be an adjustment period for the relationship, what you would hope to see over time is that attention will shift back to the marriage after the new roles of mother and father are adequately adjusted. Otherwise, typically, the husband will start to build resentment because his role has become reduced to that of making a paycheck, or the wife may resent the husband's lack of involvement at home – both sides failing to see how they each shaped it into that situation.

It is very common in today's culture to see parents running themselves ragged, driving their kids back and forth between school clubs and activities, at the cost of themselves having a personal life. They look at this in terms of the sacrifice that goes along with being a parent, but, quite often, what they are promoting in their children is a sense of **entitlement** – that the child is *more* important than the parent, and that the child getting her way is something that is *owed* to the child.

Ideally, what we are trying to model for our kids is that they *are* important, but not more important than everyone else. Also, we are trying to keep it clear that there remains a distinction between the rights of the child and the rights of the parents. The child doesn't have the right to make the rules – that is the parent's authority. Kids who are consistently put first (at the cost of the parent) often come to feel that they have equal rights to those of an adult, and sometimes even see themselves as being *above* authority.

The balance I'm promoting is that we attach a priority to *both* our children and our marriage. We're modeling for them a balanced sense of their worth as well as the worth of others. There will be times when their needs come first, but there should also be times when the needs of the couple come first.

The Relationship is not just the Things

"So, what are the goals of the relationship then?" I asked.

There was an exchanged look of confusion between Tom and Hannah.

"Well, are you referring to our financial goals?" asked Tom. "I pretty much handle the finances. I've invested wisely and I think we'll be able to enjoy our retirement. We've got enough in the meantime to enjoy our lives. I've got no complaints."

"In a couple years we're considering getting a larger home to accommodate the kids getting older and needing more space," Hannah puts in. "Right now they have to share a bedroom. I'd also like to live closer to my family at some point. Right now we have to travel too much to visit everyone."

"I'd like to get a bigger boat and have a better spot on the lake," adds Tom, with a smile. "Maybe get that car I always wanted."

It's interesting that when you ask a couple what their goals are, they typically think in terms of financial or material accomplishments. But when I ask about the goals, I'm asking about the *personal* goals that have nothing to do with wealth. And, of course, the reason why most people don't think in those terms is that most people don't have personal goals, let alone goals for the relationship.

I'm not trying to structure a relationship to the degree that it's like a business, but one of the reasons couples experience a sense of emptiness is that *they have no direction*. They are taking care of the responsibilities, handling life's demands as they occur, but it's more of a survival mode than intentionally heading somewhere.

I'll get into this a little more later on, but **a relationship is a progression**. There needs to be a sense of *growth*. Often, you'll hear people talk about having "outgrown" their partner over the years – and, while this can be an excuse, it can also be a reality. If we don't appreciate the concept of maturing and continuing to self-educate, then it's easy to take a somewhat stagnant position on life where the concept of progression is limited to the accumulation of "stuff".

For many couples who feel like there's nothing to talk about anymore, it's typically because life has become so routine that the only thing left is to re-hash overly familiar territory. If they were continuing to explore new territory (share new ideas, new activities, new interests), continuing to work on themselves and the relationship, then conversation wouldn't be an issue because there would be a wealth of new experiences to discuss.

And I'm not saying that all of those new ideas and activities need to be engaged in together. Either partner could be engaged in them and be bringing back what they've learned or experienced to the relationship.

I've worked with some couples where part of the problem was that they were doing *too* much together and so, because all of the experiences were shared, they were once again running into the problem of finding new things to discuss (a problem common with couples who both work and live together).

I believe there is a very good reason why people can become so diverted by the accumulation of "things". We all need to feel like we are moving forward in life. Whether we realize it or not, we are often looking for ways to improve. Whether it's new ways to up-scale our home, or just upgrading our technological toys, these are often the most visible ways to see improvement. While there is a sense of satisfaction that comes with this, I think it's also potentially misleading because it can become a diversion from improving our lives in more meaningful ways.

We *feel* like we're moving forward in life by using the visible evidence of our material success as the gauge of our personal success. But you can have everything the physical world can provide yet still be completely lacking any emotional or spiritual maturity - any true personal depth.

The Relationship is not a Competition

"How do the two of you decide who's right and who's wrong?" I ask.

Tom smiles. "Well, I could say the politically correct thing, that Hannah's always right, but I think that's an area where we've done some learning over the years.

"When we started to think in terms of different perspectives, and trying to understand each other better rather than just judging the surface things, we started to realize that it's not about right and wrong, that there are several different ways to get things done – it's more about what we're going to settle on as the solution we can both support."

"That's right," adds Hannah. "I know Tom's got a good perspective on things, but I've got things to contribute as well. So we stopped doing the 'blame game' a few years back and it's worked much better since then."

Which is what hopefully happens when a relationship starts to focus more on strategies and solutions, rather than re-hashing the problems over and over again. It was good to see that this was one area that didn't need fixing.

It's a common occurrence when I work with athletic couples, or couples in competitive businesses, or even couples where at least one partner has low self-esteem, that there is a competitive aspect that carries over into the marriage relationship. For some couples you see it in their having to have the last word. For others, it's the constant struggle to win an argument - who's right and who's wrong. Winning over losing, better than/less than.

This isn't even necessarily on a conscious, intentional level; it's just an undertone that happens when attempting to resolve issues. Competition is good at advertising strengths, but it doesn't promote exposing our own weakness. **If we can't afford to be vulnerable with our partner, then we can't truly experience intimacy.**

The nature of intimacy, and the grace that goes with it, is being able to acknowledge our fears, our hopes, and our dreams without the risk of being judged or taken advantage of. For the competitive couple, attempts at intimacy, other than physical, are often sabotaged because there is a constant aspect of judgment that exists in such relationships. Even in the physical relationship, performance can be overly scrutinized with cruel results.

Ultimately, the healthiest place to be is where we come to terms with both our strengths *and* weaknesses. We are trying to create a safe place for our partner where they don't feel that they have to constantly prove themselves in order to keep our love and respect; where an admission of fault or ownership is welcomed rather than mis-treated.

What Intimacy Is

"So, Hannah" I said. "**Tell me about how you define intimacy in a relationship.**"

"**Well,**" she replied. "**I guess I struggle with that. For me, it's about how I feel, which makes it hard to define. But the best way I can describe it is a sense of connectedness.**

"**I know that Tom's a great guy. I see all the positives that he has. I know he wants me to be satisfied. I know he feels that he loves me. But I just don't feel like we're connected. I feel like we're best friends. I feel like we're really good roommates. But I want more and the messages I'm getting from Tom are that this is as good as it gets.**"

1) Intimacy involves *focused* interaction.

Let me fill you in on the details I uncovered over the following weeks of working with Tom and Hannah.

Part of the problem with Tom and Hannah was that, while they were actually doing things together, they were, more often than not, choosing activities that required little to no interaction. And even the activities that *did* offer opportunity for interaction weren't being taken advantage of when they occurred.

The two would go to the movies and watch the actors interact. They would eat out together, and interact with their food. They would go shopping together and interact with the merchandise. At home, they would interact with their kids. On trips, they would interact with their families.

Part of the problem was with boundaries. Tom and Hannah, with time and familiarity, had developed some serious blind spots for each other. They were so close that they had fallen under each other's "radar". *For Tom, this "closeness" fit his expectations of a relationship, which was more about filling the roles of the relationship - so he was satisfied.* For Hannah, it felt like she had become invisible.

Part of the problem for Hannah was that she was so close to the situation she couldn't see what needed to change; she just knew that something was missing. Because she couldn't put her finger on it in specific terms, and tell Tom specifically what she needed from him, for Tom it seemed an illusory concept that was more about her being depressed.

❖ ❖ ❖

Focused interaction requires *focused listening*. It means taking the time to truly hear each other out, giving room to speak and respond. It does not have a rushed agenda, nor is it trying to force things to a quick conclusion.

It's not talking over each other, or impatiently waiting for your partner to stop speaking because you already know what you want to say.

For many, it's thinking about what the conversations were like back when you dated. Hopefully, each was given the floor to speak and be heard, and a healthy interest in each other's words existed.

Each person is conveying, through respectful communication, that they truly want to explore and better understand each other's worlds.

2)   Intimacy involves *depth* of interaction.

When Tom and Hannah *did* interact, it would often be to discuss the business of the day, the kids' day, what would they like for dinner, what was on TV, etc. While this was communication, it was relatively superficial.

Hannah's mapping out for Tom what she needed for him to do around the house was still superficial communication – mostly preferences. It was satisfying a need for her, but not the need for connectedness. All of their discussions could have been mirrored by the conversations roommates would have.

❖   ❖   ❖

I was working with a couple who had been married for 25 years, yet were considering divorce. They were still passionate after all that time, but now their passions were evidenced through the intensity of their *negative* reactions to each other. For a few months we'd been trying to get the husband to grasp his wife's meaning about wanting greater intimacy, but he kept making it all about his performance around the home.

One weekend, the wife initiated a conversation regarding the husband's prior relationships, wanting to know how they differed from the marriage. Reluctantly, the husband began to talk about them, fearing this would add new fuel to be used against him.

The husband had never gone into any detail about his past prior to this - in part, because he'd been somewhat embarrassed about some of his choices, but also because his focus was usually on what was in front of him and where he was headed with his career. It was unexplored territory and provided a wealth of new information for the wife that helped her better understand what was happening with them in the present. She didn't react negatively to it, much to the husband's surprise, but, actually, she felt closer to him than she had in years.

Again, part of this has to do with boundaries. By her husband talking about life before, she was able to see him for a while as more than just the man in front of her that she'd lived with for the past 25 years. She saw him as somebody separate from her, a person who was more than the assumptions and judgments she'd formed of him. For that moment, she wasn't taking him for granted – he'd stepped out of her blind spot.

For many, intimacy is difficult to duplicate because it's never really been experienced before. Once you've actually experienced it, you have a much better idea of how to re-create it. For this particular couple, now that they had a clear avenue identified for drawing closer, they could walk it more frequently.

It's important to note that part of what made this a success was that the information gained from the husband wasn't used against him. **Many times a spouse desires her partner to share on a personal level, but she ends up *reacting* to what is said rather than respecting it. She essentially teaches her partner *not* to share things with her, because she can't handle it respectfully when he does.**

❖　❖　❖

When we're able to talk to our partners about more than just the events of the day, when we're able to go deeper and continue to touch on each other's uniqueness, it accomplishes three things.

1)　We continue to see each other as unique and separate.

2)　It keeps us connected on a deeper level.

3)　It re-affirms our own identity.

Talking on a deeper level doesn't mean we have to keep finding new ways to re-hash the past, but it does mean spending time exploring *who we were, who we are, and who we want to be.* It means feeling safe enough to talk about our hopes, fears, opinions, and dreams. It means a willingness to be vulnerable and not have to maintain this surface shell of "I'm managing. Everything's fine."

Of course, not everyone is naturally able to do this. Sometimes we need a guide. Typically, there is at least one person in a relationship who is able to self-analyze and go beneath the surface, or express herself on an emotional level. To play the part of guide, she has to be careful not to make this a painful or negative experience for the partner by over-analyzing the information that comes out of it or judging it. She needs to be as much a listener as a prompter.

The concept is similar to that of support groups. When one person is able to step forward and be vulnerable, it paves the way for others to do the same.

If you ask somebody to talk about her past or her feelings, unless she's experienced at doing this, at first it's difficult to just make that mental shift. However, if we start talking about our own past, or move through our own feelings, it's more likely to prompt memories or responses in our partner and a conversation takes shape. Too often, we'll make demands of our partner ("Tell me something I don't know about you."), but forget to set the stage. Then we'll get upset that they struggle with going there, forgetting that it may be something much more natural for us than for them. We forget to be the guide.

For some, the problem is not that they're just uncomfortable with talking on an emotional level or about the past; the problem is that they *refuse* to go there. Whether it's a male who feels he's being asked to do a very "un-male" thing, or a person who's very uncomfortable with her past, it needs to be understood that this is an important area which needs to be explored and nurtured. This is one of the areas where we're asked to stretch, moving out of our comfort zones, in order for the relationship to grow.

The interesting thing about these kinds of conversations is that they impact *both* partners. It expands the listener's view of who we are, and it also reinforces or revises our own self-concept in exploring ourselves. It enhances both the individual and the relationship because it re-establishes our identity on a deeper level, reinforcing the boundaries that keep us visible to each other.

❖   ❖   ❖

Let me be a little more specific about what I mean when I talk about being able to "emotionally express oneself". Women, typically, are able to talk more readily than men on an emotional level. When a feeling-based woman says "I love you," there are several levels with which she communicates those words – it's in her eyes, it's in the pitch of her voice, it's in her body language. When a thinking-based man says those same words, if they're not reflected in his eyes, his voice, and his body language, it's often just heard as words without much depth of feeling attached. He's *talking* about his feelings, but he's not *feeling* them as he's expressing them, or perhaps not allowing the feelings to actually be reflected on the surface. He may *feel* like he's expressing his feelings to her because he *meant* the words when he said them, but if the words are being expressed only on an intellectual level, then it's going to be difficult for her to give them credibility.

I'll spend more time in Chapter 8 defining what I mean by **feeling-based** and **thinking-based** (or reason-based). The only additional comment I want to make about it here is that there are both feeling-based men and women, and thinking-based men and women.

Part of learning how to **emote** (emotionally express) is to recognize that it's often more of a process for emotionally-repressed or thinking-based people.[1] Because being emotionally expressive isn't their nature, they can't just switch it on. They often have to be talking about an emotional subject for the emotion to have time to come to the surface. And because their contribution to a conversation often tends to be shorter and more succinct, it doesn't tend to allow for the time it takes to access the deeper feelings.

I had to re-learn how to cry as an adult. It's not something that I could do just by myself. It would too quickly become an intellectual exercise

---

[1]   Emotionally repressed is not the same as thinking-based. An emotionally repressed individual can still be feeling-based; they just excessively manage the emotions.

trying to allow myself to find the tears, feel the pain, and the feeling would get lost along the way. I had to be talking about something painful to someone I trusted, and keep talking past the point that I wanted to step back and manage my emotions. Because I was discussing that painful experience, letting it out, the emotion would eventually come out as well.

In counseling, this is why you will often hear therapists ask, "How does that make you feel?" They're not trying to be sadistic; they're just trying to get somebody to move through the emotions, *experiencing* them rather than distancing themselves intellectually.

For those people who repress painful feelings, learning how to express them, give them a voice, is often an important way of learning to let them go because they're finally getting them *out*, rather than keeping them inside where the feelings continue to eat away at them.

Part of the reason for having deep, focused conversations for the couple is to give time for a couple to access the *positive* feelings – how they feel about each other, the things they appreciate in each other, how they'd like to develop together, their particular vision of a shared future, their passions, etc.

We connect to each other more deeply on an emotional level when those emotions are being shared – we are more aware of each other's humanity and heart. If all we see of each other is the "performance face" that we show to the rest of the world, it becomes hard to see the real person underneath and hard to find something in that person that we can relate to other than the masks that we share.

3) **Intimacy is sharing *new* experiences.**

Tom and Hannah had gotten used to doing a few common activities. While those activities weren't "bad" activities (if they'd actually spent more time with deeper interaction while doing them), the problem was that those activities had become so routine that there was nothing special about them any more.

Because we're trying to keep from falling into those routines that put the relationship on an unconscious, invisible level, we need to be choosing activities from time to time that break the routine.

Activities that are also focused around self-improvement such as taking classes or workshops together, learning new skills or languages, going to the gym, all reflect visible efforts to try to stay fit and grow together.

Traveling to new places, trying new restaurants, reading good books, cooking something different together, can all be ways of avoiding falling into routines. Even just changing the routine of doing chores solo versus folding a load of laundry together can become a meaningful interaction.

Sometimes it's a matter of remembering old, fun things you used to do when you were younger. Sometimes it's a matter of breaking new ground, trying the things you always dreamed of but never had the time for. But the underlying idea is that you're trying new adventures together – keeping your relationship interesting and meaningful.

Those new experiences reveal new facets of ourselves that might have otherwise been hidden or unknown, even to ourselves.

There is also a visible statement that is being made about the relationship that affirms its value to each partner, "This is us taking care of us in a healthy way."

4) **Intimacy involves a *common* purpose or vision.**

Hannah and Tom *did* have a common purpose in raising the kids and taking care of the home. Neither was so self-involved that they excluded the other, or the family. However, the common purpose was focused on filling particular roles, not on maintaining intimacy - and it was focused on "them", not "us".

The majority of marriages share the common goals of raising a family and/or doing well enough in the careers to successfully reach retirement. Even though those may take many years to accomplish, in the scheme of things they are still "short-term" goals. And the dilemma with both of those goals is that neither is focused on the marriage itself – the focus is on the kids and the jobs.

As a result, once the couple experiences the "empty nest" stage, having accomplished the goal of raising a family, if the relationship had not been tended to during that time, there is no longer a sense of identity for the couple, because their focus was completely around the roles of being the parents.

The same with retirement. Once the couple reaches that point in time where work is no longer necessary, they often go through an extreme transition because they don't know what to do with all of the extra time together. Their focus on the roles of husband, wife and career may have helped get them there, but they may now be strangers to each other at that point, having to get to know each other all over again.

If there had been a "long-term" vision of maintaining a courtship during all of those years, continuing to grow together, then accomplishing those shorter-term goals has no significant negative impact for the relationship, since there is a deeper level of relationship present, a larger focus for their lives. As a result, moving through these times of transition isn't that much of a transition.

❖   ❖   ❖

I can never get too far in the mental health realm without bringing Scott Peck into it. In my "conflict" books, in regards to the ABC's of mental health, I talked about his "Road Less Traveled". In terms of *depth* of relationship, I automatically think about Peck's "The Different Drum".

Peck recognized that many people have never actually experienced true community (true relationship). Community is where a group of people are connected on a meaningful, intimate level. The Amish would be a good example. Every one in an Amish community has a purpose, and everyone is interdependent on everyone else.

Veterans often experienced a sense of community with the men that they had to depend upon in their unit for their very survival. Police officers and firemen will often relate a sense of community to their fellow servicemen. Even gang members will sometimes relate that what attracted them to the gang was a sense of community; a sense of belonging.

Once you've experienced true community, that level of intimacy, it's hard to ever settle for less, because you know what it means to live life at that level, and how empty it can feel to live without it.

Peck identified four stages to reaching true community/true relationship:

1) Pseudo-community

2) Chaos

3) Emptying

4) True Community

Pseudo-community is where most of us live socially. It's when you interact with other people, but the communication remains on a superficial level. We talk, we laugh, and we smile. We do everything that's appropriate and acceptable to get a "passing grade" from whomever we're talking with before we move on. There's an *appearance* of closeness to it, but it is a shallow interaction.

If we choose to go deeper, we must pass through the **chaos** stage. Chaos is where we begin to actually recognize the differences between us, and voice our opinions about those differences. There is a greater amount of honesty, but it can be having a negative impact. People going through the chaos stage typically attempt to *convert* whoever they're in relationship with. There is usually an aspect of judgment that goes along with this – "I'm right, you're wrong" or "You should be more like me".

There are three ways to get out of chaos:

1) Retreating back to pseudo-community

2) Moving on to "emptying"

3) Structuring the chaos

Many couples never move past the chaos stage. They go back and forth between pseudo-community and chaos. They may feel like things have gotten better, but it's only because they're no longer addressing the issues – the issues are still there, they're just being avoided by making the communication once again superficial. If the issues once again rise to the surface, chaos returns, and the couple retreats back to a pseudo-relationship.

Emptying, the third stage, is actively working at *letting go* of our need to convert others to our way of thinking. It is working against judging, trying to exercise grace, where we can agree to disagree.

Emptying isn't avoidance. For a relationship to go through the emptying stage means that the couple has actually let go of the issues that drove them apart. This usually involves either:

- intentional forgiveness

- learning to agree to disagree

- staying focused on the greater purpose of being together

Emptying is usually focused on letting go of the *preferences*, the things we would desire our partner to change that are annoyances, but not deal-breakers.

Most of the work that I do with couples and conflict resolution is around *structuring the chaos*. I teach couples how to follow certain rules and guidelines for working through issues in respectful ways that prevent chaos from setting in. Because it is a mutually-embraced approach, it becomes a common focus for the couple to seek solutions, versus remaining mired in obsessing about the problems.

Typically, the things we are trying to "work through" are those issues that are *need-related*. I can't empty myself of a need, since I need it!

Resolving an issue by attaching a structure to the chaos (conflict resolution) isn't the same as emptying. You are able to let go because the problem was solved. If hard feelings remain attached, however, despite having resolved the issue, emptying would still be necessary. So, while we can sometimes short-cut the trip to true community through resolving our issues, rather than just accepting the differences, in the long run, everyone still needs to know how to go through both processes.

True community is moving to that place where I'm able to accept the differences of the others in my community because there's a greater purpose that we all are sharing. For the church, that greater purpose is to worship and serve God. For the workplace, it's to efficiently accomplish whatever the service is that that workplace provides. For the couple, the greater purpose is to grow and thrive together as a couple – to move past self, while at the same time valuing each other as individuals.

Part of the tightrope walk every individual has to maintain in a relationship is trying to balance self with other – trying to support and inspire the partner's dreams, while not forgetting about her own. Too often, we give up our dreams for our partner's, or for our children's. Too often, we lose direction because we allow life's demands to be the only voice that steers the ship. While there are going to be times when we need to shelve our own dreams temporarily, because other things have to take priority in that moment, hopefully, we don't let them set for too long or we risk allowing our own identity to grow vague, possibly becoming lost.

Because they have such a clear idea of where they want to go (what "healthy" looks like), the focused couple is less likely to get side-tracked. Any behavior that doesn't fit that forward-focused picture is more easily spotted and expunged because it is so obviously inconsistent with the shared vision. Just like it becomes easy for someone who is serious about her physical regimen to pass by an unhealthy food – she has worked so hard towards a particular weight, fitness or strength goal that anything counter to it holds no desire for her. To go backwards at that point would be noticeably self-destructive; going against the forward momentum that she has created. It no longer fits her lifestyle.

And because the couple now has those common goals that intertwine, moving towards those goals, helping each other get there, continues to draw them close.

5)   Intimacy is a *physical/emotional* connection.

Tom and Hannah's sex life had definitely been reduced to an occasional "two ships passing in the night". While sex was still pleasurable, it had become primarily a physical activity for the two of them, devoid of an emotional connection.

It's interesting how many people will conclude that if the sex is still good, the relationship must be okay. But it's probably more accurate to say that good sex can do a very good job of masking just how bad a relationship has become.

In the same way that doing positive activities such as dining together can become too routine, the couple's physical relationship can also fall prey to the same issue. As the relationship encounters different transitions – new job demands, kids, aging – the cost is often seen in the frequency and quality of the couple's sex life.

For some couples the routine of the sex life is problematic before any "transitions" even occur, and often this has to do with how individuals perceive sex. For some, sex is a marital duty. For others, it's an erotic experience focusing solely on physical pleasure. Yet for others, it's a deeply emotional experience that is centered around a personal connection with the partner.

When it comes to intimacy, there is a distinct difference between "having sex" versus "making love".

"Having sex" is about the physical act. Its goal is to move each partner to climax. The agenda behind it is primarily about feeling good in the moment.

"Making love" is about the relationship, not the individual. Making love is not about climax but a shared, mutually intimate experience. It involves foreplay and exploration. In the same way that you are trying to progress in other areas of your relationship, this part of the physical relationship is also something that needs nurtured and developed to remain meaningful.

Perhaps I should add that foreplay isn't the five minutes of kissing prior to the act. Foreplay is setting a mood. It's a build-up that can last an hour or a day. It's showing your partner that you value her by the intention and energy that goes into the build-up. It lets her know that it's not all about you.

Immediately some people are saying, "We don't have that kind of time," which, while being a partial reality, still raises the question of priorities. More often, it has to do with not recognizing the time that there is. To set a mood for an evening can simply start through a loving call or e-mail at the beginning of the day which underlines your feelings for your partner, your appreciation of her. It can be a random act of kindness such as a card, or flowers, or a backrub after you come home from work. **It's usually the small unexpected things that can have the biggest impact**.

For some individuals, there is no awareness of the difference between sex and making love. Part of the problem for them is that there has *never* been any depth to this potentially very intimate act. Sure, it feels good. It feels personal. But that doesn't make it intimate. Certainly most young males don't educate each other about "making love" to a woman. To them, it's a rite of passage, a conquest to brag about. The majority of today's TV shows and movies (the family's primary source of education) illustrate sex as being about momentary passion and impulse.

For individuals who haven't experienced it on a deeper level, there has to be a willingness to learn a different way, and, hopefully, a partner who can teach them.

Remember the couple I mentioned earlier in the chapter that had been married 25 years and the husband didn't know what intimacy was? It was interesting to note that, after they had that breakthrough conversation, what followed was the best sexual encounter they'd had in their entire 25 years.

It's revealing to note that many of the sexual dysfunctions that develop with couples revolve around personal focus. Impotency and premature ejaculation, for example, are often aspects of an individual who has become over-focused on his own performance. In cases that aren't shame-based (guilt), once the focus moves back to the *interaction* with the partner, focusing on the *partner's* pleasure rather than over-monitoring his own, the body tends to naturally go back to doing what it already knows how to do.

Most married couples shift back and forth between times where sex is sex, and times where it is making love. Time and energy limitations with work and family are obvious realities. The concern is for the couple that has gotten so distracted by other things that "making love" has become a forgotten art.

6) Intimacy can have a *spiritual* component.

Spirituality refers to our personal faith or belief system, whatever that may be, and the depth that we go with it – how we make sense of life beyond the physical world. Frequently, couples who share the same religion still fail to use their common faith as an opportunity to grow in intimacy. Spirituality, though, because it is an *inner* experience, by nature is personal and private. So why would we ignore exploring it with our partner if we desired to feel closer to them?

For many, a spiritual life is not explored further with their partner because their faith itself is an undeveloped one – so what is there to share? An individual may have been raised in a Catholic home, but always remained at the outskirts of the faith itself – never truly embracing it, or exploring it further.

Most belief systems have rituals attached to them that typify that particular faith. Part of our *identity* attached to that faith is then reflected in which of those rituals we choose to engage in, and which we don't. Just engaging in a ritual, however, does not ensure any degree of depth to the faith, even if the ritual is done frequently. The ritual needs to have purpose for us as we carry it out. It is those deeper meanings that we are trying to share with our partner.

I do separate *religion* from *spirituality*. Religion tends to consist of the rituals associated with a particular denomination or group, and the basic beliefs and particular doctrines attached to that religion. Spirituality is more about the *depth* that we go with our faith. I can be religious, but not spiritual; and spiritual without attaching myself to any particular religion.

For some, because there is so much of the unknown attached to spirituality, they have a "what's the point?" mentality about it. ("Why talk about something that I don't have the answers to?") But the exercise of sharing one's faith, even if it isn't one that has acquired a foundation or is still mostly conjecture, isn't about what you "know". It's about what you "think", and "feel", and "hope", and "wonder" and maybe even "fear". It's about sharing your personal experience in living out, or failing to live out, your faith. It's about the "why's" you bring to what you believe or don't believe – without an attitude of judgment attached. It's the *respect* that we show for our partner in those conversations, regardless of the differences in some of our spiritual perspectives.

If there are any worship services or sermons that we attend, do we take the time afterwards to discuss the experience with our partner? Do we explore how the message could actually be applied to our lives? Do we debate the teaching, comparing it to our own knowledge and experience? Do we pray or meditate together? Study or have devotions together? Learn together?

Intimacy, in part, is how we put our faith into practice *with* our partner.

7) Intimacy is not approached in the same way with every person.

While there are certain pathways that are common to everyone in establishing or maintaining intimacy, it's also important to recognize that there are also individual preferences in approaching intimacy.

For Tom and Hannah, the preferences for how love was expressed were somewhat different. Because Tom valued intentional acts of service, he was already somewhat content, since Hannah was very good about fulfilling her wifely (and motherly) duties around the home. This was part of what had Tom stumped, because he was also very good at fulfilling his "duties", yet it didn't have the same impact for Hannah. Hannah's desire was for quality time; the duties were secondary.

Chapman's "Five Love Languages" does a nice job of exploring the different ways we often look to give and receive love. He delineates: 1) words of affirmation, 2) quality time, 3) random acts of kindness (such as gifts, cards, etc.), 4) acts of service, and 5) physical touch. In the same way that we can be putting energy into meeting each other's needs, but doing so in a way that fails to impact, so, too, we can be trying to show our partner love through a particular "language", but fail to recognize that language isn't theirs.

We tend to show love the way we want to get love.

At the same time, just because you may be proficient at speaking your partner's "love language", which would naturally lead to a sense of contentment in the relationship, it doesn't assure that *depth* of relationship exists. If both partners' preference was for physical touch, and they had an active physical relationship, it wouldn't guarantee that any degree of quality time was occurring that would promote a deeper connection. Considering that, you can see how some couples can be content in their relationship, yet the relationship itself can still be relatively shallow.

Knowing your partner's "love language" is the *entry point* to establishing greater intimacy. It's what *opens the door* to the heart, but it's not the entire path.

8) Intimacy goes beyond respecting differences; it *incorporates* them.

As I mentioned in Chapter 1, we unconsciously tend to seek out partners who have qualities that help balance our own. Over time, those qualities either draw us closer together or push us further apart, depending on how much they are successfully allowed to balance the relationship (or how out of balance they are to start with).

There is an additional dimension to this. For the relationship that may grow to learn to accept and respect each other's differences, there is still a significant step yet to be taken. **Ideally, what you are hoping to see in a relationship over time is not just staying with our own strengths, but learning to adopt some of our partner's strengths as well**. It's going beyond balance, and moving towards *wholeness*.

There is the tendency in most relationships that, when a role is filled, we don't feel the need to have to duplicate it. Because one person has already assumed that role, there is a sense that it's being "taken care of". But what good is it to rely on my partner's ability to be disciplined, if it means I remain dependent on her for structure? At some point, shouldn't I be learning some of that skill for myself?

When it comes to strengths, beyond being partners, we are also each other's mentors. While we want to be seen as equals, we will always possess strengths and weaknesses that are different from our partner. **Remaining humble that each of us is gifted in different areas, means we also remain open to respectfully letting each other speak from those strengths**.

It's another thing we both contribute to the relationship that is uniquely, intimately us that, ideally, over time, becomes shared.

9) Intimacy is about both the present *and* the future.

Healthy love takes into account both the present and the future. It makes its decisions considering the future impact our present choices will have.

Unhealthy love is focused solely on the present, at the *expense* of our future.

In making our choices in the present as to what increases intimacy for us, where we're focusing on the work and why we're doing it, the future good needs to be our guide. If our struggle for intimacy is focused only on the present moment, then there is no direction to it other than what feels good now. Yet, what we may be choosing for the present may actually be out-of-synch, or in direct contrast, to what we would ultimately like to have. We've either forgotten the big picture, or we fail to connect how what we're doing now is going to negatively shape things down the road.

Internet porn is one of the most recurrent addictions being treated today, in part, because of its easy accessibility. Pornography, for a couple, is often used to enhance the sex life. We use arousing images of others to create or increase our own arousal in the relationship. It feels good in the moment. It's a sexual connection and so, supposedly, a means of greater intimacy.

But there are several problems with this.

1) Pornography isn't increasing our intimacy with our partners; it's increasing our connection to a fantasy image. While we may be incorporating it with our partner, it's still having to use an outside source to increase our desire for our mate. There is the risk we run that continuing to use that image strengthens our connection to that image, and weakens our desire for our partner.

2) Pornography involves fantasizing about being sexually intimate with someone other than our marital partner. While it may be fantasy, there is still a degree of practiced rehearsal of what "crossing that line" would be like. While it may not predict having an affair, it certainly can weaken the boundaries that would otherwise be more firmly in place.

3) There can be a progressive nature to pornography. In the same way that alcohol and marijuana are "gateway drugs" which increase the likelihood of using something "harder", pornography sometimes requires an increase in exciting content in order to continue to arouse. The stronger the imagery, the greater the arousal, the more potentially dependent we become. Addiction is dependency.

4) Even if its use is not progressive for us, it can undermine self-esteem. Even if we have our partner's approval to use it, and we use it together, there is often a longer-term impact on each partner's sense of self. Over time, since our own bodies can't compete with the images of perfection we are often focused on, it plants questions concerning our own desirability that don't need to be there.

This "rule" isn't isolated to pornography. Substance use, sexual experimentation to the point where it's become destructive, a narcissistic relationship, over-focus on play to the degree that important responsibilities get neglected, are all examples of this. The couple needs to be able to consciously ask themselves the hard question, "Is doing this now likely to cost us further down the road?" There will always be things that create an *illusion* of increased intimacy that can actually be destructive to it.

10) Intimacy is *initiated* by both.

One of the most common dilemmas I see with couples regards who actually tends to the relationship. Usually there's just one person in the relationship that is the "thermometer" for the relationship. And usually that role goes to the wife (or whoever is the most relationship-based).

Tom and Hannah's relationship was driven by Hannah. As Tom said, his focus was on "trying to do the things she asks of me".

This trend often begins on a seemingly positive note during the dating stage. Traditionally, the man is actively attempting to please the woman while he's "courting" her. She's giving him the cues as to what she likes and how good a job he's doing. This is the medieval, romantic ideal – the knight winning the favor of his lady.

When they cross the marital boundary, this same pattern tends to persist, since that is the expectation that was established prior. Yet, over time, one of two things (maybe both) is going to predictably happen. Either the woman is going to start resenting the fact that she's the one who has to always be identifying what the needs of the relationship are, or the man is going to resent feeling that the wife has an ongoing list of demands.

There is a distortion that takes place in this, because, *since it is the wife identifying needed change, the changes are seen as being all about the wife.* No doubt there *are* some things she's asking that are her own desires, but, since she's the official "relationship thermometer", she's also identifying things that are about the relationship, not just her. The inaccurate picture that's created is that the man's content and the woman never is, when it's often that she's pulling double duty.[2]

Often times, the only reason the wife's putting in that much energy is because she feels, if she doesn't, no one else will. If she sees he's paying attention as well, she typically won't feel as much of a need to continue to take it all on herself.

Countless times I'll work with a couple where the man automatically looks to the woman to initiate getting the marital "homework" done (to do a "sit-down", to schedule a date night, etc.), not recognizing that that's a big part of the problem that got them to counseling in the first place.

The unhealthy pattern can persist simply because both sides are caught up in continuing to do what they see as being *helpful* – the man feels he's being accommodating by waiting on the wife; the wife is showing her care for the two of them by continuing to point out the continued work. But, in reality, their "helpfulness" is making things more and more stressed. He's seen as being passive and unmotivated, while she's a nag.

A relationship is supposed to be about *two* individuals, *each* playing a part. It's not about one person constantly trying to make the other happy. It's about two people attempting to put in equal energy in satisfying the needs of the relationship; a *mutual* courtship where there's both a princess and a prince.

I hesitate to use the term "equal energy" because, suddenly, a couple starts to over-monitor the percentage of just how much each is putting into things, which leads back to the "blame game" of over-attaching

---

[2]   Yes, there *are* situations where the woman can be "high maintenance", having too many expectations. And, sometimes, it is a combination of the two ("high maintenance" *and* double duty), so you have to sort out the realistic from the unrealistic. But the situation I'm referring to here is where the *appearance* of being overly demanding is actually something else.

fault. What I am trying to draw attention to is that when a relationship has become too one-sided in *any* direction, something needs to change to shift things back to balance - and this shouldn't be the responsibility of just the one.

Yes, if one person's more "in-tune" with the relationship it makes sense that they are going to be the one to be more aware of what needs to change. But the problem is when that pattern *never* shifts, when it's *always* one person who takes on that role.

Because there is that tendency to not duplicate roles, when one partner has already taken on the role of "relationship thermometer", it is easy for the other partner to think they don't have to be doing that as well since it's already being "taken care of". While that may be true for some of the other roles, it *doesn't* apply to initiating intimacy.

It's important for a man to retain his identity in the relationship by not expecting the woman to be the most vocal or active about the relationship. I'm not saying that he needs to have his own "to do" list, or attempt to dominate the relationship, but that it's important that he continues to do his share of monitoring what's working and what's not (looking at both the maintenance work *and* the intimacy needs).

An interesting phenomenon to measure this is what happens when one partner has to go on a trip and the other stays behind. If it's a situation where one person's will has been repressed, what you will often see when the other partner's not there is a sudden surge of energy – they're running around doing all the things they want that they couldn't normally do with the other present. Suddenly, they have all sorts of opinions and ideas about what they want to do, where they want to go, what they want to eat, etc. that normally just aren't there. It's a visible sign that they've been taking a backseat in the relationship.

Now let me balance that by saying there are things we don't do when our partner's around just because we know they don't like to do them, or would disapprove of them if we did. I'm not suggesting we try to force those on our partner. Nor am I saying to suddenly become so opinionated about everything that the relationship becomes a constant power struggle. What I'm talking about is that, if the relationship is to be a balanced one, it needs to have both voices present, both identities recognized and affirmed. If it's going to be a future both can be excited about, it needs to be a future that incorporates both visions about what kind of a relationship is desired.

For intimacy to develop, it requires both sides to be:

- sharing from their hearts
- assessing their own needs
- thinking of creative ways to meet the partner's needs
- thinking of and committing to new territory to explore
- nurturing and initiating a creative physical relationship
- attempting intentional, meaningful conversation
- accepting responsibility for the relationship's continued growth

Discussion Questions:

1. **When you assess your own relationship, is the focus more on how well the marital roles are filled, or on the quality of intimacy?**

2. **How well are the job roles of the relationship satisfied? The parenting roles?** How much do you gauge your personal success by the quality of things you've acquired? How much of your relationship is about getting chores done? If you were going to better balance any of these areas, what would that look like?

3. **Do you feel like you have a competitive relationship?** Does one of you have to always be right, or have great difficulty with admitting fault? Is there a sense of being "less than" in the relationship? If the two of you were going to stop competing with each other, what would that look like?

4. **Does your marriage:**

- **have *focused* interaction?**
- **have *depth* of interaction?**
- **explore new experiences together?**
- **have a common purpose for being together beyond filling the relationship roles?**
- **have a physical/emotional connection?**
- **have a spiritual connection?**

- **know each other's "love language"?**
- **attempt to incorporate each other's strengths?**
- **practice healthy love?**
- **mutually initiate and nurture intimacy?**

5. **Which of these areas do you need to put more effort into?** How are you going to do that?

Chapter 3
Priorities and Focus
(the Deception of Distraction)

The fact that couples get distracted from focusing on the relationship is a legitimate point to be made for a marriage essential, but I think we often lose sight of its magnitude. To me, **distraction is the one of the biggest contributors to not just a failed marriage, but to leading an unfulfilled life**.

The only way to have a great marriage is to be able to maintain a focus on keeping the relationship healthy. In the same way that to do well with a career you need to stay focused on where you're headed. The surest path to living contentedly is by maintaining your focus on using your particular skills and talents in the most meaningful ways.

Of course, the more we over-focus on any one thing, the more we have to take our focus off of something, or everything, else. To manage this, we have to learn how to balance our focus. For the married couple, ideally, they each have the advantage of the partner's perspective to help them do so.

Distraction and Motivation

Peter and Ruth had been married for over 10 years and had one child. They were considering having another child, but Peter was concerned the marriage wasn't where it should be and didn't want to have another child until things were in a healthy place.

"So, why don't you consider things to be at a healthy place?" I asked.

"Over the last two years Ruth took a job that's really gotten in the way of our home life," Peter said. "We knew at the beginning that it was going to demand a lot so we'd planned for a 6 month transition – time for Ruth to bury herself in her job and get things organized. But the problem has been that that was several years ago and things are still the same. Even when she's at home, her head's still at work. She'll come home at the end of the day and be immediately on the phone talking to colleagues. If we go on vacation with family, she's talking about work."

"Did you work before this job?" I asked Ruth.

"Yes. I've worked since I was in high school," she replied.

"It's the fact that this job is more demanding than the ones she's had before," added Peter. "Ruth's always afraid of her performance falling short. As a result, that's where her focus is. Also, she's in a position now where she has to fire people and has had to learn how to harden herself emotionally in order to do that. But, at the same time, I think it's also hardened her in every other area as well – including our marriage."

"This isn't just about me," Ruth inserted. "Peter is addicted to video games."

"What makes it an addiction?" I asked.

"It *used* to be an addiction," Peter stepped in. "But that was back at the start of our marriage. It gave me some distance from over-obsessing about some of the personal problems I had going on at the time."

"It's still an addiction," insisted Ruth. "You're still at it whenever you're at home."

"Just because I still use it, doesn't mean it's still a problem. An addiction would mean that everything is out of balance in my life because of it," asserted Peter. "I exercise. I have time with our son. I don't neglect my work. I read. I have hobbies. If I'm playing games, and it's not on my own personal time after you're asleep, it's because you're occupied elsewhere. If you weren't on the phone, I wouldn't be doing it. And if you need me for something, I get off of it. You can't expect me to just hover around, waiting for you to give me a free moment. If you're busy, I'm going to occupy myself - and I'm not going to just passively sit around and watch TV."

"You could be getting work done around the house, instead of playing all the time," said Ruth.

"First off, it's not '*all* the time', it's '*some* of the time'. And it's not like you're getting all that work done while you're on the phone. Besides, the chores do get done, just not as fast as you'd like them to be," Peter shot back.

He looked to me. "I recognize that games were a problem in the past, but now it's just become her scapegoat. Whenever I try to address her loss of balance with the job she uses it to parry my point, rather than own it."

"You won't own that games are a problem," said Ruth. "Why should I own anything about work?"

"My life *is* in balance, Ruth," responded Peter. "Yours isn't. You don't exercise. You find excuses to be out of the house doing 'chores' rather than at home with your family. You have only one good friend, and you have no side interests. You work, you come home, you watch TV, and you go to bed. Day after day. I'm not willing to live the rest of my life like that, and I'm certainly not interested in bringing another child into that."

A big part of remaining focused on a marriage has to do with maintaining our motivation to keep it a priority. The more we take our relationship for granted, the more comfortable we are with its success, the greater the likelihood that our attention is going to drift to the other priorities that are more visibly in jeopardy of being neglected. For us to keep that focus we can't allow ourselves to ever see our relationship as such a "done deal" that it can't be undone by neglect. We have to choose to remain uncomfortable (though not miserable) about its stability.

The source for healthy motivation always comes back to *healthy love*. Why are you trying to stay motivated to continue to focus on your marriage?

Because you care about it. Because you care about you. Because you care about your partner. Because you care about your kids. If there is a sense of future focus to the relationship, seeing it as a progression, while it adds an aspect of adventure to it, it also underlines the need for a clear direction. To maintain that direction requires paying attention to the landmarks you pass along the way which tell whether or not you're getting off course.

Peter and Ruth's relationship had definitely started to drift. There was the question of whether or not Peter's past over-use of video games had become a "wound" for Ruth, a deeper issue with deeper meanings attached, and so his continued use of it set off old hurts for her, even if the frequency of his use in the present was being moderated. Of course, there was also the possibility that her bringing it into the conversation was an attempt to distract the conversation from focusing on her. And, there was the possibility that he still used it more than he realized.

❖   ❖   ❖

There are two different types of people who read this book. Those who are looking for me to make the read exciting enough, and easy enough, that they move through it with as little effort as possible. And then there are those who are motivated to get through this book primarily because of their own desire to benefit their marriage and glean whatever they can from what I have to offer.

For the first type of reader, it is questionable whether they will finish or not because it all depends on me, the writer – how well I did at motivating them to finish, how well I kept them on-task with my structure, etc. For the second type of reader, they will most likely finish the book one way or the other, because their motivation was internal, it came from within - so it really only depends on my part to a degree.

The first type of person has what is called an *external* locus of control. She looks for her motivation to come from *outside* of her.

The second type of person has an *internal* locus of control. Her motivation comes from *within* herself.

In a marriage, **a person who has an external locus of control depends on her partner for her motivation**. Her positive participation lasts only so long as her partner continues to positively motivate her.

For a person with an internal locus, the marital behavior is dependent on no one but herself. It's her own personal standard of being a positive partner that she is living up to. Certainly, the partner's behavior still *influences* her, but it doesn't *decide* things for her.

Having an internal locus does not make you a doormat; it simply manages the degree of your reactivity. You stay in control of yourself because you don't give your control, or motivation, away like a person with an external locus would. For an internal locus there is no "eye for an eye" mentality. There is no vindictive standard of "You hurt me, so I'm going to hurt you", or "I'll do better when you do better".

When I do couple's work, a lot of the initial effort is getting people to stop "muddying the water" by continuing to keep things stirred up. For such couples, they can't help but continue to do or say just one more negative thing, whether out of spite or reaction. Someone with a restored internal locus no longer muddies things – she's turned the focus back on her part and doing what she needs to do in order to regain her own sense of integrity, rather than continuing to compromise it because of the partner's choices.

The person with an internal locus doesn't depend on the partner to make her "step up" and assume responsibility for the relationship, since her motivation isn't dependent on externals.

At the same time, people with an external locus aren't doomed to remain externally focused. If they're going to feel more in charge of their lives and more effective in their relationships, they need to grasp the difference between an internal and external locus of control. They need to work on making that shift. They need to be vigilant about making conscious choices that match personal ideals rather than life, and the people in it, making all of the choices for them.

Ruth's locus of control appeared to be more external. If Peter's perception was accurate, her boss's demands dictated her choices. And, quite possibly, she was distancing herself in *reaction* to Peter, rather than focusing on who she should be in the relationship regardless.

Peter's locus of control appeared to be mixed. Peter himself identified that he was reacting by retreating to his video games, but he also seemed to have more overall balance in his life than Ruth.

Ideally, we are trying to develop an internal locus across the board in our lives simply because it is the most balanced, the most conscious, and the most positively "in control" place to be.

Distraction and Mental Health

"One of the complications with this is that Ruth possibly has Attention Deficit Disorder. She goes from one task to another around the house. She'll start something and then something else will catch her attention and she's off on another path. She'll easily lose track of time on the phone or in a conversation, while others are waiting for her. And she's constantly forgetting to tell me about things she's planned until the last minute," continued Peter. "I often feel like she gets lost in the middle of our arguments when I'm trying to make a point; that she has difficulty tracking my logic, but can't admit it when she does.

"The problem becomes I don't know how much slack to cut her – it's easy to see all of these things as just more examples of how self-absorbed she is, and how unimportant I am to her. If this is ADD, how much is she responsible for and how much do I have a right to expect her to change?

"On top of that, she expects me to not take issue with these things, because it's supposedly just part of her ADD. But, if I do those same things to her, she's upset because she does see it as selfish or disrespectful if it's coming from me. So there's this double standard."

"What it comes down to for me," inserted Ruth, "is that I'm not getting my needs met at home. My work is very affirming. I know I do a good job. I get consistent praise. But, at home, I get criticized."

"How can I praise you for something that's killing us?" persisted Peter. "When you cook, I praise you for it, but you don't really cook much anymore. I see you gaining weight to the point that you're developing health problems – how do I praise that? Even the doctor says you need to start exercising, but when I invite you to come with me even just on a walk, you turn me down. I never put you down because of your weight, but I've a right to be concerned. How can I praise an absence of things to praise? Should I be thanking you that you're there when I get up in the morning or that you come home from work at all? I'm seeing things getting worse and worse, but you won't hear me on any of it. Instead, you just shut me out."

Ruth said nothing in return.

While the core of mental health has to do with how people handle emotional pain (accepting responsibility for working through the legitimate pain that is yours to deal with, and letting the rest go), distraction also plays a very significant part.

With conditions such as mood disorders (depression and anxiety), we become distracted by depressed or anxious thoughts. The more we feed and dwell on those thoughts the more they remove us from staying focused on living our lives effectively.

Panic attacks are a great example. Panic attacks happen for a reason. However, it can often be unclear as to exactly what it was that first set them off. The focus of the problem, because of its intensity and visibility, becomes the panic attacks themselves, *not* what started the attacks. So, *the panic attacks end up being a distraction from the real problem.* Solve the underlying problem and the panic attacks usually go away.

Obsessive-compulsive problems revolve around ritual behaviors or tracks of thought that become incredibly distracting. There is a relief that is experienced in giving in to the compulsion, but the more it is entertained, the more powerful it becomes, often branching into other rituals and other obsessions – leading us further and further away from a healthy life.

With addictions (such as drugs, sex, food, gambling or shopping), we become overly focused on engaging in a particular behavior, even though that behavior is now costing us in important ways.

The majority of mental health disorders share the common theme of the individual becoming distracted from a healthier path.

Each of these conditions has an underlying legitimate, healthy need that is driving them, but the individual has lost sight of how to meet that need in a healthy way. They have become mesmerized by their negative rituals and are having difficulty finding their way back.

For many, part of the treatment for such issues attempts to find healthy ways to distract the sufferer from being overly obsessed with her own issues, but it's important for the client to make the connection on a deeper level that *the issues themselves are often the distractions, or outcomes of being distracted.* Rather than trying to do *more* (distracting herself from the distraction), it's about doing *less* – not even expending the energy that it takes to be distracted in the first place. And restoring the primary focus to what she would be doing *without* the negative distraction, back to actually living her life.

❖   ❖   ❖

In relationships, we have to work at staying focused on the positives, and not overly distracted by the negatives.

With actual issues, we have to remain focused on the issue at hand, seeking balanced solutions rather than distracting each other with judging, bringing up the past, or side issues.

The surface, petty issues tend to get all of the focus and we fail to recognize that they're really just distractions from deeper, more meaningful things going unsatisfied. **Solve the deeper things and the surface issues fall back into perspective**.

When it comes to emotional wounds, the reaction to something that sets off the wound is always disproportionate - that's how you can tell it's a wound in the first place. That over-the-top reaction is advertising, "You just pushed my button."

The couple has to be willing to recognize that those incidences aren't about the surface issue that set things off. It's what that surface issue represents; it's something deeper. ("Okay, what is this *really* about? Why is this such a big deal for you?")

Peter and Ruth had a lot to explore. Peter's concerns about Ruth's possible ADD were legitimate, but even though the actual presence of the condition might better *explain* some of her behavior it didn't put her above accountability for working on changing that behavior. It was clear that *neither* Ruth nor Peter were getting their needs met any longer in their relationship.

Peter's concerns involved all three core needs:

1) He was feeling unimportant to Ruth (significance).

2) He was feeling a lack of control over what was going on in the relationship, not knowing what was within his rights to take a stand on (security).

3) Because they weren't having any "play" time together anymore, the quality of life was suffering (fun).

Ruth's expressed concerns, so far, seemed to be primarily about significance and security. She was feeling criticized rather than accepted – about her job, about her weight, about her emotional withdrawal, about all the things that could be ADD related. And she saw his video games as her competition.

The difference between the two was that Ruth was pulling away from Peter, and Peter was still trying to pull her back in. Ruth was getting her needs met elsewhere, through her work, and, while Peter was attempting to satisfy his own need for fun through video games, he was still wanting and seeking to involve Ruth in his life.

There were all sorts of distractions going on in this case: Ruth's work, the possible ADD, Peter's games, the phone calls, Ruth's weight, and Peter's criticizing. Everything was justified by something else, so it kept the focus off of the central problem: "**What are we going to do to make this relationship work?**" The focus needed to be on finding solutions that worked for both, rather than rehashing who did what to whom.

Healthy Distractions

"Is there anything to add to this picture that hasn't already been brought up?" I asked.

Silence for a bit between them and then Ruth spoke up, "I think he's having an affair."

Peter rolled his eyes. "It would be pretty hard for me to have an affair when I'm at home every evening."

Ruth ignored him and looked at me. "There's a girl at work that he has lunch with, and she's also in a yoga class he takes."

Peter held up his open hand, like a stop signal, looking over at Ruth. "Wow. When are we going to move past this? I walk with her while I'm at work, because you won't walk or exercise with me when I'm at home, so it doesn't interfere with my home time," said Peter. He looked at me and added, "I've gone over these explanations numerous times with her and it never sinks in. This girl is a good friend and that's it. She's married. I've asked Ruth for us to do things with them as a couple so she can see the girl's okay, but she refuses. I don't have dinner with her, or go to movies, or anything that would have the appearance of a date. At most, we've had lunch during the work-day and that's it."

Ruth replied simply with, "He's always making friends with women."

"That's a distortion," replied Peter. "I work in a field that's predominantly women, so I'm around women a lot. But, up until now, for as long as we've been married, all the women have only been colleagues. I've never done anything with any of them outside of work. This is the first time, while married, that I've ever actually had a female friend."

"So can you understand why that might be uncomfortable for your wife," I said, "especially now when things are stressed for the two of you?"

"Well, there's another level to it as well," said Peter. "Prior to me, all the men in her life disappointed her in some pretty serious ways. She was cheated on and physically abused. At one point, even her father significantly betrayed her. She's told me before that she can't help but feel sooner or later I'm going to do something to hurt her as well – and now she thinks she's found it.

"But, to answer your question, yes, I certainly understand how she could take it as a threat. But you would think that would make her want to work on the marriage more, not less."

"You may not be having sex with her, but it's still an emotional affair," said Ruth.

"That's a new term Ruth's picked up," Peter said to me. "Which is convenient, because how do you prove or disprove the existence of an emotional affair?" He looked back to Ruth. "Sue's been a support to me when you haven't. She's been a good friend when I've had no one else to talk to. But I don't think of her in a romantic sense. Physically, I've never done more than give her a hug to say thanks. You want me to give up my social supports but then leave me with nothing. I'm supposed to give up one of my best friends, even though you're not willing to be my friend. Besides, it's a double standard. You have male friends at work. I'm not making an issue about that."

"Those aren't emotional affairs," replied Ruth.

"Do you ever have lunch with any of them?" Peter asked.

"Not on a regular basis," said Ruth.

"I don't have lunch with Sue on a regular basis either," said Peter. "If anything, I've got more reason to think you're having an emotional affair simply because you're avoiding us. It's clear you're getting your needs met somewhere else. I'm not. I want to have more time with you. I want to do things with you. I'm not okay with less."

Both Ruth and Peter had legitimate points about what was going on with the relationship, yet *neither* side was doing a very good job of validating the other. They would provide a rationale for their own behavior, excuse the behavior, or add an additional piece to the picture, but nobody was taking the time to really relate to what the other was saying. They kept *distracting* each other from what really needed to be said, and so the overall experience was, "We keep talking but it's only making things messier, not clearing anything up".

In session, so far, it was clear that Peter was providing the majority of the conversation, giving much more content than Ruth was. Perhaps Ruth was holding back because Peter was explaining away every criticism she came up with, or perhaps this was another example of how Ruth had withdrawn from the relationship overall.

Even with the added complications of a possible emotional affair, my greatest concern was still with Ruth. Everything she was instinctively choosing to do, even if it was just in reaction to her fears about Peter, were moving her *further away* from the relationship, not closer. And it was costing her as much as it was Peter – costing her her health, her balance with priorities, and any opportunity for truer intimacy.

Most minds require stimulation. And if our lives aren't stimulated in positive ways, our minds will attempt satisfaction through finding negative focuses, just like a child who doesn't get positive attention from the parents will ultimately seek out negative ways to gain their attention.

Core needs (security, significance and fun) are legitimate. They *have* to be met. The problem is never with the need itself, but always in how we go about meeting the need. If we need to feel more significant in our marriage but fail to identify to our partner that that need's not being met, we remain vulnerable to other things outside the marriage that will meet that need. Our own needs start working against us because we haven't been finding healthy avenues to satisfy them.

Distractions help alleviate some of the distress that unmet needs create. However, they can also band-aid the fact that our needs are gradually starving. Legitimate pain exists for a reason; to draw our attention to what needs fixed. Distractions can alleviate the pain enough that we end up losing our motivation to solve the real problem. That relief may even convince us, for a time, that the problem is solved. If I feel bad about my lack of physical self-care, the emotional pain that I experience exists to motivate me to get off my butt and go to a gym. But people will distract themselves with other things to make themselves feel better (eating, shopping, socializing, over-committing), while the health problem remains. We only feel good so long as we stay absorbed in the distractions, avoiding legitimate suffering – and possible healing.

❖   ❖   ❖

There *is* such a thing as a *healthy* distraction. Too much work *needs* the distraction of play. Too much time thinking *needs* the relief of being able to just be in the moment. Healthy distractions help balance us.

Healthy distractions are often where we have our fun. Fun, balanced distractions are vital – they serve a purpose even if their immediate utility isn't always obvious. Not all healthy distractions, of course, are related to the need for fun but most of them provide a necessary relief from stress.

One thing that decides the severity of a problem is the *frequency* of its re-occurrence. **What can often decide whether a distraction is healthy or not often comes down to how often it's engaged in in comparison to everything else.**

At the point a healthy distraction starts to interfere with keeping other healthy priorities balanced, it's now becoming unhealthy. That doesn't mean you have to give up that distraction completely, but rather see if it can be *moderated*. If, over time, you find that it's too powerful to moderate, you have to accept that it holds too much of a draw for you to be able to continue to keep it in your life.

Peter had supposedly learned to moderate his over-use of video games. Since this was up for debate with Ruth, the only option they had to prove or disprove the theory (if they wanted to expend the effort), would be to attempt to track its frequency.

It was questionable whether or not Ruth's over-commitment to work needed to be tracked, since she was not denying it. It was more important that, if Peter was accurate, she could come to see that his seeking time with games was a result of her still being occupied with her job while she was at home, rather than the other way around.

Peter's possible "emotional affair" was also in question in terms of whether his friendship qualified as an unhealthy distraction. It certainly was becoming an unhealthy distraction for his wife. He was making some healthy choices with it by limiting the amount of time spent with this friend and the type of activities they participated in. Also, he wasn't giving up any "home time" for it. However, there certainly was the potential for it to turn into something more, especially since his relationship needs weren't being met in the marriage.

Peter's fears were certainly understandable that, if he gave up that working friendship, Ruth still might not be any more emotionally accessible and he would be without any significant support. As with tracking frequency, we would have to spend more time exploring the extent of this outside relationship in order to decide what needed to be done to safeguard the marriage.

A Singular Focus

"So why is work so important to you?" I asked Ruth.

"Well, my father was always a hard worker. And I was always uncomfortable with my mom's situation. She only worked when she was younger, and it put her in a very vulnerable place. If their relationship had ever gone bad, she wouldn't have been able to take care of herself," answered Ruth.

"So work isn't just about significance for you; it's also part of your security," I added.

"Well, yes. I know I don't have to depend on anybody to take care of me," she replied.

"So, is it also a way to keep from being vulnerable?" I asked, wanting to explore an idea.

"I don't know if I'd say that," said Ruth. "More like dependent. It pays enough that we can afford the house we're staying in."

"Does Peter not have a job?" I asked.

"Yes, he works. But we couldn't afford our house on his salary alone."

"Coming from a home where your dad provided for your mom, was that your expectation going into this marriage?" I asked.

"I wish that Peter would make more money, or do more with his career, but I don't expect to be taken care of."

Peter added, "Before we got married, I told Ruth that I wanted a partnership, where the responsibility was shared. I made the expectations clear going in. I've always maintained steady work, but I don't think I've ever made enough for Ruth to be content. During the early part of our marriage she admitted to me she was jealous of her girlfriends who could just hang out at the golf course and talk while their husbands worked.

"Her dad was a workaholic. Though she doesn't directly say it, I know she compares me to him. It would be nice if she took into account my positives, and just stopped comparing altogether. I don't have any interest in trying to compete with her dad – I don't desire to have the kind of life that he does.

"Somebody pigeon-holed it for me a few months ago," continued Peter. "They said that Ruth lives to work, and I work in order to live. And I think that's very accurate. Everything, even fun, turns into a task for her, while I want to find ways to make work fun."

"Would you label your dad as having been a workaholic?" I asked Ruth.

"Yes," she said simply. "He was."

"And would you say he had a happy marriage with your mom?" I continued.

"No, I wouldn't say they were happy. They just learned to live with each other," Ruth acknowledged.

It was interesting to note two things about this piece of Ruth and Peter's conversation. First, Ruth's job really was a protection for her. It kept her financially secure, but it also assisted in not making her dependent on Peter. On a larger scale, her withdrawal from him and attachment to the things that were "safe", things that she had control over, were all a reflection of her need to self-protect – protect herself from a possible affair, protect from financial dependence, protect from criticism, protect from pain.

Second, Ruth was re-creating her parent's marriage, or at least her father's role in it. Her father had also "checked-out" of his own marriage through his work. Her parents had learned to get by through filling the "roles" of husband and wife, but with a lack of intimacy. By not looking at this more closely, Ruth was unintentionally allowing those past models to guide her present.

Many tend to see attention deficit, in terms of its distractibility, as a person who has too *broad* a focus. She is attending to so many things at once, she can't maintain focus on any one thing. But it's actually the opposite. Attention deficit tends to be a *singular focus* – a form of tunnel vision. Because she can only focus on one thing at a time, anything that turns that focus away removes the initial object of focus from her sight.

For many people, the problem with distractibility is that what may start out as a healthy outlet can turn into a negative distraction if it goes unchecked because it has now become a singular focus. What makes this so difficult to see is due to the positives that can be coming out of the chosen activity. Say someone gets involved with the local church. She's overjoyed that she's found a meaningful way of contributing to the community that fits her personality. But, over time, she starts to take on too much. It may not even feel like too much to her, but now it's starting to take time away from the family; she doesn't have time for exercise – it's costing her in other ways.

What can make these healthy outlets such powerful draws is that they are satisfying legitimate needs for the person and, because the choice of the distraction is such a positive one, it's easily rationalized.

For people like Ruth, who get lost in their careers, how can you argue with providing for the family? She's being responsible by holding down a job. She's advancing in her career which provides even more options for her family. But, yet, the career is only one priority – what about all the others? And just how much of her career was really about family, and how much was really about self?

It was also Peter's struggle with considering letting go of a good friend. Why should the marriage cost him a positive support? How could that be healthy? Yet, if it would cost him his marriage, was it worth it? It certainly wasn't going to make everything better, but what if it was one less significant obstacle?

It's everyone's struggle in a marriage, having to weigh out just how much sacrifice is necessary, and at what point we are making too much of a compromise.

❖   ❖   ❖

"Taking care of the relationship" is about balancing *all* the priorities because each of those priorities can either add to or detract from the relationship, depending on their degree of balance.

What makes this harder is that, as we age, the list of "to do's" gets a lot longer. There's a lot more that needs to be juggled. When I was a kid, going to bed wasn't a complicated task. Brush your teeth, get into your pajamas, and go to bed. But as an adult, it's more like: check the locks on the doors, make sure the stove's turned off, make sure all the lights are out, make sure the thermostat's set, get dressed for bed, brush your teeth, floss your teeth, take a Tums, change the sheets and pillow cases, set the alarm, get up again and put some moisturizer on because your dry skin is making you itch, do some push-ups because you didn't get enough exercise during the day and now you've got too much energy that's getting in the way of sleeping, etc. Self-care, by itself, can be a full-time job!

When you add self-care to all the other responsibilities as partner, parent, employer or employee, family and friend, it is very easy to feel overwhelmed and guilty for not being able to maintain any kind of balance for very long. For every "to-do" that's added you're also adding a new potential distraction from everything else.

So, I understand that there's a lot to juggle. **What is vital is knowing the difference between what is most important and least important to be done within each of those priority categories, and not letting the small stuff distract us from the big.**

If I only have a certain amount of time, forgetting what would *feel* the best, what would be the most important things to get done? That's what needs to be my guide while remembering that, *sometimes*, the most important thing may also be what would feel the best.

One shortcut to balancing is how we can over-lap priorities. Rather than treating all of our priorities as separate, we can actually take care of a number of them at the same time. For example, involving our kids in our hobbies, having our partner exercise with us, doing things with other couples that also involve the children, taking the family to church, etc.

A Very Personal Trap

"So, in a way, each of you found your own personal distraction trap," I said.

They both looked at me, confused.

"Peter, for you, the trap was the games. They gave you necessary relief from thinking anxious thoughts about your life. They got you through a hard time, but they also took you away from your wife," I explained. "And, Ruth, your work, though stressful, makes you feel significant and secure, but at the cost of being emotionally available for your husband. Each satisfy significant needs for you, but, ultimately, distract you from what's more important – the marriage.

"Let me ask you this. How do you hold each other accountable for change in the relationship?"

There were a few moments of thought.

"I think we voice our concerns to each other," said Peter. "If anything, we over-talk things. But it's a lot easier for us to get angry with each other now than it's ever been. The least little thing can get me upset. But while we might make requests of each other, I don't think we tell each other what to do. I haven't demanded that Ruth quit - though, come to think of it, back when I was lost in the games she did tell me that I needed to get rid of them, just like initially she wanted me to get rid of my friend. But I felt those were extreme solutions."

"I think," said Ruth, "that we've given each other so much room to make our own choices that there haven't been any firm lines drawn. I think neither of us feels like we should have to make the other do anything – they should just want to do it."

Personally, **I believe that every person has an Achilles' heel in at least one or two areas that they will have to remain vigilant against throughout their lifetime**. It may be a hobby that becomes obsessive, unhealthy relationships, a drug that takes away their control, a career that distances them from the family, over-involvement with the kids to the neglect of the marriage, or even a problematic way of thinking about themselves or about life. And, for each person, that Achilles' heel is their personal distraction from living life well.

The sooner we have recognized for ourselves what our particular weaknesses are, the better we can strategize and safe-guard against them taking control of us.

In terms of accountability (Chapter 7), this is where the marriage relationship helps keep each other in check in necessary, healthy ways. The accountability routines keep the relationship focused and guarded against drifting too far astray. But accountability requires ownership.

A big part of the problem in Ruth and Peter's relationship was that it is very difficult to hold somebody accountable for something they're not willing to take ownership of. The blame game kept the two of them from arriving at workable solutions, and so the pattern for the relationship became just recycling complaints as resentment grew.

When it came right down to it, everything that Ruth and Peter said made sense. Their choices and conclusions weren't necessarily healthy or balanced ones, but you could understand their thinking (or feeling).

Looking at Ruth's history, it made perfect sense that she was acting the way she was. She'd been betrayed or rejected by the men she cared for throughout her life, and now she was being rejected by Peter (due to his criticism) and possibly even betrayed by him (with his female friend). To cope, she withdrew into what still accepted and praised her - her job.

For Peter, who truly felt he was managing his game time and really didn't see his female friendship as being an emotional affair, Ruth's continued focus on those subjects came across as just excuses to turn the attention away from her own work obsession, and neglect of everything else. His continued invitations to involve her in his life seemed only to result in her drawing further away. Whatever he tried to do to convince her he still cared, her focus seemed to remain solely on the things that supported her conspiracy theory that he wasn't sincere. His attempts to approach accountability with her only provided new ways for her to experience being rejected by him. Positive efforts with negative results. So, of course, he would feel distressed and angry.

They weren't incredibly damaged people. In fact, they were both pretty normal people who excelled in many different areas of their lives. But they had hit a hurdle in the relationship that was becoming progressively more complicated the longer the problems continued. To move through it would take focused work, and there were certainly numerous distractions in their lives to keep that from happening.

Ultimately, for every couple, what decides whether or not a relationship perseveres comes down to: 1) how much damage has been done, 2) how motivated the couple is to make necessary changes along the way, re-focusing on the relationship, 3) knowing how to go about making those changes, and 4) maintaining those changes over time.

Discussion Questions:

1. **How much does your partner's behavior decide your own?** If they're upset, are you able to stay positive? If you're upset, do you insist that they be upset as well? Are you able to stay focused on who you need to be as a husband or wife, or does that depend on how great a job your partner is doing? If you were living up to your personal ideal of being a loving partner, how would that differ from what you're actually doing in the present?

2. **How much of a positive focus does your marriage have?** Do you feel that it gets sufficient attention? Do you feel like you address the important issues that arise? Is there a tendency to avoid issues because it might stir up conflict? Are there distractions that are

threatening keeping the relationship as a priority? What steps do you need to take to keep the distractions in check?

3. **In your marriage, how do you decide what are healthy or unhealthy distractions?** Are there any distractions that you've had difficulty moderating in the past or present? Any distractions you've had to get rid of? Are there any distractions that are currently problematic for the relationship that require accountability? If so, what would healthy accountability look like for that particular distraction?

4. **How balanced are your priorities?** When you consider work, the marriage, being a parent, time with other couples, relatives, hobbies, a spiritual life, and your personal health, which get the majority of the attention? If you were going to shift your attention to better balance those categories, what would you be doing different? Between you and your partner, is feedback welcomed regarding unbalanced priorities, or is it avoided?

5. **Do you know what your particular "Achilles' heel" is, when it comes to relationships?** How do the two of you attempt to protect the marriage from it becoming a problem?

6. **How much time do the two of you take to really talk – where problems, hopes, needs and fears are truly explored, supported or resolved?** How much of a voice does your relationship have compared to all the other demands in your life? If these are lacking, what are you going to do to make it right?

Chapter 4
Healthy Boundaries

Boundaries are the invisible relationship lines you draw for yourself, consciously or not, that separate you from your partner and the rest of the world. With different relationships, different depths of relationship, the boundaries are, or should be, noticeably different. For example, how you treat your best friend should be different from how you treat a stranger. How you treat your partner should be different from how you treat your best friend. The closer the relationship, the greater the depth of sharing and more privileges shown.

This was, for both Eli and Tonya, their second marriage. They'd been married for about 5 years now. Both were in their late 30's. They were coming in for couple's work for a variety of reasons. Tonya was feeling that Eli was overly critical of her. Eli was insecure about Tonya's behavior with other men. They weren't talking about divorcing, but they didn't want a repeat of their first marriages and were hoping to stop things before they got much further.

"It's true," Eli said, "that I can come off as being overly judgmental of her. It's almost a reflex, I guess, because, often, I don't even realize that I'm doing it until I'm halfway through it, or when she continues to point it out."

Tonya was nodding. "And that's my concern. It comes so easy to him. There's no asking me what's going on; he's already making these conclusions about my motivation for why I'm doing what he thinks

I'm doing. So it's these accusations that seem so inappropriate and hurtful."

"Well, you've got to admit, you do overdo it with men," commented Eli.

Tonya paused, pursing her lips. "I'm friendly, not a flirt. There's a difference."

"I don't think the men see the difference," replied Eli.

Tonya looked directly at me. "His first wife cheated on him and now he's paranoid that it's going to happen again. He knows I've never cheated on anyone in my life, but he's still insecure about us."

"You're gorgeous," said Eli. "Men are naturally going to want you. And when you're friendly, it gives them the wrong idea."

"I'm not your ex, Eli," said Tonya.

If I hold my finger out in front of me far enough away, I can see it clearly. If I move it further out, it loses focus. If I move it too close, it also loses focus. For many couples, the problem is not that they're too distant, but too close - in the same way that I am often too close to my own issues to have a clear perspective.

When I say "close", I'm not referring to intimacy, but rather "close" in terms of boundaries. The range of my vision and perspective extends to those people who are *outside* of my innermost boundary, but over time my partner will start to slip inside that boundary.

Unless we are consciously engaged in maintaining healthy boundaries with our partner, over time, those boundaries that are initially there begin to fragment. We come to see our partner, and sometimes even our kids, as no longer "separate", or "other", and no longer filter or edit the things we say or do in front of them. We expect them to think and feel like we do and judge them for it if they don't. We no longer give the benefit of the doubt that we would to our best friend, and we treat them with less regard than we do others. Our issues that we normally manage, now leak out onto them. They have fallen "under our radar" and are at risk of being taken for granted because we no longer see them as separate.

So what causes this shift? A number of things:

- Familiarity
- A failure to "edit"
- Defining reality
- A lack of benefit of the doubt
- Our own woundedness
- The formation of conspiracy theories
- Reactivity

Familiarity

Since familiarity is built into any long-term relationship, making it a likelihood that boundaries will diminish over time, what's a couple to do?

Much of the initial solution has to do with *awareness* of what's going on. Because we know familiarity is going to lead to recurring blind spots, we can keep its occurrence from becoming personalized when that blind spot shows itself. There's enough emotional perspective intact that we can stay focused on the problem as a momentary loss of our own boundaries rather than something that's uniquely wrong with us or our partners.

"So, when you talk about Eli being judgmental, is that only concerning you giving men the wrong impression?" I ask.

"No, not at all," answers Tonya. "He's critical about how I take care of the house, the things that I cook, how I spend my time. He's convinced I don't really care about what's important to him. He doesn't like my job and feels it takes time away from us. He'd prefer that I don't work at all, though we still have plenty of time at home together."

"How much time do you spend at work?"

"The typical 40 hours. And it's not like I go out a lot, either."

I look to Eli. "Do you agree with what Tonya's saying?"

"Yes," he nods. "It's a regular full-time job. I just like the idea of her being at home when I get home."

"So how much do you miss each other by?"

"She gets home about 30 minutes to an hour after I do," replies Eli.

"So, Tonya," I continue. "About how long into the relationship did the criticism start? Did you see it when you were dating?"

"No," she says. "It didn't start until about 6 months to a year after we married."

"Was there anything that changed at that time that you can think of?" I ask.

"No, it just changed and I have no idea why."

When a couple buys a home together they are typically drawn to it because of all the special perks and qualities that make it unique and a good fit for them. Two years later, in that same home, you will often witness a shift in what the couple is attending to. Now the focus is not on the perks, but on the projects. *What is noticed is everything that needs fixed - not what's working.* We have to consciously stop and focus on those perks again in order to start appreciating them anew.

It's the same with couples. Because of familiarity over time, a couple starts to lose touch with the things that drew them together, and begins to over-focus on the problem areas. They stop doing the very things that drew them together in the first place – one of which is treating each other respectfully. At some point, if this goes unchecked, and all that's discussed is the ongoing work, the overall perception of the relationship becomes biased due to over-focusing on each other's faults.

It doesn't even mean that anything drastic has changed in the relationship, or *to* the relationship - all that has changed is the focus.

Another example of focus would be the depressed or angry client. For her, the glass is usually half empty. No matter what the situation, she'll find the negative in it. For somebody else who has a glass half-full mentality, he is always finding the good. The point is, if you are looking to find the negative, it's always there. But so is the positive.

❖   ❖   ❖

Often we may be doing a good deed in the moment, but because it wasn't what our partner needed most, it's seen as a negative. Because of familiarity, it becomes easy for our partner to assume that because we *do* know them so well, if we didn't give the help they needed, the way they needed it, it must be an intentional choice on our part - therefore we're being insensitive or uncaring. The good deed, or the underlying positive intent goes completely missed, or misjudged.

For example, a husband comes home and sees the lawn needs mowed, so he takes care of it, but the wife's upset because it was more important to her to have some help with the kids. Now if she'd told him that, and he went for the lawn anyway, it would be one thing. But if she hadn't, she'd just expected him to know what she needed, that's a loss of boundaries. He isn't in her head. Him mowing the lawn was still a positive because it was tending to the home as well. It would be wrong for her to conclude that he didn't "get" her, or that he wasn't interested in the family. Now if there was an ongoing *pattern* of doing everything else but being with the family when he was home, there may be something more to address, but it still comes back to educating each other about what we specifically need rather than just expecting it to happen.

Many times couples will be complaining that the partner doesn't do "anything" around the house, yet when it comes to itemizing things, there are several things that they do, just not the specific ones that the other is focusing on. So there are still positives that deserve recognition if the issue is going to be addressed in a balanced way.

Now, some people, even though guided to what's needed most, will stubbornly continue to do those things that *don't* work for the relationship, insisting that their positive intentions still be credited. They have to recognize that, good intentions or not, if it doesn't work for the relationship, they need to work at changing that particular behavior. (If she's only looking for a listening ear but he keeps trying to solve her issues for her, at some point he has to step back and let go of his need to do so, recognizing that his way of helping, isn't helpful.)

Eli was a very insecure fellow, and it started before his current marriage. When Eli's boundaries started to fail, Eli's issues started to spill out onto

Tonya. Because he was no longer seeing her as separate, he was unable to distinguish his own issues from hers.

Often, an aspect of insecurity is a tendency to be self-critical. Eli began to be just as critical of Tonya as he was with himself.

A second level to this is that at the heart of most insecurity is a fear of failure, judgment, rejection or abandonment. **The problem with fear, once it goes beyond a healthy concern, is that, if we allow it to control us, we tend to create the very situations that we're afraid of.** Eli had already had one major romantic loss in his life. He was afraid of losing Tonya. But he was the one, at least in part, doing the things that were pushing her away. He was creating his own rejection, but was too close to it to see it. His positive intent, to express his concerns and hold his partner accountable, wasn't being applied in a way that worked for his partner, or for him.

A Failure To Edit

At the beginning of a relationship, when the boundaries are still clear, we have a filter in place that allows us to edit what we say. We are thinking about who we are talking to and how we can help them understand what we're trying to communicate.

Those healthy filters allow us enough perspective, and emotional distance, that we can separate our own fears and insecurities from reality. But filters need enough time to process what we're going to say before we say it. For many couples, the problem is that they no longer allow much time for any filtering to take place.

People with poor boundaries don't take the time to self-edit. They say what's on their minds whenever something's on their minds, assuming that everybody's going to take what they're saying the way they meant it. The term **egocentrism** applies to such situations where we think everybody thinks like us, or should. Their expectations in relationships are that everybody else should just adjust to, or understand, their unedited statements and behavior rather than accept that it's their actions that might need some changing.

The tendency for most people is to take short cuts, whether it's in the name of efficiency or laziness, and a couple is no different. Over time, we don't wait to hear our partners out. We don't listen as intently. We don't put as much thought into our responses. Because we feel so comfortable with our partners, we believe that we don't have to put as much effort into editing - they'll just automatically understand us, or *should* understand us.

When they don't respond the way we want them to, when they misunderstand, rather than considering that it's how *we* were trying to communicate that might be the problem, we automatically look at them as being at fault.

Eli's comments to Tonya were partly problematic because his criticisms were across the board – her public behavior, her cooking, her homecare. He may have been in the habit of making random observations without recognizing that there was a critical nature to all of it – and how much those criticisms were piling up for Tonya.

❖   ❖   ❖

Aside from familiarity, what makes editing more difficult is when outside factors take our attention away from our necessary internal filtering. As life circumstances get piled on (new job, kids, a move, family problems), we become distracted from the finer details of communication.

Since most of us weren't even aware we were using a filter, we tend to be at a loss as to why things are suddenly not working as efficiently. We know we've become more stressed by things and people are starting to tell us we're becoming short or blunt with them, but often we're too caught up in what's going on outside of us that we're really not attending to what's going on on the inside.

Because we're no longer taking into account the differences between us and those closest to us, we're now talking in ways that no longer respectfully communicate an awareness of that difference. Because we're no longer editing ourselves, managing what goes on within, that uncontrolled flow that's coming out of us is typically all about self, since we've stopped thinking about its impact on others. And that is often what relationships deteriorate into. **Relationships usually start by being all about the relationship, but, if filters are abandoned, it ends up being**

all about self. Who's been hurt the most? Who's had to give up the most? Who's the most at fault?

Paradoxically, **we have to start focusing again on ourselves** *in a healthy way,* **on our own behavior, restoring the filters, in order to stop making it all about us.**

❖   ❖   ❖

When you consider family histories, an interesting thing happens regarding filters for those couples who are trying to *not* be like their parents. Perhaps the couple grew up in families where the model they had of how to be a husband/wife or a parent was a very negative one. In their own present-day marriage, if they're aware of those negative family influences and are working at keeping them from re-occurring in their own, that information has been consciously added to their filters of how to not behave.[3]

However, when the relationship gets stressed or becomes distracted (either because of things within or without the marriage), and the filters get dropped, the negative parent or partner model will still often show itself.

When it's just the two in the marriage, the husband and wife, the filters usually stay intact longer because there aren't as many distractions. But when we add kids to the picture, it's relatively common to see at least one parent stepping back in shock at some point and recognizing, "I'm being my mom," or, "That was my dad talking."

The filter was dropped. Time to put it back in place.

---

[3]   Let me underline the fact that I said *consciously* added. For many couples that don't pay attention to the models from their past (possibly thinking that the past has no influence on the present), because there is no conscious alteration to those filters, the negative parent/partner models of the past show themselves much more quickly because we never adjusted our filters to keep them out.

Benefit of the Doubt

"So, Eli," I said. "When you see Tonya around a guy and she's being friendly, where does your mind go with it?"

Eli gives it a moment.

"Well, I automatically think that she's giving him the wrong idea."

"She's making him think she's interested." I clarify.

"Yes," he affirms.

"And then where do your thoughts go from there?"

"Well, I get upset about what he's probably thinking about her."

"That he's judging her?"

"No, that he's starting to fantasize about her. That he's looking at my married wife like she's available when she's not."

"And what are you thinking about Tonya?"

"How could she do this to me? Why doesn't she care enough about me that she would be more careful around other men?"

"So you conclude that she doesn't care about you." I add.

"Not that she doesn't care about me at all, but that she's not really committed to us."

Not only are failing boundaries where we start to take shortcuts with our own communication, but we also take shortcuts with how we interpret our partner's actions.

Most couples, unless things have grown chronically hostile, don't actively seek to start a fight. We don't usually look for ways to hurt our partners or start a conflict.[4] Most people don't enjoy getting upset. Most couples actively try to avoid conflict. Yet many arguments start over what's *assumed* to be intentional harm.

At the beginning of a relationship, most couples are actively giving the *benefit of the doubt*. In other words, if there's room to assume something negative about my partner, I'm going to err on the side of the positive until I have better evidence to the contrary.

But, because we become so familiar with each other over time, we start to make the assumption that we know each other inside and out. And, of course, one would hope you *do* get to know your partner well. But the potential problem with this is that it leaves no room for allowing that we can still be wrong about our partners.

Many of the couples I see are in constant conflict because many of the assumptions made about each other are *wrong*. And, more often than not, where they go wrong is with the *degree* of assumption they make.

With Eli and Tonya, Eli was chronically making assumptions about what Tonya's behavior meant. In his mind, things went from the *accurate* observation that she was being friendly with a man to "She's not committed to us," which was a possible distortion. It made sense that if he was making that conclusion that he would be upset. So it was the *degree* of the assumption that was the problem, as well as the *absence* of the benefit of the doubt.

Eli's observation that Tonya was being friendly with another man was not being debated. Taking that observation to the level of questioning her commitment turned a surface issue into something much deeper, making it about Tonya's character. Tonya did not have any history of infidelity. She was an extrovert, a naturally social person, but she had never been unfaithful. For Eli to make these conclusions about her character, and her commitment, based on a surface behavior with no substantial evidence (other than his *own* history), was extremely hurtful to her. She felt that she had earned his trust, but was not being given the benefit of the doubt.

---

[4]   Though some like a good debate.

At the same time, I'm not saying that Eli shouldn't have an issue with Tonya's behavior around men. Just because Tonya had never had an affair before, did not make her immune to one. She *did* need to be careful that she didn't give men the wrong idea by being overly friendly. That didn't mean she needed to be rude or rejecting, just have an increased awareness of the difference between friendly versus *overly* friendly. Maybe Eli didn't even want Tonya to be friendly. Maybe Tonya's behavior *was* overly friendly. It would require further discussion to better define what was and wasn't "okay".

Because this was an area of woundedness for Eli, he was not going to be able to just "get over it". The discussion would need to focus on how Tonya could positively safeguard Eli's feelings in public situations in realistic ways, and, further, what Eli needed to do to stop agitating his own wounds.

In the micro-seconds before we decide that we have an issue with our partner, we are just observing what's going on around us, just taking in the moment. We may be fully focused on that moment, or just partially attending to it - which ultimately effects the accuracy of how well we interpret it. Once we start interpreting our observation, we're now forming an assumption of what it meant. The further we take that assumption, reading into it, without taking the time to seek further *external* evidence of its truth or falsehood, the greater the likelihood we're going to be reading too much into it.

Stereotypically, men don't go deep enough with their communication, failing to looking for deeper meanings or implications. Women tend to do the opposite, reading too much into simple communication.

And couples that have failing boundaries tend to read into the gaps of information the things that would be the most hurtful to them.

He says, in a neutral tone, "Are you going to wear that tonight?" wondering whether or not she's going to need time to change before they go out.

She verbally reacts in a hostile tone with, "What's wrong with what I'm wearing?"

The gap in the conversation, what went unsaid, was her immediate assumption that he was criticizing, when he wasn't.

"Benefit of the doubt" says that if something was said or done that was hurtful to us, we should take the time to *ask* and *explore* before we *conclude.*

The benefit of the doubt entertains the bigger picture that there are always any number of reasons for why we do what we do. Rather than cling to one rigid assumption, we need to be recognizing that there are other potential factors than the ones we most quickly hang onto.

Because in the past there may have been times when the assumption was correct, now that assumption is applied *every* time whenever there is room to read into things. Just because it was true once, doesn't mean that's always going to be the correct conclusion.

Woundedness

I mentioned the word "woundedness" when I referred to Eli. When a couple talks about "walking on egg-shells", they're often referring to a relationship that is trying to survive by focusing solely on not agitating the wounds, which is different than actually trying to help heal the wounds.

A wound is recognizable by the severity of the reaction. When a partner over-reacts to an issue (more than would seem warranted), it's usually an indication of a wound.

Our woundedness typically leads us to over-react to our partners and give up our respectful communication because of how intensely we are feeling, and how personally we are taking things.

Some wounds go as far back as childhood. Some wounds are created in prior relationships. Some wounds we've created within our own current relationships.

Eli's prior marriage, the affair that ended it, was obviously a major wound for him. It caused him to be overly-sensitive to anything that was a reflection of that wound in his relationship with Tonya, and contributed to his difficulty continuing to separate her from his former partner – it affected the boundaries.

There is a strong parallel between a physical wound and an emotional one. If a wound fails to be treated, it can become gangrenous and destroy the rest of the body – just as an emotional wound can destroy a relationship.

If a physical wound continues to be re-opened, it will not get better and will likely worsen – just as a relationship wound can continue to be agitated by a partner, or even the wounded individual herself sometimes can't stop picking at it.

As with a physical wound, it can get to the point where the emotional wound has become numb. It's not that the wound is better, but it has gone through such sensory overload, too much pain, that it has lost its ability to feel. When a partner talks about having become emotionally numb, feeling like she doesn't feel anything anymore for her partner, often it is the result of having been re-wounded to the degree that the feelings became so negatively overwhelming that the wounded person simply emotionally shuts down. This is an important point to make because **there is a difference between feeling nothing for my partner, versus having become emotionally numb due to being hurt too much for too long**. With the latter, at least there's hope that if the re-wounding is stopped, in time, the feeling will come back.

Part of the initial work with wounds is identifying what wounds we actually possess. We have to know what it is we're trying to heal if we're going to be successful, just as a physical wound needs to be diagnosed in order to be appropriately treated.

We go off, we over-react, but we have no idea why. Yes, what was said or done hurt, but not to the degree that it justified that degree of response. So why was that such a sensitive thing for us? We have to be able to step back and explore it.

Once we know what the wound is about, we have to strategize what we need to do to help heal it. The solution requires two parts: 1) what we can do ourselves to keep from feeding or agitating the wound, and 2) what we need from our partners to help us heal.

The idea is to first recognize what's going on (reacting) and step beyond it – to restore some sense of perspective rather than continuing to just get sucked into the same reaction time and time again.

We need to be working at isolating negative events, trying to treat the issue at hand in terms of just the current incident. We are trying to restore perspective because otherwise each incident is taking on the full weight of all those other incidences as well, and the negative meaning we have been attaching. Because each negative event is now connected to that wound, it is easy to be emotionally overwhelmed unless we start to step back and treat the incidences individually rather than as a whole.

On the other end, if I know this is a wound for my partner, then I'm likely to be able to give a little more room for her reaction, because I know it's about something bigger than just me.

Conspiracy Theories

"So when Tonya stays firm that she wants to continue to work, rather than stay at home and be there for you at the end of the day, how do you interpret that?" I continued.

"Well," said Eli. "Part of me knows she has a right to work just like I do. But there's another part that, when she seems so rigid to not even consider the idea, the message I get is that her job's more important than me."

"And the house? When she hasn't kept it up the way you would like her to, how do you interpret that?"

"Again," said Eli. "That if she cared more about me, she'd make it more of a priority – that she's not committed to us."

"Does she actually put effort into cleaning the house?" I asked.

"Yes, I think she tries," he acknowledged.

"And the meals? Tonya said you get picky about how she cooks."

"Not all the time. It's just that, sometimes, she knows what I like and what I don't, and there are times, when she chooses not to do it the way I like. It adds up."

"So it becomes one more way of showing that she doesn't love you enough," I conclude.

"Yes," said Eli.

One aspect of woundedness is the occurrence of **conspiracy theories**. In a relationship, conspiracy theories are those conclusions we've made about our partner that either feed our own fears about our partner's true motivation, or support character judgments of them that feed our anger.

Eli's conclusion of "She doesn't love me enough," was a conspiracy theory.

Part of the problem with conspiracy theories is that, just as we can always find the negative in any situation if we look hard enough, any action our partner engages in, good or bad, can be interpreted in a way that feeds the theory.

Most conspiracy theories start out with accurate surface facts. Tonya *wasn't* embracing the idea of staying home. She *didn't* keep house exactly the way Eli liked. She *didn't* cook every meal to cater to him. So the initial observations were accurate. How Eli made sense of it all was to take each of these different pieces and find the common thread that would fit it all under one theory. But *the part his conspiracy theory left out were the details that **didn't** fit*. After work, Tonya *was* taking time for him. She *did* work at keeping the house clean. She *did* cook meals for him. He was over-focusing on the details of his preferences, rather than on her actual efforts to meet his needs.

Once the theory is in place, when we are presented with information that contradicts the theory, we tend to dismiss or minimize that information. It's not uncommon that, when a partner actually does what the other asks, the first response is "You only did that because I asked you to, not because you wanted to." But the fact is that if change is initiated, it should be recognized, not shot down. Once a theory is in place, we can become our own worst enemy - undermining the very change we desire.

It's important to recognize in assessing each other's behavior that what we do in the moment isn't always reflective of the bigger picture. Just because we have moments of selfishness doesn't make us selfish people. Just because there will be times when we don't think of our partner first, it doesn't mean we don't care.

A couple needs to pay attention to noticing destructive *patterns*, recurring negative themes, that may indicate a need for approaching accountability with each other, while making an even greater effort to keep those observations balanced with the rest of the information available – all of those times where the pattern *doesn't* occur.

Eli had a right to voice his concerns about what he saw happening with Tonya. It was his place to be able to state his *preferences* about how his food was cooked, how Tonya acted around men, etc. The problem occurred only when those preferences were given too great a priority, and were interpreted as much deeper things than they should have.

Defining Reality

One of the most frequent dilemmas with believing that we know our partners inside and out is seen when it comes to how we **define reality** for each other.

Defining reality is when we insist that we know what our partners are thinking or feeling, even when they're saying it's something different.

Now, we *do* learn things about our partners that they may not be able to see. We have the benefit of being an observer of them which provides a perspective that they do not possess. But when we place ourselves in the role of God, and start telling them what's going on inside of them, despite what they say to the contrary, we're shutting them out of the conversation.

Eli's conspiracy theory that Tonya didn't love him enough was also defining Tonya's reality for her. Thankfully, Eli was still open to hearing contradictory information. If it had gone to the extreme, Eli would have been saying "I *know* you don't love me," and there wouldn't have been anything Tonya could have done to change his mind.

Other examples of defining reality might be:

"You're just saying that because you feel guilty."

"You think you're better than everybody else."

Benefit of the doubt says "I will never know my partner completely, and I have to remain open to taking into account her perceptions of herself or I'm shutting myself off from necessary outside information that would help balance my own thinking".

Yes, in some relationships the problem has been that one partner has chronically lied to the other, and so nothing she says can be trusted. The lying has become a wound in the relationship. Yet, at some point, if the relationship is going to go forward, there will have to be risks taken to again trust the partner's word. (Hopefully, she will also be able to provide evidence to support that the truth is being told.)

Because the boundaries grow vague, often we don't even recognize that we've stopped seeking our partner's input. We're filling in all the missing pieces with our own conclusions as to why they do what they do. Yet, even if what we're guessing they feel/think is accurate, and they confirm this, it won't change the fact that it's a potentially dangerous shortcut.

No one likes being told what they think or feel. It's inherently invalidating. To take up such a position doesn't invite any actual two-way conversation. If you've already decided what your partner thinks and feels, then why even have a conversation with her? You can play out the entire dialogue without even asking her to take part. While that might sound slightly caustic, that is the message the partner hears. "Why should I even respond to what you say if you've already decided everything for me?"

If conspiracy theories persist, and we're unwilling to change our perception *despite* contradictory evidence, it can get to the point where our assumptions really don't allow for a relationship to continue. After all, if our conclusion about our partners' motivations is a significantly negative judgment of their character, how can we remain in such a relationship for very long if that is how we see them, and why would they want to remain knowing that is what we thought of them?

❖   ❖   ❖

There is an in-between with this where defining reality *can* be safely approached. When we say "I'm concerned that you *might* feel like…", or "I'm worried that you *might* think…", then we're allowing that we could be wrong, and we're inviting our partner's input for confirmation.

In terms of respectful communication (and just plain fairness), why adopt such a closed way of communicating that we ourselves wouldn't respond positively to it if our partners were doing it to us?

Reactivity

For enmeshed, wounded couples that have stopped editing, whose conspiracy theories fly freely back and forth, and who have totally abandoned the benefit of the doubt, they have deservedly earned the title of **reactive**.

When I use the word "react", I'm talking in terms of a couple going with instinct, which is either fight or flight. Either they are attacking or withdrawing pre-maturely from the conversation. And each person is allowing the other's behavior to decide what their next step will be.

Eli and Tonya were not yet reactive. They weren't happy with the situation, but they were still able to explore issues without everything deteriorating into mud-slinging.

Withdrawing may be seen as helpful, if it's avoiding a fight, but, more often, during the early part of an argument, if one person withdraws too soon they've lost an opportunity to get at the real issue. She's made an assumption about her partner's intentions/motives, but she isn't staying in the conversation long enough to find out if she was correct. Withdrawing can end up being avoidance, which doesn't solve things any better than an attack; it simply delays the issue and fosters a building resentment.

If an **attack** is the chosen behavior, it's usually an expression of anger. This may be done in terms of a judgment ("I can't believe you could be that insensitive.") or an attempt to parent the partner's behavior ("You need to get your act together.") through verbally consequenting them or trying to control them. For many, they think they are identifying the problem by voicing their anger, but anger is the *surface* emotion that covers up the *hurt* underneath. It leads the partner *away* from what really needs to be explored.

An attack rarely works because it's automatically putting your partner on the defensive. Vulnerability promotes vulnerability. Ownership promotes ownership. Attack promotes attack.

To "talk from the hurt", or the heart, is to remain vulnerable and open to new information. It is still expressing the hurt, and even the anger, but doing it in a controlled way rather than falling back on insults and judgments. It is an attempt to educate your partner about your pain in a way that she can receive it, understand it, and apply it.

Usually, why we are hurt is because we care. Yet the fact that we care is the last thing that we advertise during an attack. If we can connect our partners to the fact that the reason we are angry or upset is because we love them, and that love was just seemingly attacked, rejected or stepped on, we're likely to get a vulnerable response in return rather than an attack back.

An example of "talking from the hurt" would be, "That was really upsetting to me, and this is why..." or, "When you say/do that, this is what that means to me..." Rather than giving them something to react to, we are providing necessary information about how their behavior impacts us.

It's not talking in a detached unemotional way. You can still convey anger or hurt in your voice, getting the emotion out, without resorting to being inappropriate.

Remaining vulnerable goes *against* instinct. It is unnatural - which is why it's so hard to do. Yet if the goal is for us to be understood, rather than just hurt them because we've been hurt, we have to understand that an attack doesn't accomplish this.

Choosing to remain vulnerable is choosing to remain in control of ourselves.

❖   ❖   ❖

You have to be willing to commit to *staying* vulnerable in the conversation. Many will initially attempt to be vulnerable, but if the partner continues to attack, will fall back into an attack pattern themselves. You have to completely remove *your* inappropriate part from the interaction. If they are the only ones saying or doing the inappropriate things, it's much easier to sort out and see who's being the problem than if both of you are attacking.

Somebody might say, "Well, that's not fair. Why should I be a verbal punching bag for my partner?" Well, because a relationship should never be "an eye for an eye". It's about being an Adult, rather than regressing to the tactics of a Child throwing a tantrum or a controlling, judgmental Parent. I'm not suggesting you tolerate verbal abuse. There does come a time in a conversation, if it's not productive, where you do need to shut it down, but you do that by respectfully stepping away not by aggressing back.

❖   ❖   ❖

A reactive couple reacts to each others reactions. They are engaged in a recurring control struggle, though each is actually giving up their control by allowing the partner's behavior to decide their own.

Usually a reactive pattern doesn't develop until the couple has stopped trying to balance things. At the start of a romantic relationship typically there is one who speaks and one who listens. One who vents, and one who soothes. And, hopefully, the couple takes turns with those roles. The reactive couple is no longer able to respect that balance. Now, because both have lost perspective, they're both assuming the *same* role of reactor – and so they share the same blind spot when it comes to stepping out of the reactive cycle.

The center of reactivity is an *over-focus* on the other's behavior, and a lack of focus on our own. We step away from being the person that we need to be in the situation, because we are no longer examining ourselves. And we end up behaving in ways that cause us to lose self-respect, all because we were staying focused on the wrong person.

In a reactive cycle, since each is dependent on the other's reaction, all it takes for things to improve is *one* of the two to step out of the destructive interaction. In my books on conflict resolution, I spoke of **healthy exits**, where, when the conflict has become too destructive, one person removes herself from the conflict, but does it in a respectful way. This is something very different than *reactively withdrawing*, which is just another way of controlling the argument.

A healthy exit is telling my partner things are getting too heated, and that we need to step back and regroup. It's not storming out of the room or throwing in one last insult before I shut down the conversation. And it's committing to a time-frame when the issue will be re-approached. Further, whoever is shutting down the conversation assumes responsibility to bring the issue back within that timeframe.

For reactive couples, there is far too much attention given to finding fault. Words are being *over-scrutinized* for any hint of offense.

In terms of accountability, the couple may be trying to address issues that really do need to be addressed, but they've completely forgotten about approaching it in a respectful way and are automatically resorting to judgment and rejection. We don't inspire change this way, yet the couple has become so absorbed in the struggle, they keep forgetting that the reactive approach rarely, if ever, works.

If boundaries remain intact, a couple is unlikely to become reactive because they don't lose sight of themselves. In fact, they are at an advantage because they see the partner as separate and are able to think in terms of how that partner thinks and feels, as well as remembering what the wounds are for each. If the partner *should* react, the other has enough emotional distance from the reaction that they can think in terms of "What's really going on here?", "Where's that coming from?", and "How can I get at what she needs from me?" or "How can I communicate what I need from her?"

That emotional distance isn't so far removed that we're emotionally beyond being hurt. The words still sting, but they don't manage us to the degree that we get pulled back into the reactive cycle. We're able to stay focused on either clearing up a potential misunderstanding, move on to seeking solutions for the particular issue at hand, or shut things down if now is too emotionally intense.

My Best Friend

"So how long did the two of you date before you got married?" I asked.

"Several months," said Eli. "We hit it off pretty quickly."

"Was it a head-over-heels experience, or did you feel like you were taking your time to get to know each other?"

"I think we were both a little out of control," Eli answered.

One of the important steps for couples during the dating years is to build both a friendship as well as a romance, taking the time to get to know each other rather than running passionately full-steam ahead. There is a deeper reason for this that plays out during the married years, moreso than just assurance of compatibility. Typically, when a marriage comes under attack, if all that exists is the romantic relationship, when it fizzles there's nothing left for the couple to fall back on. The relationship is in dire straits.

If a friendship existed as well, there is a safety net for the marriage. While we're not getting along as husband/wife, we still have the friendship to act as a buffer. The distinction is that a friendship recognizes love still exists even though things might currently be stressed. There is also a greater degree of latitude/acceptance that typically goes along with a friendship.

During the times when the boundaries start to fail and we start to treat our partners like they're us, or our worst enemy, we need to have some sort of template to use that acts as a guide to restoring respectful behavior. Because my partner is in my blind spot, and often no longer a model of respectful behavior herself, I need to move her far enough away emotionally that I can regain some perspective on my own behavior.

One aid is using people that are still clear in your vision as a model of what to do. The question "How would you be treating your best friend?" becomes very relevant. (Though it makes the assumption that you have, or have had, a best friend, and treated her respectfully.)

Hopefully, the clearer boundary for a best friend is someone that you:

- Take time to listen to
- Give the benefit of the doubt
- Exercise patience with
- Apply grace to their shortcomings
- Speak to respectfully

If you have both a friendship as well as a marriage, these concepts are already intact, and tend to be applied more easily. For those without that friendship, it is having to learn to think in terms of "friend" while the marriage is being re-built.

❖   ❖   ❖

Similar to this concept is how you can use the idea of "others" to help come up with solutions. Because we're too close to the problems, we often feel lost in terms of thinking up solutions. But if we think in terms of "How would you counsel a friend or family on this kind of issue?", suddenly we can think of options that we couldn't before.

My Ideal Self

"Do you feel like the two of you have drifted from being the people you know you should be?" I continued.

"Most definitely," said Tonya. "I don't like who I'm becoming anymore than I like who Eli is changing into."

Most people have an ideal of who they should be in the relationship that goes beyond roles. If you ask a man or woman, "When you think of being a loving partner, how does that person behave?", most people have a pretty good sense of what loving looks like, and that's usually why they're upset with their partner, because of how far the partner's strayed from that. But as far as how that same ideal applies to them, they may no longer be attending to it with any conscious intent. They've become distracted.

What couples need to realize is that they lose their own sense of integrity and self-worth in a relationship by acting in inappropriate ways with each other. **If my focus remains on who I need to be in this relationship, what the personal ideal is that I'm trying to live up to, *regardless* of what my**

105

partner is doing to complicate it, then I am restoring an awareness of the positives still within my control.

There is still room for accountability with my partner's inappropriate behavior, but now, at least, *my* behavior is not a complicating factor as well. Since this is not a competition, I'm not going to be advertising to my partner how much better I'm behaving than they are (which would create another level of issues). I'm just going to be a positive model of that behavior.

This does not mean there is no anger if I'm upset. It just means I am modeling discipline over how I express that anger. My focus remains on me being a healthy me regardless.

Somebody Else's Perspective

"So what's the support system for each of you? Do you both have close friends or family in the area?" I asked.

"Both of our families are out-of-town. I have several good friends that I talk to on a regular basis, but Eli is pretty isolated. He's got work and home and that's about it," Tonya replied.

Men tend to be less relationship-based than women, and are more likely to get themselves into a corner because they have no close friends, and do not feel the need for close friends - until a crisis hits. Because men tend to be more private, and less likely to advertise their personal business, even if they have friends they will often not discuss their marital struggles.

One key to seeking out supportive friendships is choosing to consult with people that are relatively unbiased, which is why family is often a not-so-good choice. If you know your mother doesn't like your wife, then it would not be a good idea to consult with your mother *about* your wife. Similarly, if your best friend is celebrating a recent divorce, then she may not be the best person to talk to about trying to make the relationship work. Usually women have a better grasp on women, and men are better able to explain other men – but you have to be very careful here because seeking out opposite-sex friends to discuss your partner is often the groundwork for how emotional affairs begin. With emotional affairs, there is a *pattern* of routinely discussing the personal details of your marital life.

A second key to supportive friendships is having a couple in your life that has gone further than you have. In hard times, such a couple can serve as mentors to help show you the way. Hopefully, you don't wait until the hard times to seek that advice, since prevention is the preferred route to take.

For many, "someone else's perspective" means a professional counselor. Because a counselor is there to represent both sides, there is a better chance for balance. Preferably, this is also a "relationship specialist", since you wouldn't go to a general practicioner for specialized surgery.

At the point we're in jeopardy of losing perspective, typically, our partners' voices are the last ones we're willing to view as credible. But we can't afford to just rely on our own viewpoints, especially if strong emotions are involved.

Environment

"So when these arguments occur, is there a particular setting? Usually at home, out in public – does there seem to be a pattern?" I continued.

"I usually don't say anything in front of other people," said Eli. "If something happens in public, I'll wait until we're back in the car. Most of our arguments happen at home, though."

Because home is such a familiar place, it almost supports forgetting about treating each other as separate. We automatically want to just be able to relax and be ourselves, without having to worry about such menial things as "editing".

For those couples that have done well at doing the work of the relationship, there is room for this. We don't always have to be on guard with everything we say. We know our partner understands us well enough that we have room to be "human". Teasing isn't taken seriously. What could be regarded as offensive is instead given the benefit of the doubt. Mild lapses in behavior aren't harshly judged or immediately seen as issues of character.

It's when the evidence of our communication says "She's not getting me", we need to step back and re-apply better boundaries, putting more intention into our communication.

Some people will intentionally choose to have their arguments in public, *not* because they like to advertise their "dirty laundry", or are exhibitionists, but because they're in a setting where other people can observe them, and things aren't so familiar. It automatically raises a degree of boundary that was difficult to get at home. **The scrutiny of other people makes us more aware of our own behavior.**

Some might say that that is "false" behavior, because we're on our best behavior in front of others, but it doesn't change the fact that the experience in itself raises the couple's awareness of their own behavior.

While we can't solve all our problems in public, hopefully we can gradually restore a healthier atmosphere at home by paying attention to the differences between who we are when we're observed and who we become when we're not.

Issues in the Moment

"Eli," I asked. "Do you think that you tend to bring these issues up after you've been sitting on them for a while, or is it more at the time that it's happening?"

Eli considered. "Probably as it's hitting me. Often I'll be kicking myself later that I brought it up at all, because I recognize that I'm turning into a nag. I don't want to be a pain to Tonya, but when something's bothering me it just tends to come out."

One of the patterns for most couples is that there is little, if any, time taken to prepare for raising an issue, expressing a concern, or making a criticism. We are thinking about it in that moment and so we start to talk about it.

Yes, we shouldn't always have to watch every word we're going to say, but that doesn't change the fact that *there will always remain a need for healthy filters.* There always needs to be a sense of my partner as "other", just as there needs to be a sense of "us". Separateness and togetherness in balance.

The more thought we've put into possible solutions for an issue, the easier it will be to keep the conversation focused on solutions versus blame.

The more thought we've put into our concerns, as to why they *are* concerns, the more effective we'll be in explaining ourselves.

It's also taking time to choose the setting of "when" and "where" to approach a discussion.

The more thought we've put into sharing a criticism, the better we'll be able to choose the approach of best fit for our partners, the one where we'll be most likely to be heard. And, by considering what works best with our partners, we're also having to think in terms of their perspectives. If we're truly able to do this, we're already restoring a degree of boundary because we are consciously thinking in terms of the distinctions between us and them.

Some people will say, "Well, I put a lot of thought into that before I said anything. That's why it built up to the degree that I exploded." But that is an example of feeling (emotional logic), not thinking (rational logic). If all you're doing is feeding your upset, you're not really thinking it through. You're dwelling on the emotional impact of the problem, and not considering positive outcomes.

Feeding your upset is typically focusing on what's *not* in your control (your partner's behavior). Focusing on positive outcomes to the dilemma – your delivery, the relevant points, possible solutions – is restoring a sense of control, because you're looking at what you *can* do to gain resolution.

It's this tendency to not take the time to think, not allow our filters to kick in, that keeps getting people into trouble.

Changing the Routines

A primary contributor to familiarity that's become unhealthy is the routines that have become too routine. Because we do the same thing, day after day, we've become mesmerized by these rituals that ultimately lull us to sleep. We no longer see our daily choices, but follow that pre-set path established by the roles we've taken on.

What helps to fight familiarity is choosing to do things that break up the routines in the relationship. If a courtship still exists, how routine has it become? If the relationship has become all about the roles, what do you need to do to restore some focus on the intimacy? How much energy do you still put into the little things, that aren't part of the routine, that show your partner you care?

By starting to restore a degree of freshness to the rituals of the relationship, even the chores, it can also restore awareness of our partner as separate and "other" – moving us away from just taking things for granted.

If my focus is back on the present and what I can do today to add a degree of variety to things, to have a little fun, to do something different, then I'm re-introducing choice and freedom into making the relationship into something positive again, rather than being lost in more of the same old routine, or over-focusing on the work.

Discussion Questions:

1) **Would you assess your marriage as either too distant, too close, or just right?** Do you feel like the boundaries between you and your partner are distinct or have started to become vague over time? What do you do to keep the boundaries visible?

2) **Are things being too routine a problem for your marriage?** If you were going to "break up" the routines, add some new things to make it more interesting, what would that look like? Are there any accountability routines for your relationship – ways you routinely discuss necessary change?

3) **Do you feel overall like you still do a good job of self-editing in the marriage, or more thought needs to go into what is said before it's said?** What things can you do to make sure you've given yourself some time to think before you speak?

4) **Does the benefit of the doubt still exist in your marriage?** If it's lacking, what do you need to do to bring it back?

5) **Looking at your own life, are there any particular emotional wounds, any particular sensitive areas, that you bring into your marriage?** Are there any wounds that the marriage itself has created? What are the two of you doing to help heal each other's wounds?

6) **Are there any "conspiracy theories" that exist in your relationship?** What do the two of you do to counter theories forming and keep the benefit of the doubt alive?

7) **How do the two of you attempt to manage your own reactions and the reactions of your partner?** Are you able to take "healthy exits" when things get too heated? If you get some space from a heated issue, are you able to re-approach and work things through to a resolution?

8) **Do you feel like your marriage is both a romance *and* a friendship?** Have you ever had a best friend? How did you treat them? Do you treat your partner better or worse than that best friend?

9) **When you think of being a loving partner, your own standard, what does that look like?** Is that standard any different than the reality of how you actually treat your partner?

10) **Do you ever seek other's opinions about your marriage?** Are those sources of advice reliable? Do you know other marriages that you respect and admire? If so, do you ever explore what makes theirs work?

11) **Is home an overly familiar place where it's easy to be on your worst behavior?** If so, what can you do to become more aware of your own behavior in your own home?

12) **Are issues raised in the moment, or do you take the time to think things through before you approach each other?** If in the moment, how well does that work for you? If it's clear you need to take more time to think, how do you go about doing that?

Chapter 5
Respectful Communication

The core of the two books I wrote on conflict resolution revolved around a model for conflict and the "ABC's of a fair fight" (26 rules and strategies for successful resolution). Yet, if I were going to summarize the conflict model and those 26 "rules" into just a few words, it would all come down to **respectful communication**.

The Words That We Use

Richard and Susan had only been married for a year, in their late 20's with no kids, but were already having significant problems.

"We got married about 3 months after we started dating," said Susan. "It was all very intense and passionate. Our friends were worried we were going too fast, but nobody could talk us out of it. So here we are completely surprised that we're acting in ways that we never thought we would," continued Susan. "We get into these angry fights and say the most hateful things to each other. I'm supposed to be his wife, yet there's times when he talks to me like I'm dirt."

"Hey," Richard put in. "When we were dating I never heard you curse once. Now you sound like a truck driver. So don't try to put all of that on me."

Manners are often the first thing to go.

"He doesn't compliment me like he used to."

"She doesn't say 'hello' anymore when I come in the door."

"He forgets to hold the door for me now."

"I never hear a 'thank you' from her."

"He never, ever apologizes, even when he knows he's wrong."

Manners will always, always, always have an important place in the relationship. Just because this is your partner who's seen you on the toilet, cleaned up after you when you were sick, heard and smelled your worst bodily functions, will never change the fact that she will always need a visible degree of respect and courtesy. She's not your best buddy; she's your mate.

Terms of endearment tend to slip away - from the simple "I love you" to the pet phrases we use for each other, to the compliments and praises we give.

"She knows that I love her. Why should I have to keep saying it?"

Well, it's true that "I love you" shouldn't become such a ritual that the words lose their meaning, but we *reinforce* the emotional connection by continuing to make these affirming, assuring statements.

Your partner will never grow beyond needing to hear verbal expressions of love and appreciation as long as the two of you are together. I can't say it any more clearly than that.

❖ ❖ ❖

Many times harsh language, such as cursing at each other, is evidence of a deteriorating relationship. For some couples, this is part of their everyday vocabulary, something they maybe grew up with, so there may not be as noticeable a negative shift, but it doesn't make it any less potentially destructive. It's one thing to curse when talking about your job, momentary frustrations, etc. but when you start to aim those cruel words towards your partner, it's the equivalent of character rejection.

What makes it okay to talk that way to the person you're supposed to love above everyone else? Because they upset you? So the underlying theme for the marriage then is "I'll treat you nice so long as you treat me nice, but if I'm not happy, then I'll treat you however I want to treat you." That's a child's mentality! And when a couple falls into that pattern it means that two adults have regressed into child roles, raising the question of emotional maturity.

Mutual Respect

"I'm not trying to put it all on you," replied Susan, "but I need to feel like I've got an identity in this relationship. I feel like I've given up my life to live yours, and you're not even happy with your own!"

"I don't *want* you to give up your identity," Richard returned. "But a lot of your ways aren't my ways. And they end up being problematic at times. I can't act like I'm okay with things that I'm not. I should be able to point them out and hope that some of them are going to change."

"So why is it that I'm the one who needs to change? Why isn't it on you?" asked Susan, irritably. "And why is it that everything that's not okay now, was okay for you before?"

Because Richard and Susan's relationship had quickly devolved into reactivity, it now revolved around a constant control struggle. Who was going to dominate and who was going to submit? Whose "shoulds" were going to be respected, and whose would be given up? It was becoming a struggle over identity.

Ideally, with balance, there should be a visible stretch on both sides – the focus being on creating win/win scenarios where each is getting the *core* of what they need from the other, even though it may not be the desired ideal. The focus is on "us", not self.

❖   ❖   ❖

There is a tendency over time for relationships, especially ones focused on just the roles, or those that are task-driven, to view each other's efforts towards the relationship as simply fulfilling one's "duty". Yet, if the relationship is something that promotes and inspires each of us, then we need to be giving credit where credit is due. If we want to retain a balanced perception of what our partner contributes to the relationship, then we need to be taking into account *everything* positive that they do.

If we're doing things in a relationship because we care, and not because we have to, then there should be some recognition of the choice that's involved. And we should also recognize that there's a degree of choice in the things that we ask of each other.

If everything is about "have to", then it's easy to begin feeling trapped. But if I'm staying in touch with, "I'm doing it because I care, *not* because I have to" then there's room to work because the motivation remains focused on what brought the two of you together in the first place.

Somebody might say, "Well, that's not true. I *do* have to. I made that commitment."

And I doggedly reply back, "Yes, you made a commitment, but everything you do under that commitment is a choice."

You don't *have* to be nice. You don't *have* to do chores. You don't *have* to remain faithful. You don't *have* to do any of that. You do those things because: 1) you care, 2) you *choose* to do them, and 3) they're the healthy things to do.

Those positive choices are what help retain your own self-worth. You need to be able to feel good about having made them, rather than viewing them solely as demands. You need to be able to give yourself conscious credit in the same way that we look to our partners to give us recognition for our efforts.

In terms of *preferences*, there is even *more* choice. If I know my partner wants the clothes done a certain way, I can still do it my way or I can go the additional mile and try to be more accommodating. Preferences are about *opinions* of what would be best for any particular situation, not "have to's", and so are visible opportunities to show we're going above and beyond by choosing to honor a preference. Hopefully, here too there is recognition of the extra effort taken, rather than just expectation that because we want it our partner should do it.

There should be a visible balance between whose preferences are being met. If it's primarily one person's preferences taking priority the majority of the time, that's a prediction for resentment over time, or loss of identity for the person who's attempting constant compliance.

❖   ❖   ❖

The potential glitch with "I'm doing it because I care," comes during those not-so-good times in every relationship where, for that moment, for that day, for that week, we're *not* feeling like we care very much. If my motivation was *solely* based on doing it because I care, then now I've possibly lost my motivation to continue to make an effort.

Hopefully, during those moments, there's also a part of some of those choices that has to do with "I'm doing it because it's the right thing to do." So, even when the positive feelings aren't moving me forward, I'm still able to rise to the occasion because I know those choices are good ones for the relationship whether I'm feeling it or not.

The reactive couple doesn't keep that in mind. For them, the choices are all dependent on the partner. If he's not motivated, then she's not going to be motivated. If she's not doing the right thing, he's not going to be doing what's right for the relationship either.

❖   ❖   ❖

When it comes to recognition of my partner as "other", I am re-attaching respect for several things:

- Respect for their time
- Respect for their property
- Respect for their cooperation
- Respect for their opinions

Respect for Their Time

"You used to have time for me, for us," continued Susan. "But now it's your job, or the computer, or your friends. I never had to compete with those things before."

"Susan, you were my sole focus when we were dating. It was impossible to maintain that kind of attention in the real world. I have to make a living. And I *do* have a life outside of you. Nowadays, it seems like you want me to be available for you all of the time, and you take it personal when I've got other things to deal with," said Richard. "That's just life! I want you to have a life of your own as well."

We naturally expect our partners to want to spend time with us. But we may go overboard in that we seem to think that they should give us that time exactly when we want it.

The stereotype of this is the woman walking into the room expecting the man to drop whatever he's doing and give her his full attention. A *respectful* interaction would be where the woman *asks* if it's a good time to discuss something that's important to her. A respectful *response* would be, if now's not a good time, committing to a time that would work for both.

The underlying rule behind this is to *ask*, not demand. Your partner is not your property. She's not supposed to jump when you say jump. Marriage is supposed to be an adult-adult relationship, not a parent-child.

If an issue is important to you, then the solution should be just as important, and you want to approach it as optimally as you can – at a time when you have your partner's willing, conscious attention. If it's under forced conditions, you have already partially set the environment to be an unmotivated one, because the typical motivation for the partner in that circumstance is to get it over with as quickly as possible so she can get back to what she was doing.

Yes, there are exceptions to this since, obviously, there are occasional issues that require an immediate discussion, and immediate, focused attention *is* required. But you're trying to avoid the other extreme where every little thing requires immediate attention.

I may not agree with how my partner spends her time, but if I'm avoiding passing immediate judgment on it ("That's a stupid sport." "Why do you waste your time on that?" "Why don't you do something useful?"), and showing respect for some of her rightful choices, I'm more likely to get her cooperation when it comes to the time that I need from her.

There are times when accountability has to play a part if someone is avoiding her responsibility in the relationship and consistently putting herself first. If this has been a continuing pattern, then her use of time needs to be directly addressed. But **what you are trying to avoid is where one person in the relationship has become the authority or judge on what constitutes what is "worthwhile" time for everyone else.**

Respect for Their Property

"You talk about feeling like you've given up your life for mine," countered Richard. "But when I look around our home I see a whole lot of you, and very little me! Half of the stuff that was mine is now either in storage or you threw out!"

"You said you were fine with that!" replied Susan.

"Well, I thought I was at the time, but now that you bring this stuff up I'm realizing that you're using a double standard," said Richard.

One of the expected hurdles for a couple is when they first move in together. They have to decide what's going to be kept and what's going to go. Sometimes this goes smoothly, and sometimes it's the first big fight of the relationship. It often shows how the couple approaches sacrifice when it comes to things of personal value. Do they respect each other's property or are there automatically judgments over what is "stupid" and "unimportant"?

How a couple decides to decorate a home is another reflection of this. Does one person dominate decisions on how the house is decorated, or is it a joint project? Are there judgments passed on each other's taste, or is there respectful consideration of those personal differences? Some couples will move past this easily enough because one person would really love to decorate and the other person could care less what it looks like. Problem solved.

Later, in a relationship, as the boundaries fade, the respect for each other's "stuff" often shifts. The judgments of the "stuff" come out more easily in conversation. She throws his old stuff out without telling him, or asking first. He starts to resent just how much "stuff" she's accumulating. Each starts to over-monitor, unspoken or not, the kinds of stuff the other is purchasing.

Yes, accountability still applies in terms of when acquiring "stuff" gets out of control or becomes too much of a priority, but, other than that, we're simply trying to avoid making material judgments of "them" based on "us".

Respect for Their Cooperation

"It feels like you'd be more than content to just leave all of the housework to me," said Susan, changing the subject.

"That's not it at all," said Richard. "You have very strong opinions about how the house should be, so it's easier to let you do it the way you want it, rather than try to argue about it."

"So where's the appreciation for how I do take care of it?" replied Susan.

"Well, where's the appreciation for letting you do it the way you want to?" responded Richard.

Chores are a central point of conflict for many couples, often because of role expectations. Yet, we shouldn't just be *asking* for our partner's cooperation with the things that need to get done; we also need to be expressing our gratitude for the help we get. (Hopefully, the expressed gratitude goes both ways.)

I often hear couples say, "She doesn't need to thank me for that", but, again, you have to be careful of the trends that you start. Appreciation always has a place. Recognition of the positive will always play an important part in the relationship. Completing a chore, no matter how minimal, is still a positive.

Overkill would be feeling that you had to notice every little thing, and that's not what I'm suggesting. All I'm saying is to keep a tradition alive of verbally recognizing the things you like that your partner does.

Not only is it about praise; it's also reinforcement. The more our partners feel we recognize and appreciate the positives that they do, the more they're going to be motivated to continue doing them. There is a subtle positive shaping going on where we are guiding them to what we appreciate the most.

For some, the positives are *internally* recognized, but not *outwardly* expressed. While we may feel we're still in touch with what our partners do well, we still need to go that extra step and let them know. Otherwise, there is always the risk of a gradual build-up of resentful feelings because it doesn't appear that we see, or appreciate, the things that they do for us.

There are some people that make a recurring error with praise. Praise for them looks like, "I really appreciate that you did <blank>, *BUT...*" In other words, "Thanks, but you messed up." It's really important that we try to separate the praise from the criticism. The reason I say this is because **if I end a compliment with a criticism, I've just negated the praise** - not intentionally, but that's the impact. If this is the traditional approach taken, then I'm shaping my partner to brace themselves whenever I'm giving a compliment, and possibly no longer be receptive to the compliments I have to offer.

When I have a couple do a needs list, they will most easily identify the needs that are least met. For those that already are having certain needs met, when you ask about the met needs the response will often be, "That isn't such a big deal for me". While that's true in the moment, it's often not until the need goes *unmet* that we recognize just what a big need it really was. **Because we take for granted the areas that our partner is already satisfying, we often don't give the recognition those areas deserve.**

Respect for Their Opinions

"I want to feel like I have a say in what happens in this relationship, yet it feels like things are just being assumed or taken for granted, without us talking about it," said Susan, adding yet another level to the conversation.

"I think that goes both ways," said Richard. "You're right, we don't really seem to talk about what we're going to do, we just do it, thinking that the other will be okay with it."

"I think it's crazy that we *both* see the other as controlling and selfish," continued Richard. "One of us has got to be wrong. We can't both be like that."

"Why does every opinion have to have a judgment attached?" asked Susan.

In new relationships, young couples such as Richard and Susan's will often not openly share information about what they do, or are planning on doing, because they don't yet practice accountability with each other. It's only over time that they realize that relationships require ongoing communication and comparing notes – at the beginning they will typically see the partner asking for information as being over-controlling rather than something that is a right and should be respected.

When it comes to sharing opinions:

Competitive couples constantly compete for whose opinion is best, or right.

Reactive couples constantly invalidate, dismiss or judge each other's opinions.

Passive couples constantly *avoid* giving their opinions.

Many couples will say that a big part of what attracted them to their partner was that they had so many opinions in common. Others might say they were so physically attracted to each other they never bothered to pay attention to what the opinions were. But it's not really about how many opinions you mirror for each other. What's more important is whether or not your partner's opinion helps balance your own, and how you continue to show respect for an opinion that's not the same as yours.

As I said earlier in the book, most of us, quite unintentionally, choose partners who have qualities that we lack. We're attracted to them because of how they balance us, or how they bring out something in us that we can't easily do on our own.

As time goes by, and the boundaries fade, those *necessary* differences become labeled bad, usually because at least one of the members in the couple is becoming rigid. The more entrenched a couple becomes in "his way" or "her way", the further they move away from remembering they're supposed to be finding "our way".

It's the mutual respect for each other's opinion that keeps each person feeling valued.

We may haphazardly tease each other about our opinions, but we have to be careful that we don't go too far. It's easy to create a tradition of teasing that can gravitate to something more rejecting, and less forgettable.

What makes it so dangerous to negatively judge our partners' opinions is that it will be perceived that we're rejecting them. The power of that rejection typically has to do with 1) how strong the judgment was, and 2) how important that particular opinion was to the person who held it.

The most valuable contributions our partners bring to the relationship, aside from what they do on a behavioral level, are their thoughts and feelings. If these aren't treated respectfully, it's going to directly impact their behavior towards us.

This isn't to say that we have to agree with everything our partners think or feel, but we will always need to be respectful of their thoughts and feelings. If we verbally invalidate or dismiss their opinions as being "silly" or "stupid", we just called our partner "silly" and "stupid". An opinion is an extension of the owner of the opinion.

Our partners will always have a right to their perspectives. They are not always going to be accurate or profound, but they are theirs to have, just like we have ours. We want ours to be respected, just like they do. Fair is fair.

And the reality is that *we need their perspective*. It's one of the reasons why they're there. We may not always like to hear another opinion, especially if it contradicts our own, but that is what matures and balances us as a couple.

Certainly there are going to be times when we do or say something that really is stupid. And, hopefully, we each have enough self esteem that we can admit it, or allow ourselves to be teased about it. What I am warning against is developing a negative tradition, especially when we are judging a thought or feeling that is close to our partner's heart.

❖   ❖   ❖

Now, in the same way that we need to respectfully *receive* opinions, we also need to be mindful of how we *give* our opinions.

I often hear complaints that "My partner doesn't listen to what I have to say." But two things need to be understood in these situations.

The first is that **listening to an opinion shouldn't obligate you to have to follow that advice.** Some people who give opinions feel that, "He didn't really listen to what I had to say because he didn't do what I suggested." But, your opinion is your opinion. It doesn't require being acted on to still be valued or heard. And just because it isn't acted on doesn't mean you should take offense and stop giving it when it's asked. After all, if they really didn't care about your opinion then why would they be asking again?

Note that I said "giving it when it's asked". Sometimes we *force* our opinions on our partners ("Here's what you need to do…") rather than asking if one is wanted first ("Can I offer a suggestion?"). If I try to force my opinion on my partner, I am already bordering on being unintentionally disrespectful, since it has the flavor of a parent attempting to control my choices.

The second thing is that **often our opinions aren't heard or respected because of *how* we express them.** If we want our opinions to be treated with respect, we need to state them in a respectful manner.

"You need to stop being so lazy, and get off your butt," while an opinion, is also a judgment. If my opinion is a judgmental one, why am I expecting that I'm not going to get a judgment in return? Because they shouldn't judge me in the same way I judge them?

We often sabotage intimacy by inviting opinions but then react to them once they're given. She asks him about his job. He expresses being stressed and not knowing how much longer he can keep doing it. Out of her own insecurity, she reacts to this and says something like, "You'd better not quit! You have a family to take care of!" to which he becomes defensive. He needed the room to vent and possibly discuss options, whereas she just taught him it wasn't safe to share such things with her.

Opinions are the pathways in to understanding our partners better - to drawing closer. If we rigidly have to find approval for every one, or can't get beyond our own issues to hear them out, we are keeping ourselves from the very closeness we say we desire.

Discussion Questions:

1. **Do manners still exist in your relationship?** Do you ask rather than demand? Do you feel like the two of you can still talk respectfully to each other even when you're upset?

2. **Do you feel that you get respect from your partner for:**

   - **your time?**
   - **your property?**
   - **your efforts?**
   - **your opinions?**

If not, *specifically* how are they not shown respect, and *specifically* how would you like to see respect restored?

Chapter 6
Timely Validation

When it comes to communication, the one mistake I see couples making most often is forgetting, or not knowing how, to validate each other. For those of you who think I'm talking about parking tickets, let me step back and explain what I mean by validation.

Validation is being able to acknowledge my partner's perspective, even if I don't agree with it. It's giving it "validity" by recognizing or being able to successfully communicate to her that her opinion counts.

Theresa and Henry, a couple in their late 30's, could never arrive at a resolution. They kept getting stuck on his viewpoint versus hers.

"She grew up in a family that had a lot of conflict," said Henry. "And I think it really traumatized her. She's constantly telling me I'm angry at her when my tone goes up just a little and so I don't have any room to speak unless everything stays very neutral. It's really frustrating."

"For me," said Theresa, "I feel like Henry doesn't acknowledge how I feel about anything. He's constantly telling me I shouldn't feel that way, or that I should just 'get over it'."

Theresa is pointing out that she doesn't feel that Henry validates her opinion, though she is referring specifically to how he doesn't acknowledge her feelings. If our feelings aren't acknowledged, respected, then we don't feel validated.

Validation is one part of a four-step process in working through issues that looks something like this:

1) Identify
2) Validate
3) Explain
4) Resolve

Obviously, at the start of an issue, if there's going to be resolution, you have to know what you're trying to resolve, so somebody has to go through the first step of *identifying* what the actual issue is ("I'm upset and this is why…"). The biggest dilemma with this step is your *delivery* – being able to present an issue in a respectful way that invites a conversation rather than pushes your partner away.

The second step depends on the circumstances. If there's a potential misunderstanding, an *explanation* is usually the best second step since it's likely to clear up whatever was misunderstood. If it's not a misunderstanding (there's an issue that needs worked through), then *validation* is the best second step.

Typically, the logic behind an explanation is that, "If I just explain myself, she'll understand what I was thinking and be able to let it go" – which means he's still assuming a misunderstanding is at the root of things. But if there *is* an issue, an explanation *by itself* is not going to resolve it. An explanation may enhance her understanding of why he did what he did, but it doesn't change the fact that what he did is still a problem for her.

After identifying an issue, the first thing she's looking for from him is to *acknowledge* her side, not counter it with his. If he steps in too soon with his perspective, rather than taking the time to understand hers, he's *unintentionally* invalidating hers.

This is where couples become polarized. She restates her issue, and he restates his perspective. Because each is waiting for the other to acknowledge *their* viewpoint, *neither* is taking sufficient time to listen and respond to the partner's. Each is making it about self. She's making it all about her. He's making it all about him.

The *sequence* of things becomes very important.

Respectful communication acknowledges that whoever raised the issue gets the platform first.

If it's her issue, once she feels her position has been heard, it frees her up to listen to her partner's side. If her partner's explanation invalidates her position ("It's really not that big a deal...", "You do the same thing...", "I only do that because..."), it deflects the issue back on her, which forces her to restate her case or add more information to make a better case. She isn't looking for a deflection. She's looking for validation and a resolution which he keeps stale-mating.

❖   ❖   ❖

In resolutions of bigger issues, where *both* sides need something from the other, there usually needs to be *two* strategies, one for each partner as to what they can do to keep the problem from re-occurring. This is because, in a relationship, every individual issue now becomes an issue for the relationship - each contributes to the existence of that issue in a positive or negative way. If things are being approached as a team, then there's something that *each* partner can do to improve the situation, even if it's mostly one person's fault.

❖   ❖   ❖

Since, many times, the problems that develop in a relationship are in *reaction* to what each partner does, for one partner to positively change her behavior it automatically helps the other to remove his contribution to the reactive cycle. In other words, one of the easiest ways to stop the cycle is to remove the behavior that creates the reaction.

❖   ❖   ❖

For people who focus on black-and-white solutions, sometimes they have to recognize that the identified problem behavior may not have to change *completely*, but simply alter the *part* of it that is problematic for the partner. (For example: He says, "She doesn't like me to go out." To which she says, "It's not that I think he should *never* go out without me, I just have a problem when he goes out and doesn't check in to let me know when plans change." She just wants the respect of him staying in touch with her when he does go out.)

❖   ❖   ❖

Many people approach an argument with the assumption of right and wrong. ("I feel I am right, therefore she must be wrong.") But most arguments are actually about differing perspectives. We invest time in explaining ourselves because we each have a reason for *why* we did what we did. For most people, if you track the logic behind the choices made, they make sense within the limited perspective that they had in that moment. It's not until you get to the big picture, with *all* of the information on the table, that you can see it might not have been the best choice for the situation.

She says: "I felt you were being short with me, and so I was upset with you."

He says: "Well you were acting upset with me, and so I was being short with you."

Since we can each justify our behavior, it really doesn't help to waste energy trying to convince each other whose logic is superior, or which side more important. That leads to competition and a control struggle. If we're just trying to *understand* each other's logic, trying to reach a solution that takes both sides into account, the focus remains on exploring what would have worked better if we had to do it over again, rather than getting lost in who was more right or more wrong.

❖   ❖   ❖

If you catch the conversation going round and round usually one of five things is going on:

1) The couple is continuing to side-track each other by bringing up additional issues that keep the conversation distracted from the initial focus.
2) Someone is refusing to accept responsibility for her part of the issue.
3) The couple is continuing to refuse to budge from "his way" or "her way"
4) At least one person isn't feeling validated enough to move on to a resolution
5) At least one person's agenda is just to complain. At that moment, they care more about venting than resolving.

Forms of Validation

"Well, let's start with something in the past week or two," I say. "Pick a recent issue that went unresolved."

"Okay," said Theresa. "I'd received a phone call from my mother. Henry is uncomfortable with calls from my mother because they usually get me upset. At any rate, mom called and she upset me. I wanted to talk to Henry about it, who really didn't seem to want to talk about it, but when we did, he very quickly fell back on 'I shouldn't let that get me upset' - which made me even more upset."

Henry steps in. "It's frustrating for me because I see it happening over and over again between her and her mother. I realize that it's her mother, but if you know something's going to upset you, why do you keep going back to it? That's why I don't like to talk about it with her anymore, because she's just going to keep getting hurt and there's nothing I can do. I don't know what she expects of me."

Listening is the most basic form of validation. With our tendency to take short-cuts with communication, one of the easiest things to forget is to listen. Typically, we're already ready with our reply before our partners have even spoken. We're rushing through the conversation because we think we already know everything our partners are going to say. And, even if that's true, it still doesn't change the fact that, if we want them to feel satisfied with the interaction, we need to give them the opportunity to speak, and the time to be heard.

Theresa was just looking for Henry to listen to her. She didn't want him to solve her problems with her mom. She didn't want him to even attempt to discuss it. She just wanted his support by letting her vent. Because he wasn't understanding that, or, perhaps, even knowing what exactly that looked like, Theresa was feeling unheard.

This is one of the big reasons why it's important to identify the *intent* of a conversation to our partners (to listen, to understand, to vent, to resolve or to suggest) at the start. If we can let them know what we need from them with the conversation on the front end, we're much more likely to get it.

It's important to note that Henry wasn't being *intentionally* invalidating. He cared very much about Theresa. He wanted to help. He just didn't know how to go about it. Yet his *positive* intentions were interpreted as "controlling" and "insensitive".

There is a bigger picture to this particular problem. While Henry did need to learn to better validate Theresa in these kinds of situations, Theresa's problems with her mother *were* having an impact on the relationship. At some point, simply because Henry was Theresa's partner, he would have been neglectful if he didn't try to address this with her. Part of being a team is to be able to assist each other with our personal dilemmas, not just sit idly by and watch. I'm not saying that Henry should try to control the situation for Theresa, or force a solution, but part of his healthy role as husband was to share his insights and concerns, just not when Theresa's looking to simply be heard. And Theresa needed to remain open to that. That is part of what a couple does in order to maintain balance.

One of the dilemmas with listening, when it comes to seeking resolution, is when you have a partner who tends to monologue. You try to listen but there's just so much to keep track of that you get lost in the speech. A partner who talks in speeches usually brings in a number of different issues and past events, making it difficult not to get side-tracked. We need to remember to talk in *digestible chunks*, making sure that our partners have time to "digest" the identified issue.

❖   ❖   ❖

Questions can be validating because it shows we're interested in understanding our partners. It shows respect for their opinions because we're valuing them enough to explore them further.

If your partner's "conspiracy theory" of you is that "He doesn't care", asking questions, rather than attacking or dismissing her, are evidence that you value what she has to say and interested in what she's thinking.

Much of effectively asking questions comes back to 1) the tone we ask them in, and 2) the appropriateness of their content.

The best question you can ever add to your vocabulary is "What do you need from me right now?" It addresses the fact that seriously upsetting issues usually revolve around an injured or threatened need, and you're saying you're willing to do something about that. It also keeps things in the moment because it focuses on what you can do right now, the only thing you really have control over, versus what thing you did wrong 10 years ago. And, it focuses the conversation in a positive direction, specifically, on a possible solution.

Stereotypically, men tend to jump too quickly to a solution, forgetting about validation, so you have to be careful not to ask this question too soon in the conversation or it gives the impression that you're just trying to shortcut the issue, rather than taking the time to move through validation. But when you see the conversation start to become problem-obsessed, that becomes a great time to reach for this particular question and change the course away from that negative whirlpool.

❖   ❖   ❖

Acknowledgment is validating. If we're attempting to understand our partner's viewpoint through listening and questioning, ultimately, at the point we know what they are thinking, it's important to validate it. ("I can understand, if that's how you were putting it together, why you would feel that way.")

As I already commented, just about everyone, if you track their logic, arrives at conclusions that make sense within that logic. They may be making those conclusions based on faulty assumptions, or not enough information, but it makes sense that if those are the assumptions being made, or the only pieces of information being considered, why they concluded what they did.

If a husband has not been coming home on time for a while and has not given any substantial explanation of what's going on, if other areas of the relationship are suffering, it would be predictable that the wife might start to worry about what he was doing with his time. The husband, being over-absorbed in his work and not cheating (aside from his work being his mistress), knows exactly what he's been doing so his wife's concerns seem ridiculous. Yet, at some point, he needs to step back and acknowledge that she has a point with her concerns, and take the time to fill in the blanks for her rather than just dismiss her as being insecure.

Acknowledgement is *not* agreement. Just because I understand my partner's viewpoint, doesn't mean I have to agree with it - just show respect for it. If she thinks this is a big deal and I don't, I don't have to agree that it's a big deal. All I have to acknowledge is that it's a big deal *for her*. Hopefully, because I know it's important to her, I'm going to consider attaching a different priority to it, even though *my* perspective doesn't change.

In other words, if calling her in the middle of the day just to say "Hi" is a very big thing for her, even though I think it's neither here nor there, it would probably be wise for me to call her - not out of fear of punishment, but because it's such a simple thing to do. If that little amount of energy is going to make such a big difference for her, then why not?

❖   ❖   ❖

Ownership is incredibly validating. For couples caught up in competing, who finally learn to let go and humbly embrace fault, it makes a big difference. If this is your partner with whom you're supposed to be most "human", what makes it so difficult? Whether it's ego, pride, or that we're punished when we do own blame, this is just another situation where we sabotage what we want from each other.

Ownership is admitting fault. It's being able to say, "You know you're right; I was wrong for doing that." Sometimes it is such a relief to be able to just acknowledge a mistake, or even an intentional wrong, rather than have to exhaust ourselves with defending and rationalizing our behavior.

What people often get stuck on is *percentage* of fault. The thinking is, "I'm not going to accept the blame because I wasn't the only one at fault." But you can still own *part* of the fault, and still not get into a debate over the degree of how much was you and how much was them. It's accepting that most issues involve mutual responsibility. ("You're right; part of that was mine.")

At some point **ownership loses its weight if nothing ever changes**. If we've said, "I'll never do that again," but it keeps happening, ownership has now become just lip-service. Beyond ownership, at that point, we have to commit to some actual strategies for how we're going to go about change, and be willing to hold ourselves accountable to our partners for maintaining that change, in order to regain their trust and/or respect.

❖   ❖   ❖

Apologies are validating, and a form of partial ownership - "I'm sorry for what I did."

You can apologize for the *outcome* of a situation without having to agree on fault. If she's saying you did something on purpose, but you didn't, you can still take partial ownership for the pain that it caused, without agreeing on the intent. ("While it wasn't my intent, I'm sorry that that hurt you.")

After all, sometimes we can do things that cause hurt but they were still necessary things to do. For instance, those that take honest criticism as judgment or rejection may want us to say we were wrong for hurting them, and maybe there was a better way to approach them, but it doesn't make the criticizer wrong for attempting to share a painful, but necessary truth.

Apologies often come far too late in an argument – *after* the point that they would have made a difference. Now, since so much more damage has been done with what's been said by either side, it's too little too late and there's now much more that needs to be apologized for.

Apologize early and often. Sincere apologies show simple respect and are a model of our own humility.

❖   ❖   ❖

The act of resolution, committing to a specific strategy for change, is validating. That you attach enough weight to an issue that you're willing to act on doing something differently is clear evidence of how you value both your partner and the relationship.

If you find that you have to repeatedly apologize for a recurring issue, you most likely need to go *beyond* an apology or ownership and arrive at a specific strategy to keep it from continuing to happen.

Detail versus Content

"What I want from him is to just hear me out. He doesn't need to solve it for me and he certainly doesn't need to tell me to stop feeling the way I feel," said Theresa.

"But, for me, it doesn't seem to work whichever way I try," added Henry. "She says I'm not listening as much as she wants, but when I do listen she gets upset with the questions that I ask."

"That's because you're always questioning my logic. I don't need you to pick apart what I'm saying, I just need you to hear me out," replied Theresa.

"Can you give me an example of Henry picking things apart," I said.

"Well, it's simple things. I'll say, 'I got a lot of work done this weekend' and Henry will say, 'You didn't get around to planting the flowers yet.' It's true that I didn't get them planted, but I did get a lot of other stuff done."

Because there is this tendency to over-compensate, going from one extreme to another when trying to initiate change, a couple tends to also lean towards the extremes of *under-listening* and *over-listening*. Over-listening is usually about **detail versus content**.

"Detail versus content" is when we get so caught up in the details of what our partner is saying that we're missing the big picture. We get so bogged down in the accuracy, or inaccuracy, of her every word, that we're no longer paying attention to the *content* of what she's trying to get across.

We have to be able to let the small inaccuracies and the side-tracking statements pass, in order to stay focused on what she is trying to communicate.

For a reactive couple, they are overly-watchful of every word. There is no room for error. Every little thing becomes a potential fight. The most neutral comments can be twisted in a way to find offense because each has become hyper-vigilant of the other. It becomes a situation where each partner, unintentionally or not, is looking to start a fight. They may not *want* to fight, but they keep choosing paths that take them there.

It's ironic, because you can be putting a lot of energy into hearing what your partner is saying, but what's conveyed by getting lost in the detail is "He still isn't hearing me."

Validating What Can't Be Validated

"When we try to talk and he isn't able to give me what I need, I'll end up getting angry because I don't think we've got a future if this isn't going to change," continued Theresa.

"So what do you do when you get angry?" I asked.

"I'll start to yell. And sometimes I'll throw out ultimatums, if he seems unwilling to change," said Theresa.

"By what Henry was saying, it's not okay for him to raise his voice. Is that accurate?" I interjected.

Theresa nodded. "I tend to be sensitive to his tone of voice."

"But it's okay for you to yell?" I added.

Theresa became a little uncomfortable, but she answered, "Sometimes I get that upset, yes."

Choosing to ignore the double standard, I continued, "So what do you expect from Henry when you yell?"

"I hope he understands what it is I need from him; that he recognizes how upset it's making me," Theresa said.

Sometimes what your partner is asking of you *can't* be validated. Don't get me wrong, there are always things you *can* validate, but sometimes the *specific* way she is asking to be validated can't be done.

There are several situations that fall into this category:

- Mistaking validation for agreement
- Validating a misunderstanding
- Validating inappropriate behavior
- Validating an unhealthy priority

For a lot of people the problem is that they don't get the difference between validation versus agreement. They are insisting that you agree that something is a big deal when, for you, it's not. Or they're insisting that you say they're right, when you think they're wrong. They will step back and say "You're not validating me," but that's not validation. Or, rather, "agreement" and "ownership" *are* forms of validation, but they're not the only ones. You shouldn't be verbally agreeing with something you really don't agree with, or "owning" something that you don't truthfully feel is your fault.

For the partner who is insistent on constant agreement, I have to say that's not being realistic. You don't have to agree on the details of an issue to still come up with a workable solution – in the same way that you can share the same faith but still be from different denominations. **A relationship can still be healthy even if you don't see eye to eye on everything, so long as the differences are viewed with respect, and the solutions are balanced between the perspectives.**

There is an unhealthy dynamic that sometimes develops where one person will just agree, even though she doesn't really agree, because she feels it's not worth getting into a struggle over it. While in milder situations, this can just be a form of trying to be accommodating, you have to be careful that it doesn't become a pattern to the degree that who you are, and who your partner thinks you are, are actually very different. It can create a gulf between the two of you because of the lack of honesty. Better to be honest at times and risk a conflict, than to chronically acquiesce and start to resent or grow apart.

❖   ❖   ❖

If your partner is obviously misunderstanding an incident or interaction, it's difficult to consider an apology or ownership as the approach to validation. She may be saying "What I need from you is not to lie about that any more", but, if it wasn't a lie in the first place, to agree to that solution would be endorsing a false premise.

One workaround in these situations is to validate the underlying need, not necessarily the surface request, and then step back to attempting to clear up the misunderstanding.

She says: "I need you to treat me more respectfully than that."

He says: "I will certainly do my best to be respectful of you. I understand you've got every right to want to be respected. Can I stop a second, though, and try to clear something up? What I meant by what I said was...."

Let's take Theresa and Henry's situation. If she's saying to him, "I want you to apologize for raising your voice at me like that," when he didn't feel like he was even past frustrated, rather than falsely owning that he was angry when he wasn't, it might be better for him to simply apologize for hurting her feelings because that wasn't his intent. Whether or not he tries in that moment to educate her about the difference between degrees of anger is up to him, but one way or another, at some point, Theresa is going to have to adjust her reaction to conflict. Henry *does* need to have room to get upset so long as he handles it responsibly.

When it comes to "defining reality", which I mentioned earlier in the book, a partner can insist that "You just think I'm a failure", and the other not feel anything of the sort. It would be wrong to try to validate this unhealthy conclusion, or the partner be insistent that the other support an inaccurate assumption, but one could step back and validate some of the thinking that led up to that. For example, "You're right that I said that/ did that, and I understand why that was hurtful for you, how you could interpret it that way. But there's a difference between my being upset with a choice that you make versus seeing you as a failure. I don't consider you to be a failure; I just saw that as a poor choice."

❖   ❖   ❖

Sometimes the problem is that the partner is wanting to be validated, but how she tries to get validation is inappropriate, which goes beyond being hurtful.

Theresa was operating from a double-standard – Henry wasn't "allowed" to get close to angry, but *she* could, and did. Not only did she get angry, but she would become inappropriate – calling him names, passing judgments and throwing around ultimatums. Henry had a pretty tough skin and was tolerating a lot of this, but, for many others, this kind of an attack is death for a relationship.

Let's say a wound is being re-opened, which is often what leads to such an exaggerated reaction, and the partner's "losing it", screaming and pitching a fit, but expecting you to acknowledge her pain. There are a couple of ways you might consider approaching it.

1) You could still attempt to validate her pain ("Honey, I understand that was really hurtful for you. What do you need from me to help?"), remaining vulnerable, ignoring the tantrum, and hoping continuing to do so is going to be enough water to put out the fire. (Though you would still want to exercise accountability at some point for the inappropriate behavior, just probably not in that heated moment.)

2) You could attempt to restore some boundaries with the inappropriate behavior ("If you're wanting to have this conversation, you need to talk to me like I'm your partner and not your enemy."), and hope she has enough control to re-group. If she can't, then it might be time for a healthy exit.

But the better point for me to make is for the partner. **Don't expect to be validated if you're asking for it in inappropriate ways.** Don't verbally wound your partner, and then expect her to be vulnerable in return. That's abusive. It just doesn't work well that way. It puts too much on the partner to make the conversation work.

It's like having an affair, and then trying to blame your partner for pushing you into it. Or coming home drunk and wanting your partner to sympathize. You may be hurting, but it doesn't justify treating your partner in a way that you wouldn't want them to treat you.

For some people this happens because they don't get the meaning of "inappropriate". As I'm using it here, inappropriate doesn't mean poor manners, getting upset, or saying the wrong thing from time to time. **Inappropriate means destructive to the point of being emotionally wounding.** The person who engages in tantrums to the degree of attacking the partner's character may feel like she's just "blowing off steam", but, if it's killing the partner emotionally in the process, it can't continue.

Inappropriate behavior cannot be tolerated in a relationship. There's no room for it. If we feel behavior is that extreme, we need to be clear with our partners as to how hurtful it is, making the connection that, if they want the relationship to continue, it has to stop. Initially, it's approaching the partner in terms of accountability, but, if it still persists, it forces an ultimatum.

❖   ❖   ❖

There are times when priorities get out of balance. For instance, when someone is spending too much time at work and neglecting the home life. She may want the partner's support for her hard work, but the partner finds it difficult to validate the effort because, as far as the partner's concerned, work *is* the problem.

Part of it, for the partner, is still finding what he *can* validate. There is a positive in a partner trying to be responsible with her career. So it might still be wise for the neglected partner to make note of that, while approaching accountability for the part that is out of balance.

The workaholic needs to be realistic that her partner cannot be supportive of something that is hurtful to the relationship.

Granted, there are times when the demands of work will eat into relationship time, and the relationship needs to be flexible with those occasional shifts. But, if those times become chronic to the degree that it is more the routine than not, at some point there will probably have to be some hard questions asked as to "What's more important, the job or your family?" For many, the true problem isn't that those at home should be more understanding about the job, it's that the particular job (or how time with the job is being mismanaged), isn't a good choice for also having a family.

Finding the Point of Agreement

"So what do you agree about then, with what we've been discussing?" I said.

They both looked at me, confused.

"We don't agree about anything," said Henry. "That's the problem."

I shook my head. "Do either of you like conflict?"

"No," they both said.

"Do both of you care about each other?" I added.

"Yes," they both said.

"Do both of you want to be able to communicate better?" I continued.

"Yes," they both said.

"Do both of you want to be better supports for each other?" I persisted.

"Yes," they both said.

"Then you do have some things you agree on, don't you?" I finished.

What moves a couple smoothly through conflict often depends on whether they are over-focused on the problems versus positively seeking solutions. In the same way that any situation contains negatives if you're willing to look for them, there are always points that a couple can find to disagree on when discussing perspectives. The key to any discussion is always looking for the **points of agreement**. Finding that commonality is where you can start to build a solution.

Sometimes the simplest commonality is "We both care about each other. We both want this to work. So what would be something that would work for both of us?" Or, "If what we want is to draw closer, is continuing on this path accomplishing that? If we were staying focused on that, how would we be handling this differently?"

The commonalities are usually connected with the big picture, versus being lost in the details of the argument. The big picture always presents a better perspective.

Henry and Theresa were so lost in their problems that they had no idea which way was out. The relationship had become far too rigid, and needed to become more flexible if it was going to be able to start breathing again. They had created a quick ritual of automatically moving into "his camp" and "her camp", and not being able to recognize any middle.

Part of the problem was that Theresa was over-controlling the options in the relationship when it came to discussion. She wanted to be able to hear from Henry, but she was so restricting his delivery that his choices were incredibly limited. For things to get better, she needed to allow him more freedom to talk with emotion. And, at the same time, she needed to give herself *less* freedom to go as far as she did. The point of agreement was that they needed to be able to better communicate – in order to do this, they would have to give up some of the restrictions placed on the relationship that were preventing this from happening.

❖   ❖   ❖

Since the root of all problems comes back to how we're attempting to get our needs met, or how we're attempting (or not attempting) to meet our partner's needs, the point of agreement often has to come back to the core needs, which are always healthy. My partner needs to feel secure. She needs to feel significant. She needs to feel like she has room to enjoy her life. And I need all of the same.

So, sometimes, a couple has to work from the ground up. If she wants to feel secure, but her approach isn't working for her, or for me, then what are some other ways she, or I, can try that would accomplish the same thing – satisfy the same need?

The point is, there's more than just "his way" or "her way" to find a path to meeting the core needs for both. Remaining willing to bend, so long as it doesn't overly compromise a personal standard, is vital.

In terms of validation, you're always looking for what parts of the conversation you *can* agree with. If you can't agree with your partner's conclusions, can you agree with any of the logic that led to the conclusions? If you can't agree with the logic, can you at least agree with the initial observation that started the issue - how it could be taken wrong or have been the wrong thing to do/say? If you can't agree with any of that, you can always fall back and support the injured need underneath it all.

❖   ❖   ❖

A big part of staying focused on the point of agreement is identifying what you want, not over-concentrating on what you don't. Theresa wanted to feel validated, and Henry wanted to effectively validate her. But Theresa focused a lot on how Henry was failing her, stating example after example of when he fell short, but she wasn't doing a very good job of identifying for him what she saw as success. There had to have been times when he did a decent job or they wouldn't have been together as long as they had. It would have been helpful for him to have those past examples of success used as guides for him in the present.

Even if there had been no past examples of success, it didn't change the fact that Theresa, who seemed to have an idea of what she was looking for, didn't really specify "this is what works for me." If she had been able to give him some clear examples of what showed her he was listening, rather than just saying "He doesn't listen", it would have been easier for him to duplicate what she needed – otherwise it just came across as confusing and unfair since, to him, he thought he was already doing that.

This is true when it comes to issues of skills in the relationship. Sometimes what we're asking from our partners is a skill that hasn't been developed yet. Because we may already possess that skill, we tend to assume that our partners also know what to do and how to do it - so we think that they're just refusing to do it.

If such is the case, that a partner lacks the particular skill, then it falls on us, the partner *with* the skill, to lovingly educate our partner on how to do what we're asking. I'm not saying to parent them, which can be somewhat condescending. I'm saying to educate them, peer to peer. "When I say I need to be validated, this is what that looks like for me…."

This is a common "bad habit" when it comes to how we fail to ask for what we want. We often wait for our partners to give us what we need, rather than to just ask if we're not getting it. Why let them flounder or fail, if we have the answers? She's thinking "He's not validating what I'm saying", and ends up just walking off upset. Why not, in that moment, just say, "Is there anything in what I'm saying that you can take some ownership of?" (If ownership is the desired form of validation.)

Some would argue, "Well, if I just spell it out for him, it's not going to be sincere if he does it." Loving education is always necessary for a relationship to progress. If my partner is willing to comply with my specific request, it doesn't matter that the request came from me, all that matters is that she was willing to comply. Now if she complies but she does so with obvious sarcasm, then she really didn't comply - which may mean I try again later when she's in a better emotional state. There are those partners who really do want our happiness, and they just need a map to making that happen - if we refuse to educate, then we become part of the problem.

We always have a choice of what we focus on when it comes to cooperating. She asks him to take out the garbage though he's obviously already feeling rushed. He does it, but he's not skipping and smiling as he does. So was this a positive or a negative outcome? It depends on what you focus on. He complied, which was a positive. His attitude could have been better, but ultimately it shouldn't completely take away from the fact that he did what was requested. It was a successful exercise in emotional discipline that he didn't let his feelings dictate what he ultimately chose to do. However, in some situations, especially the more meaningful, personal ones, we need both - respectful cooperation *and* a positive, loving attitude.

We need to be better mirrors to our partners of what we need. Not only by modeling it, but asking for it when we're not getting it.

Discussion Questions:

1. **Overall, do the two of you feel validated by each other?** When it comes to the different forms of validation (listening, questions, acknowledgment, ownership, resolution), which are the ones that you have the most difficult time with? Which are the ways that you prefer to be validated the most?

2. **When it comes to resolving issues and the four steps (identify, validate, explain, resolve), is there a particular place that you get stuck?** Can you slow the conversation down in order to be sure that you're being heard and giving time to listen? Do you work towards two-part solutions with your resolutions?

3. **Do you tend to be accused of under-listening more, or over-listening?** Do your understand that if you under-listen, you need to be more openly validating? And if you over-listen, you need to be less focused on details and side-tracks and more focused on the content of what is trying to be said?

4. **Are there things your partner wants you to validate, that you find difficult or impossible to do so?** Are there other points with her issue that you can find to agree with, or validate?

5. **Do you feel like you and your partner do a good job of identifying what you need from each other when you talk?** If your partner isn't identifying what she needs, do you take the time to ask?

Chapter 7
Accountability

The bottom line for any long-term relationship of depth, be it friend or partner, comes down to two things: grace balanced with accountability. In the majority of the troubled relationships I see, the break-downs are in one of these two areas. Either they don't know when or how to apply grace to the things that need to be accepted, or they don't know how to exercise or receive accountability for the things that need to change.

Grace is being able to accept my partner for who she is. I'm able to see past her flaws and eccentricities, loving the core of her person. It is being able to separate my personal *preferences* from my personal *needs*. Grace accepts the fact that my partner's preferences are not my own, and that that is okay. Grace accepts the fact that both of us are human, and we're going to be making mistakes. We're not always going to be on our best behavior or know the right thing to do or say all of the time. The application of grace creates an equal partnership where each of us is flawed, but each of us remains committed to the health of the relationship.

Accountability pertains to how we lovingly hold each other responsible for the health of the relationship. It is how you respectfully hold up a mirror to your partner to help her see that her actions are negatively impacting your personal needs, destructive to the relationship, or harmful to herself. Accountability is the balance point we bring to the relationship because *each* of us has a necessary piece of the picture. I need my partner's perception of me because, without it, I'm partially blind. I'm too close to myself to always see my part in things clearly. I need the help of others to help me see how I'm perceived by the rest of the world.

Accountability is also where we lovingly confront each other on those things we've committed to that we haven't followed through on.

❖   ❖   ❖

One essential for a healthy marriage is the skill of knowing how to approach each other when change is required. For some, asking for change, or offering a criticism, can mistakenly be perceived by the partner as the equivalent of character rejection. Saying that the partner needs to change is automatically heard as "You're not good enough". Yet change is something that's ongoing in a life-long relationship on one level or another. You may not have any life circumstances such as children, job changes, or major moves in your lifetime, but time itself is a factor in how each of us changes over the years.

There *are* aspects of a person that don't change dramatically, even with aging. In the same way that our core needs never change, our core personalities tend to remain consistent despite the passage of time, unless there is a significant trauma. What typically *does* change is our understanding of life, and how we go about living (getting our surface needs met).

I am sometimes amazed that dysfunctional people can remain dysfunctional all of their lives. You would think that, at some point, a light would go on, or things would become so uncomfortable for them that they would be forced to look at themselves and approach necessary change. But, for many, part of that dysfunctional make-up is the result of *avoiding* self-analysis, and *resisting* change. So long as I see every one else as the problem, why do I need to change?

Yet, learning implies that, as we go through struggles in our lives, or witness it in others, how we see the world, and interact with it, should mature with new knowledge. So, *not* maturing is the equivalent of refusing to learn.[5]

---

[5] For some, the problem is that they've made their lives so isolated from the rest of the world that they are seldom exposed to any new information that would challenge their thinking.

There are two aspects we bring to a relationship: 1) our core personality and 2) the role that we take on to accommodate the relationship. When couples request change they often make the mistake of taking it as a demand to change *who they are*, rather than recognizing that often what is being asked to change is simply *how they are going about filling the role of partner*. The relationship roles can go through many changes across a lifetime.

❖　❖　❖

Jenny was in her early thirties and about one year married. Matt, her husband, was about five years older. Neither had been married before. They were drawn together because of their different qualities. Matt loved how "in the moment" Jenny was – how she worried very little and seemed to be able to enjoy life so easily. Jenny loved the fact that Matt brought order to her sometimes-chaotic lifestyle. He brought a clearer focus to her life due to being naturally structured where she was not.

"We're not moving forward," said Matt. "We had this plan of getting our finances together, with Jenny stepping back from some of her work, so we could start to have kids. But, instead of that happening, she's taken more projects on."

"They were good investments at the time," said Jenny, quickly. "I would have been stupid to pass them up."

"But it wasn't what we agreed to," added Matt. "And it doesn't get us any closer to what we said we want. Jenny says she wants to be married but I think she also feels trapped by it. She's used to doing her own thing. So when she feels she has to sacrifice, she starts feeling closed in - which is when she's most likely to do something impulsive."

I looked at Jenny. She shrugged, "It's true."

"Are the finances the only issue?" I asked.

"No," said Matt. "The issue isn't about finances; it's about discipline. Jenny also likes to party a little too much. When we dated we used to go out a lot, but now that we're married I'm not as interested in staying out late. But she hasn't changed. She wants to continue to go out."

"I'm just used to going to bars to socialize," said Jenny. "Matt thinks everything should change just because we're married, and I don't think it should make a difference."

"Yes, but, there needs to be limits," added Matt. "If I don't go with you to make sure you get back home, you'll stay out all night. And when you do get back home, you're so plastered that it takes you a day to recover."

"That's why I need you to come with me," said Jenny.

"I don't like being around you when you get like that," replied Matt. "It's embarrassing. I don't want to have to police how much you drink, and it never stops just at drinking. Drinking's just the door to you doing harder drugs."

"That doesn't happen every time," Jenny defended herself. "I've gotten better at not going too far."

"It just happened last week," said Matt.

"Yes, but it had been a good two months or so before that," answered Jenny.

Perhaps jumping the gun, the easy diagnosis here is that Jenny needs to grow up. Matt, older and more responsible, while attracted to Jenny's fun side, was now experiencing the problem aspect of it since it wasn't really balanced. The more chaotic Jenny became, the more it forced Matt into being overly-structured in an effort to balance her. Neither of them liked him being in that role. He was being forced to be the Parent to her Child. He was struggling with how to apply accountability for something that was potentially destructive to their relationship.

We need to have a common gauge of what's fair in a marriage. The problem for many couples is that they have two different sets of "right" and "wrong", and never arrive at a mutual standard for the relationship. What actually works for *us*? How much time apart is too much time? How much time in my hobbies constitutes being excessive? How much investment in my job is enough? How far is it safe to go if we're angry with each other? What is considered emotionally abusive?

One of the simpler reasons that couple's counseling works is that it attempts to get everybody on the same page. The counselor guides the couple to embrace a common approach to conflict resolution, where both sides try to uphold the same standard. The guidelines and rules are made very clear, not intellectually abstract, so it's no longer about "his way" or "her way" but supporting "our way".

At this point, Matt and Jenny hadn't established clear limits. And even when Matt thought he had, Jenny would cross them. At the same time, I was surprised that Jenny wasn't getting more visibly upset with Matt's confrontation of her behavior. She was defending herself, but she wasn't emotionally escalating. Typically, an immature person doesn't handle criticism well. Even if it was just her being disciplined in public, in front of me, it was still *some* degree of discipline.

Giving Criticism

"So you see the issue as Jenny not being disciplined enough?" I asked Matt.

"Definitely," said Matt. "She's like a kid who refuses to listen to anybody."

I looked to Jenny. "Jenny, what would you like to see change in Matt?"

"Matt needs to give me some room. Marriage has been a big adjustment for me. I know I can be impulsive, and I know I shouldn't be staying out all night, but he acts like it's the end of the world," replied Jenny.

"So how have the two of you tried to work this out?" I asked.

"We talk about it. We agree that things need to change. Jenny agrees to not do anything impulsive, and then it happens again," said Matt.

"I told him I'd do *better*, I didn't say I was going to be perfect." said Jenny. "I'm an adult and I don't need another parent lecturing me about what I do."

The core of accountability comes down to giving and receiving criticism. So each partner has to be open to accepting that there is such a thing as *positive* criticism, and it's *necessary* in order to keep a relationship balanced.

As with any strategy we use to attempt to maintain balance, there are always the unhealthy extremes. With accountability, as with personal communication styles, we can separate these in terms of passive, assertive, and aggressive.

Passive accountability, the positive extreme, would be allowing the relationship to drift dangerously far before requesting any change. This often happens due to good intentions – not wanting to control the partner, not wanting to hurt her by confronting, etc. Still, it's an extreme, and creates problems because it's actually neglectful of the relationship.

Assertive accountability, the balanced position, would be confronting things as problems arise, not letting things go too far. It is very concerned about each partner's personal rights and what is fair for both. It looks more at the things that are destructive to the needs, not so much the petty issues that are really just preferences - most often addressing the broken commitments or desired change. It focuses on the destructive actions, not the character of the person engaged in them. It looks to find a "win" for the two, not the one.

Aggressive accountability, the negative extreme**,** would be overly criticizing to the degree of being chronically judging. It typically doesn't separate focusing on the act versus the character of the person who committed the act. An aggressive style makes little distinction between the little and the big things; everything tends to be addressed like it's a big thing. It has an aspect of rejection and control to it rather than support.

❖   ❖   ❖

Part of why some people have a hard time accepting accountability is because their definition of love promotes the motto "true love is unconditional". They then twist that concept into, "You should accept me no matter what", which in reality is not unconditional love; it is grace *without* accountability.

Mature love is *unconditional* in the sense that it says, "I love you *despite* your flaws". It does not say, "I will only love you *if* you change this,

this, and that" – which is both withholding and manipulation. Because everybody is human, we will all make mistakes, some bigger than others. Some wrongs are even intentional. But mature love persists over time. It isn't here one day and gone the next. It doesn't waver just because I've been disappointed or hurt. The relationship doesn't end just because I or my partner didn't get our way.

Mature love is *conditional* in the sense that, while love will continue, there are still behaviors that are unhealthy for the relationship, and, if the relationship is going to continue as a healthy one, or, sometimes, continue at all, these behaviors need to change. Typically, these behaviors occur when self is chronically getting in the way of "us". While you still love your partner, there are things in a relationship, such as emotional abuse and neglect, that can't be tolerated. So the statement becomes "I do love you, but there are particular behaviors that I cannot tolerate in a relationship."

Jenny's behavior (having agreed to a solution but then disregarding her commitment to that solution) required accountability. While, to her, it was just about doing what felt good, it was without the larger perspective that her selfish actions were starting to come before the health of the marriage. The solution wasn't for her to give up her fun altogether, but to start disciplining herself in order to learn *moderation*. If she didn't have the discipline to exercise moderation, then she would have to consider giving up some of her sources for fun and find healthier ones.

It is certainly possible to kill the love in a partner's heart. We all have our limits. If enough destructive behavior has occurred, you may still desire to experience love from your partner, but your behavior has effectively extinguished it. Sometimes the reason for marriages not working out, even when there *was* a chance for reparation, was because too much emotional damage was done and now, even though the partner may *intellectually* want it to work, there's nothing left *emotionally* on which to build.

Accountability versus Judgment

What most couples struggle with is recognizing and respecting the line between accountability versus judgment. There are three aspects to keep in mind that help underline the difference between the two.

First, let's talk about **conviction** versus **condemnation**. If I feel *convicted* of something (not in the legal sense), that I've done something wrong, then I'm feeling uncomfortable enough about it, but, also, *inspired/motivated* to do something to correct it, or make amends for it. While there is ownership that accompanies conviction (recognition/admission of fault), it's the *weight* of that conviction that motivates me to do something positive about it. **Conviction motivates change.**

With *condemnation*, I'm buried by guilt. Either I'm doing it to myself, or somebody else is forcing it on me. **Condemnation robs us of our motivation to change.** We are so overwhelmed by the negativity, that we feel helpless to do anything about it.

Accountability is a positive thing. It requires change in *necessary* ways. If lasting change is made, the relationship improves.

Judgment is the equivalent of condemnation. It is such a powerful rejection that it moves us further from change, and further from our partner.

We may be approaching our partner in what we feel is a positive way, but, for them, it can still come across as judgment. In such situations we need to be able to ask, "How could I have approached you with this in a way that you wouldn't have felt judged?" If they have a workable suggestion for how to approach them more effectively, then we've gained a new tool. If they say there's no way to approach them about the subject, they have to realize that, for any committed relationship, there has to be room for healthy criticism.

❖   ❖   ❖

The second aspect is reflected in Eric Berne's **transactional analysis** approach, something that was popular back in the 1970's and '80's. I've already made references to it in earlier sections of this book, without identifying the source. One of its principles is that there are three communication roles we assume in an adult relationship – the Adult, the Parent, and the Child.

The **Child** role's focus is around play – being in the moment without responsibility. But the Child also throws tantrums, manipulates and insults when she doesn't get her way.

The **Parent** role attempts to manage the partner's behavior – through punishment, judgment, lecture, and attempts to control. Needless to say, none of us, as adults, like to be parented.

The **Adult** is the most mature of the three, because this role doesn't engage in any of the control strategies that the other two attempt. The Adult is only concerned about maintaining control of themselves. The adult role supports the relationship as a partnership based on mutual respectful behavior.

There *are* positives to being the Parent and the Child. Sometimes we need the role of educator that the Parent provides, so long as it is done respectfully. Sometimes we need to be able to step away from responsibility and be a Child for awhile, enjoying just being alive. But we are trying to avoid the *negative* aspects of these roles as well as staying in those roles past the point that it's appropriate.

When it comes to accountability, we typically attempt to motivate our partner to change by becoming the Parent. The problem with this is that it is negative reinforcement, not positive. The focus tends to be more on punishing for the negative behavior, without giving any recognition for the positive. It can be a very condemning approach that comes off as direct judgments.

The Child role will also attempt accountability through its manipulative tantrums, passive resistance, or direct rebellion. It destructively demands change - or else.

The Adult role avoids both of these failed strategies, yet still addresses the issue. It doesn't attempt to manipulate or parent. It stays focused on the choices, and accountability to the relationship. For example:

"We need to talk about your drinking. You've said in the past that it wasn't a problem, but it's continued to be a problem because of (example), and (example). I care about you, and I care about us. And this is getting in the way of us. We need to talk about how this can change other than just you, by yourself, trying to manage this, because that isn't working."

The Adult identifies her own hurt, remaining vulnerable, rather than getting lost in venting her anger. She is able to make the connection that her hurt exists because she cares, and verbally make that connection for her partner - she's not the enemy. She's also able to identify when the issue goes beyond her own personal preferences, and becomes an issue for the relationship. She stays with the facts, not getting lost in conspiracy theories or her own woundedness. She is able to give credit for past successes, allow for time and the benefit of the doubt for new efforts to be made, but also knows how to step in when it's evident that greater change is needed.

Now, hopefully, the partner is also able to be an Adult, and is mature enough to accept ownership that a better solution is needed for resolving the issue. If the partner, in reaction to being lovingly confronted, attempts to Parent (control, judge or punish) or be the Child (manipulate or rebel), and this continues to be the pattern with refusal to change (refusing to be held accountable), it will move things to a point where ultimatums need to occur. He needs to be mature enough to be able to see that this isn't about the partner trying to control him; it's about his degree of commitment to the health of the relationship and the self-sacrifice, or self-discipline, that that requires.

Preferably, ultimatums are reserved for those issues that don't leave room for compromise.

I would say that the vast majority of couples that end up in couple's counseling are there because they keep falling out of Adult roles, or don't know how to step into them.

❖   ❖   ❖

Lastly, accountability is focused on the problem *behaviors*, not the person.

One unhealthy parenting style is failing to make the distinction, when attempting to parent a child, that there is a difference between what we do and who we are. Because we make a foolish choice does not make us a fool. Because we fail to be disciplined in one area does not mean we're undisciplined in *every* area.

People who grow up in homes where there is no separation between the act and the person, or who fail to learn this distinction for themselves as they get older, tend to bring this into their adult relationships. So, when accountability is attempted, they either 1) judge the partner rather than addressing the problem behavior, or 2) if the criticism is directed at them, automatically take it as a judgment or rejection.

We have to grasp at some point that rejection of character is rejecting who our partner is. And if we're essentially saying "I reject you, because you're a (judgment)" then how can we continue to have a relationship? If we truly believe the judgment we're passing then we're saying that this is a defective person. And even if the partner doesn't believe herself to be "defective", why would she want to stay in a relationship with someone who thinks she is?

The problem for many is that they pass judgment but, to them, it is simply harsh words said in the moment. Unless we have a partner that is able to just pass this by as "She's just angry. She doesn't really mean it," damage is done. Maybe we went too far with what we said and now feel a little silly, but most partners can only handle character rejection so many times before it becomes intolerable.

❖　❖　❖

It is true that, when a consistent pattern of negative behavior persists, it does start to say something about the person, not just the behavior. If I make impulsive, hasty decisions on a regular basis and it continues to cause problems for the relationship, at some point I've earned the label of "impulsive". In terms of accountability, it's having to point out, "The reason I'm bringing this up again is that this isn't just a one-time thing. This is happening again and again."

I'm not saying that judgments never have a place, especially if they've been earned, but I think it often depends on who you're dealing with. Some people are so sensitive to judgments that, even when a judgment is deserved, it's too overwhelming for them to go there, so you have to stay focused on the behavior. For other people, sometimes it's only when things get to a place of judgment that they're willing to take ownership and change. You have to pay attention to what works best for who you're in relationship with.

Receiving Criticism

"Aside from feeling parented, what makes it difficult for you to hear Matt's concerns?" I asked Jenny.

"I just wish he wouldn't make me sound so horrible for just wanting to have fun," she said.

"Do you think, if he was being loving, that he should just leave you alone and not say anything?" I persisted.

"No, I understand that it bothers him. I just don't know what he could say that would help, rather than make me feel judged."

If things were going to move forward for Jenny and Matt, Jenny was going to have to learn to accept Matt's criticisms as necessary for her own balance. She was still minimizing her behavior as "just wanting to have fun", and not really acknowledging her actions as problematic other than that "they bothered Matt". At some point, ideally, she would have to come to see her impulsive choices as being unhealthy for herself, and not just a problem for Matt – the idea being that if change is going to last, it's because we're doing it not just for our partner, but for ourselves.

If we truly understand and can apply grace to our lives, it automatically allows us to accept criticism. Because we've already accepted ourselves as human, and fallible, the fact that our partner also recognizes that we are is no big deal.

The more we have to pretend we're above making mistakes, the harder it becomes to accept it, and own it, when we have.

If part of who I am is somebody who wants to improve and grow, then positive criticism holds no threat. It can only help me consider changing in a necessary way since I need to understand my mistakes in order to learn from them.

The thinking behind defensiveness is usually focused on how our choices in the moment are justified, because there's always a reason behind why we do what we do. ("I did that because you made me angry.") But *even though we had a reason in the moment that led us to that choice, it still doesn't make the end choice okay.*

In this particular situation, it wasn't so much a matter of Jenny not being able to apply grace to herself – if anything, she applied too much grace. It *was* possible that the partying really wasn't a big deal to her, and that was why she did it. But it was also possible that she didn't want to admit to herself that it was a big deal because 1) of what that would say about her, and 2) if she admitted that it was a big deal, then she would have to accept responsibility for change. Matt's concern was that if he treated her actions the way Jenny desired, like it wasn't a big deal, then the problems would just continue to occur.

❖   ❖   ❖

Part of *discretion* with receiving criticism is knowing when to accept it and when to let it go. Positive criticism, something that can help us grow, needs to be embraced and explored. Negative criticism, something that is only there to hurt and wound, needs to be allowed to pass rather than take up residence and begin to poison us.

Since even positive criticism is based on observation, it isn't inherently truthful. My partner may be concerned about my behavior, and interpreting it a certain way, but that doesn't make her conclusions correct. But if I'm treating the criticism respectfully, I'm going to give it consideration, express my appreciation for the concern, and attempt to respond to the criticism in a way that either expresses some ownership or, hopefully, helps my partner alter her interpretation of what she sees, if it's inaccurate.

If I'm getting similar criticisms from other sources as well, at some point I may need to either step back and question my own assessment, or explore why I'm giving such a wrong impression.

One of the personal criticisms I've had directed at me more than once in my life is that I will often take time to respond to a question before I give an answer. The impression that this can give certain people is that I'm not being truthful because I don't have an immediate response. While it is true that I am editing, it is not to hide the truth, but to express what I have to say in an accurate way. It is my recognition that other people think and talk differently than I do, and if I'm going to be best understood I need to express myself in a way that they will be most likely to hear it accurately. My own experience is that when I don't take the time to edit, I'm more likely to be misunderstood. So, while the positive criticism itself was useful in terms of how I can be perceived, the conclusions that were being made about my behavior were inaccurate.

◈　　◈　　◈

I would be hard-put to say whether it's more difficult for somebody who's usually wrong, or somebody who's usually right, to admit it when they are wrong. People who are usually wrong are often so tired of being wrong that they aren't receptive to hearing about it any more. Yet, people who are usually right are often so confident in their "rightness" that it sometimes becomes difficult for them to back up and entertain the notion that they might be wrong this time.

To remain vulnerable, open to hearing critical advice, is not easy - however, it is an aspect of healthy love and a sign of maturity. It is healthy love our partner is showing towards us; being willing to risk upsetting us by offering necessary criticism that may ultimately improve our quality of life or relationship. And it is healthy love we show ourselves by being willing to hear concerns, sift them for truth, and change what needs changing.

Accountability Routines

"You said the two of you agreed to a plan for a family," I said to Matt. "How does this plan get enforced?"

"Well, that's part of the problem, I guess," said Matt. "We both agreed that we wanted to prepare for having kids, but, aside from Jenny cutting back on her work, I don't think we have any other details."

"And how was Jenny supposed to cut back on her work? Were there any timelines attached or planned steps?" I continued.

"No, not really," said Matt. "She just agreed to start cutting back."

In the same way that healthy "out-of-the-routine" routines keep a relationship from becoming stale, one of the best ways to keep a relationship fit over the long term is to have some form of an **accountability routine**.

One such routine is the weekly sit-down. Even though, for a fit couple, the sit-down doesn't need to occur on a weekly basis, the fact that the couple is regularly taking time to look at "us" keeps the relationship on a very conscious level. Because it's addressing both what's working and what's still "in process", it provides a continuing accountability without casting it in a negative light.

Often a spouse will approach her partner seeking accountability for something, but because she's attempting to do it on her own, without any agreed-on approach to address issues, it immediately is interpreted as *her* issue. If this occurs repeatedly over a period of time, there is a tendency for this to cast her in the role of being a "nag". Her issues may be legitimate, but the repeated attempts on her part to address them end up being labeled a problem in itself - she is seen as a complainer.

The existence of an accountability routine automatically creates a platform for approaching each other without it being nagging, since necessary criticism is part of the expected agenda. It removes the weight off any one partner to raise an issue, because the time together is supposed to be talking about "us".

Every couple needs to know how to separate the issues from everything else. There needs to be a time to talk about the relationship projects, and times where those things are left alone. Without an accountability ritual, the tendency is for issues to creep into every discussion, rather than having a separate time reserved. This way, things such as date nights, can respect the rule that "the only rule for date night is we don't talk about problems".

Sit-downs give the couple practice with how to share criticisms in a constructive way – having had time to think about possible solutions and approaches ahead of time, rather than just impulsively jumping into arguments. With sit-downs, you don't overwhelm each other with everything that's "wrong", but, instead, you focus on what you would like to see each other improve on, and discuss strategies for how that's going to happen. You're trying to keep things on an information level, rather than taking feedback personally. The focus is not on the problem behavior, but, rather, the desired healthy behavior – what you want, not what you don't.

Sit-downs are balanced in that they address both what's working as well as what still needs work. It's taking focused time to underline the small successes in the past week, restoring some degree of recognition for the efforts still being made for each other.

Sit-downs aren't supposed to be marathon discussions, simply 20 to 30 minutes of re-capping the week and staying on top of what the couple continues to work on.

Many couples will express concerns with lack of success at maintaining change over time. They will state that things improve due to a crisis, but after the crisis passes, things gradually go back to the way they were before. If an accountability ritual exists, this is much less likely to occur, because the work (and the successes) stays visible.

Matt and Jenny had no specific plans for meeting their long-term goals. They needed to come up with actual steps to getting there and needed an accountability routine to keep on top of the progress, or lack of. Everybody needs gentle reminders of the things that are being overlooked or forgotten in the relationship. The key is doing this gently, respectfully, while expecting that each side will remain accountable to what they've agreed on in the past.

Doing a Replay

One of the tendencies for a couple, when they *do* bring up issues, is to over-talk the issue. They keep re-hashing the problem, adding more and more information, but not moving closer to a solution. Pretty soon they've overwhelmed each other with how complicated they've made what could have been a simple misunderstanding or incident.

When I talk with couples about incidences from the past week that might have gone wrong, I'll ask them to do a "replay". **A replay is a simple, structured review of the problem event**. Its focus is, each person taking turns, identifying only 1) what went wrong for you, and 2) what you'd like from your partner that would prevent it from occurring again. Simple as that.

Each person points out what they saw as problematic and what they need for change. What could be a long, drawn-out conversation can be moved through in the span of less than ten minutes.

By staying focused on the information, and sticking with solutions, we keep from attaching all the extra emotional baggage, and are able to resolve things efficiently.

Couples tend to judge themselves based on whether or not these negative encounters occur, but the reality is that they're going to happen. What's *more* important is, when they do, how a couple recovers from it – how quickly they pick themselves up again and do what's necessary to set things right. The problem isn't the argument itself; it's the two or three days of tense silence afterward that creates the rift. If couples were better at doing timely replays of the events, without all the extra punishing and lecturing, staying focused on the end line (arriving at mutual solutions), it would circumvent a world of hurt.

Now, for the bigger issues, a replay will probably fall short. You have to remember that part of working through the bigger issues is the validation and explanations that are necessary to help re-connect us, help restore intimacy. The smaller issues can be approached with simple solutions and refinement, but the bigger issues require more discussion.

Allowing for the "knee-jerk"

"I just need to feel like I've got some room to fail," said Jenny. "Because right now I feel like everything I do is wrong."

Part of the problem for Jenny and Matt was that the areas Jenny was failing in didn't leave much room for continued failure. Her impulsive choices were having too much of a negative impact on the security of the marriage. If Matt was a partier as well, there would have been more room for her to make these types of mistakes. But part of her attraction to Matt was her awareness that he was good for her; that he brought a greater maturity to her life.

For Matt, Jenny's staying out late was a very big thing, and Jenny needed to accept this. Because it was more than just a preference, and something potentially destructive to the relationship, she needed to take it seriously. The solution wasn't for Matt to just back off and tolerate the occasional all-nighter.

At the same time, Jenny's need to have fun was legitimate. What she heard from Matt was that, if she was going to be married she'd have to give up her fun, but that wasn't what he was saying. He was simply saying she needed to learn how to live within limits and be accountable to the things she agreed to.

There's a part to Jenny's comment, though, that's important for me to address because sometimes couples *don't* give enough room for each other's mistakes.

When couples look at change, they need to have realistic expectations that **change is a process**. It doesn't often happen overnight. Jenny was not going to learn discipline in a day or two, but, hopefully, she could exercise enough in the moment with the "big things" that she could be given more room for the smaller things.

In some situations, things *aren't* going to change. If such is the case, we have to decide how important that lack of change is to the relationship.

One of the things that isn't going to change is that each person in the relationship will stubbornly continue to be human. In other words, mistakes *will* be made. Whether the relationship continues depends on just how big those mistakes are.

Let's say that my partner has a recurring problem with saying stupid (insensitive, not well-thought-out) things - not editing in the moment. Now let's say that that problem has been identified and everybody, my partner included, agrees that that is a problem and needs to change.

So a couple of days go by. We're caught up in a conversation and she says something stupid - again. There's an awkward moment. She catches herself, steps back and apologizes.

Was that a failure or a success?

In my mind, that was a success. Yes, she did it again, but she addressed it, owned it, and corrected it. That's change.

Ideally, you would hope it doesn't happen at all, but this is the real world we're talking about. There needs to always be room in the real world for the "knee-jerk". When I say the "knee-jerk", I'm referring to reflex - something that's done without thinking.

While I can try to learn to think before I act, we all have reflexes. We all have instant reactions to things our partner says or does that we don't always step back and manage. It would be unrealistic to expect that we should not have those reactions at all. The important thing is that we learn to better handle them when we have them.

A couple comes to a session and says, "We didn't do very well this week. We got into a big argument."

To which I say, "So, did you resolve it?"

And they say, "In the end, yes."

Then I say, "Then it sounds like you had a successful week."

If they say, "Well, we still argued", my response is, "Yes, but couples *do* argue. Whether it's a success or not is decided by whether you were able to resolve it effectively."

"She didn't validate me again," he says.

"She didn't validate you at all?" I ask.

"Well," he replies, "I had to point it out to her, and then she did."

"Then that's a success," I respond. "Ideally, she can catch it for herself, yes. But, realistically, she's going to miss opportunities to validate, and that's to be expected. But that she was able to do so when it was pointed out can still be regarded as a success."

Reflex and instinct both occur without thinking. **The "knee-jerk", for most people, happens because, in that moment, they haven't yet fully**

thought things through, and, as a result, aren't editing. They're not yet taking into account anybody but themselves. Once they've actually had a moment to *think* about what they just said, to hear themselves, they are often able to catch it, step back, apologize if necessary, and appropriately re-state what they were saying using better words.

We all have selfish aspects, but the concern is for those who are ruled by them. For reactive couples, it takes a while to learn how to stop reacting. For them, *initial success isn't to stop the fight before it starts, but to stop the fight before too much damage is done.* Allowing for the "knee-jerk" with them, is allowing that, initially, they are going to continue to react, but every time they back away from "burning down the house" (walking out, hanging up, etc.) it's a measure of success.

While some would say that editing shouldn't be necessary, that that *lack* of filter is more truthful, they are ignoring two important points: 1) that we *are* separate individuals and have two different languages, and 2) even if we had the exact same language, when we don't edit we often express ourselves in ways that even *we* wouldn't be able to receive.

Editing and truth *can* co-exist. Just because I'm editing myself doesn't mean I'm lying. I'm simply choosing my words wisely and taking into account the needs, and language, of my partner. That requires thought, moreso for some than others.

A success for any interaction is when I'm able to move past self and do what's best for "us". But I need to be given the room to make that transition, rather than instantly being punished for the first thing that comes out of my mouth.[6]

There are people who aren't good at forming their thoughts before they speak. In fact, they organize their thoughts by talking it out. For someone like that, they have to have the freedom to "say it wrong" before they can

---

[6] Let me add to this that there is a difference between "making mistakes" and doing something destructive. An affair is more than a "mistake". Physical or verbal abuse towards my partner is more than a "mistake". Substance abuse is more than a "mistake". Those aren't incidences of "oops". Those are choices that aren't tolerable in a relationship because of how incredibly harmful they can be, so there is far less room for error.

"say it right". What comes out first is rough and undeveloped and needs a chance to be discussed in order to be refined into something accurate. More than allowing for the "knee-jerk", this is allowing for that particular *style* of communicating.

The partner, knowing that is the other's style, knows the initial work for her is not to react to what he's said, but attempt to clarify it first ("Is this what you're saying?") and better flesh it out. Otherwise, an argument starts over what was simply poorly chosen words.

"People-Pleasers" and Insecurity

For somebody who is considered to be a "people-pleaser", there's an additional layer of difficulty in accepting criticism. In order to get along in society we all have to learn to be people-pleasers to a degree. But there is a group of individuals who will often put pleasing others first to such an extent that their identity is more wrapped up in maintaining those positive impressions than being honest and letting it be known when their own identity or opinions are being compromised.

Because a people-pleaser's focus is primarily about pleasing people, when it comes to criticism, the people-pleaser is being faced with the dilemma of being told that she hasn't been successful in being pleasing – she's failing at her primary mission. It creates a particular dilemma for her when confronted with fault, because she is working so hard at trying to project that she has no faults.

We are graded in school for how often we're right. We move further in our careers based on how many past successes we've had. We go from dating to marriage partly because of how much approval and acceptance our partner shows us. Because so many of us are brought up to present positive images to the world in order to be accepted and promoted by others, we are naturally hesitant and uncomfortable when it comes to being wrong, or when our flaws are revealed. The natural gut-level reaction would be that if I'm seen to be imperfect, then I risk being no longer accepted or successful.

The people-pleaser often has an over-simplified view of love and approval. Because their black-and-white interpretation of *any* personal criticism is rejection or judgment, it's often confusing for the people-pleaser to see a partner who attempts to positively criticize as still loving them. "If they loved me, they wouldn't criticize (reject or judge) me."

Part of this limited perspective often has to do with insecurity. As I mentioned earlier in the book, an insecure individual's sense of self is often constructed around a fear of failure, rejection or abandonment. Even if she doesn't see herself as a failure, she's afraid that others might. So she will expend a lot of energy to either continually prove her worth, or avoid/destroy/deny any information that attempts to cast a critical light on her behavior. For her, even small criticisms are very difficult because they automatically set off those deeper fears.

I'm going to be mixing the terms here, but I should add that not all "people-pleasers" are insecure, nor are all insecure individuals "people-pleasers" – however, both groups typically have problems with giving and receiving criticism, and, when you are both (an insecure, people-pleaser), the problem becomes magnified.

The people-pleaser "deals" with her insecurity by attempting to control everyone's perception of her, creating different "masks" for whatever she thinks that particular person wants to see. This can be a self-protective measure for the people-pleaser. If her faults or weaknesses are kept safe from the world, then they can't be used to judge or hurt her. If she only allows others to get so close, then she's only so vulnerable.

What the people-pleaser often fails to truly grasp is that there is an aspect of deception that goes along with wearing the masks. While she wants to be loved and accepted, or in control and safe, she is making this difficult to directly experience because of the masks she wears – after all, it's *the mask* that is being accepted, not her.

Wearing the masks can be viewed from two different perspectives. One point of view is that the people-pleaser wears a different mask for whomever they're with (tailored for that particular person). The other perspective is that the people-pleaser wears the same approval-seeking mask with everybody. Whichever way you look at it, the end result is that nobody ever knows where they really stand with the people-pleaser because the people-pleaser actively avoids voicing any direct opinions that might be seen as hurtful. They may voice negative opinions about *others*, but they typically won't express negative opinions about the person they're with.

If the masks are discovered (often because people within the same circles compare notes), the people-pleaser still ends up with the negative reputation they were trying to avoid. Their own positive efforts to be accepted lead to their rejection.

The vocations of salesmen and politicians are often equated with the concept of people-pleaser - with the same end result. We question where they really stand, and really can't help but feel that it's all about making the sale, or getting the vote of approval.

❖   ❖   ❖

You would think that because people-pleasers see criticism as rejection that they would be hesitant to criticize others, however, internally, they can be very critical. Part of their being driven to be pleasing is because of their own internal self-criticism. They can be their own harshest judge. But they also tend to judge others with a similar harshness, though they are unlikely to directly express these thoughts.

What makes it sometimes difficult to identify a people-pleaser within a marriage is due to the fact that the people-pleaser often no longer puts the energy into pleasing the partner the way that she does for the rest of the world, and that internal critical world she usually reserves for herself, because of weakening boundaries, starts to seep out onto the partner. It becomes an additional issue for the relationship, because the partner of the people-pleaser sees everyone else getting the specialized treatment that he used to be getting, and still desires.

Even then, while the people-pleaser may be more vocal and openly critical to her partner, she will still often avoid voicing her deeper negative thoughts and feelings about him. Part of this may be necessary self-editing, but sometimes this avoidance creates a gulf in the relationship where the things that really need to be discussed are never brought to the surface.

Because both people-pleasers and insecure people, paradoxically, *fear* criticism while, at the same time, *over-indulge* in it, they usually don't do a lot of deep self-analysis. Self-exploration for them is often too painful – it's easier to stay on the surface. After all, for them, self-criticism is the same as self-rejection.

For the people-pleaser to move past this mindset, she has to be willing to live in a way that challenges the inherent fear of being criticized. She has to risk being herself in order to ever feel truly accepted. The healthy truth is that not everyone's going to like you – and that's okay. You need to like yourself enough that your satisfaction with you doesn't depend on the rest of the world. And you need to have people in your life that accept you, knowing who "you" is. At the same time, "accepting you" means that they (your friends) will still offer constructive criticism because that is part of caring.

In terms of the marriage, the people-pleaser needs to intentionally approach being honest with her partner about her thoughts, fears and feelings, while still remaining sensitive about her delivery. And she needs to nurture getting the same in return, without reacting or taking it as a judgment.

For many people-pleasers they've worn so many masks, they really don't know who they are underneath it all. But better to face that and begin to build a true identity that you can grow old with, than to remain dependent on the identities that everyone else would have you assume. For many, getting to this point is their first "mid-life crisis".

Since change is often attempted by going to the other extreme, let me add that becoming "you" shouldn't occur to the degree that you no longer care about "them". Because you do care, you still attempt to please others, but you learn to do it with a healthy balance that doesn't compromise self to an unhealthy or deceptive degree.[7]

❖   ❖   ❖

---

[7] I want to be sure that I don't portray insecure individuals or people-pleasers as being incredibly troubled – the degree of dysfunction depends on how extreme the issue. By nature of the dysfunction they are often very likeable, endearing individuals.

Insecurity, because it is fear-based, and therefore feeling-based, is often wrapped up in certain thought distortions, which I'll get into later in Chapter 9. Unmanaged fear tends to bring about the very things that we're afraid of. If we're afraid of being rejected, and, as a result, unable to accept criticism, we invite *more* criticism (and rejection) because of our refusal or inability to hear it. Ultimately, we may even orchestrate our own abandonment because our partners can't live with a person who's never wrong, or never able to be up-front with us about how they really feel.

As with the extremes of control issues (under-control and over-control) and validation issues (under-listening and over-listening), **insecure people often leap back and forth between self-condemnation** (where they see themselves as a total failure)**, and displacing the blame** (putting it on everyone or everything else) **when the self-condemnation becomes too overwhelming**. There is no balance, no grey territory, where they can just see themselves realistically as flawed but still "worthy".

❖   ❖   ❖

Insecurity is shown outwardly in different ways, depending on how extreme the issues are.

For some, they openly advertise their weakness through chronically-expressed self-doubt, self-criticism, or seeking of compliments.

For those who over-compensate for it, what is displayed to the outside world is an image of strength, confidence, and "having it all together". They project the opposite of what they feel inside. For the over-compensating types, it's often only those that they are closest to that know the public mask protects the insecurity underneath – and many times even those closest are unaware.

Rather than entertain the useful information a positive criticism contains, for the insecure it's easier, and less painful, to find ways to cast off the criticism than consider its validity - easier to put it back on the criticizer as being negative and rejecting than actually attempting to help her improve.

If I'm going to thrive in a relationship, however, it means that I'm going to have to be open to learn how to let go of my insecurity. I'm going to have to be willing to be vulnerable and embrace the idea that my partner loves me, and that her love will not go away just because she sees me as less than perfect, or has a criticism to share.[8]

Discussion Questions:

1. **Do you see change as a good thing or a bad thing? When you look back on your life do you feel like you've changed a lot or a little?** If so, in a good way or a bad way? Do you feel like either of you have changed over the course of just the relationship? Again, in what ways?

2. **Is there a common standard around what's fair in the marriage – in terms of the chores, in terms of spending, in terms of how you approach conflict?**

3. **How do the two of you attempt to hold each other accountable?** Is it a passive, assertive or aggressive style of accountability? Is it more judgment than loving criticism? More focused on the person than the behavior? More Parent/Child than Adult?

4. **Understanding the ideals (assertive, loving criticism coming from a behavior-focused Adult), if you were going to improve how you approach accountability with each other, what would you change in your own approach, and what would work better coming from your partner?**

5. **Is there any kind of accountability routine in place for the marriage?** If so, is the routine a working one? If there is not one, do you see the need for one? Do you ever do "re-plays" of events, which simply focus on what we each could have done different for a better outcome?

---

[8] This is one of the reasons why it's important to "talk from the hurt" when we are attempting to confront each other. If I'm identifying that I'm sharing this because I care, because of how much I love her, and it's hurting me, or us, it makes it a little more palatable and at least attempts to keep the partner from assuming a negative motivation. Whether or not the insecure person can buy into the partner's positive motivation for the criticism depends on 1) the partner's delivery, 2) the history of the relationship, and 3) just how insecure (how wounded) she is.

6. **Do you allow for the "knee-jerk" in your relationship - is there room to make mistakes?**

7. **Does either insecurity or being a people-pleaser play a negative role in your marriage?** If so, what can each of you do to start moving past it, or help to heal it?

Chapter 8
Forgiveness

Part of grace is the application of forgiveness for past wrongs. If we can't forgive then we're no longer truly accepting – and a sense of acceptance is part of the foundation of any marriage.

The aftermath of accountability is, when change occurs, being able to let go of the hurt that the lack of change prior to that had caused. If we nurse that hurt, despite our partners having corrected the problem, then *we* are now the ones holding the relationship back.

The daily minor mistakes, oversights and faults that occur in a marriage require a forgiving attitude. So it's necessary, if a relationship is going to progress, that a couple incorporates forgiveness as a relationship ritual.

When couples seek help, saying they want to work on the relationship, what often holds them back from being motivated to actually whole-heartedly do the work is that they have yet to forgive. It's in their voices. It's in their body language. It's in the lack of the benefit of the doubt. They're waiting for something to happen that will allow them to open their hearts again.

It becomes a problem of sequence. They are waiting to see change in order to feel like it's okay to forgive, but, in the meantime, there's no motivation to invest in change themselves. Each waits for the other to let go and invest. And so, nothing changes.

Counselors, themselves, debate the sequence that therapy should take for such issues. Some say you can't work on the issues until forgiveness occurs. Some say you can't work on forgiveness until the issues causing the unforgiveness are dealt with. Others try to address both at the same time.

The surprising thing to me is that there are some couples who have no intention of forgiving. They seem to think that they can resolve issues while hanging on to the anger that burns inside. **What is supposed to be an attempt to draw closer cannot occur so long as they hold on to what keeps them apart.**

There are many marriages that morbidly exist where neither partner really likes the other anymore. They trade insults instead of compliments, condemn rather than seek to understand, and sabotage rather than support or inspire. It's almost a shared hatred, rather than a shared love. That is what happens, over time, when the poison of unforgiveness sinks in. It doesn't just corrupt the heart; it corrupts the soul of the marriage.

Part of the issue revolves around emotional discipline (not letting the emotions make the choices), part of it is about understanding healthy love (doing what's best for the future of the relationship), and part of it is understanding what forgiveness is really all about.

Little Things and Big Things

Colby and Tyler had been married about six years but were currently separated. They were coming for counseling now because, for the past year-and-a-half, they had rapidly grown distant from each other. Colby had just recently moved out of the house.

"I left because we've stopped having sex," said Colby. "I told her that there's no way I'm going to remain in a marriage when I can't even have sex with my own wife."

"How long has this been a problem?" I asked.

"About a year now," Colby replied.

"We're not having sex because he's not willing to put any time into romance any more," Tyler said. "He just acts like I should cooperate whenever he wants to get physical."

"That's not true," Colby responded. "There are times when I do try to court you – I take you out to eat; I'll go places with you; I'll be physically affectionate..."

"Yes," said Tyler. "But I know that your agenda is trying to get me to have sex."

"Colby, why is sex so important to you that you'd be willing to leave the relationship over it?" I asked. I wasn't trying to downplay the importance of sex, but if what I was guessing was right, Tyler needed to hear what Colby was about to say.

"It's my connection to her," he replied. "It's how I show her that I care. And it's how I reassure myself that she cares about me, that she still desires me. Yes, I'm human, so part of it is that it feels good too. But that's not the only reason why it's a big deal for me."

"So it's one of the big ways you look to Tyler to know that she loves you," I re-stated.

"Yes," he said.

"And so, by her not being willing to go there with you, the unspoken message she's giving is 'I don't love you anymore'?" I asked.

"Exactly."

Part of the discernment that goes along with forgiveness is knowing the difference between what you should take offense to in the first place.

For some, the problem is that every little thing is an offense. This is difficult ground since part of respecting different perspectives embraces that what may be a little thing to you is a big thing for me. But there are still larger truths, one of which is that sometimes the issue is that a partner does not have a balanced perspective.

For instance, I had a client who was going to end her marriage because she discovered her husband had been looking at "soft" pornography on the internet. In her eyes, it was the same as if he were having an affair. That's not to say that pornography is a minor issue, but the severity of this particular case fell into the category of "misuse", not an actual addiction. But, for the wife, the idea of stepping back and applying accountability, instead of ending the marriage as she intended to do, was seen as being an ethical compromise that couldn't be considered. There was no room for forgiveness.

Part of the reason for the conflict resolution rule, "**attach a priority to the issue, so there is some sense of how important or unimportant it is**", goes beyond helping our partners understand how big certain issues are for us. The rule also exists so we have to sort through for ourselves, "Thinking of the big picture, just how important is this really?"

In the moment, when we're upset, even small things can be seen to be big. But, hopefully, with a little distance from the incident, there's some degree of re-assessment that goes on, and we can recognize that it was an over-reaction and we need to either make amends or demote the status we've given to the issue in our minds.

Because of rigidity, there are those who never re-assess. They are either too prideful, too stubborn, or too afraid to question their own conclusions. The message they give to the partner is, "I'm beyond reasoning this through. There's no working this out. I'm not going to get over this."

On the surface, Colby and Tyler's situation seemed to be a logic loop. Tyler was withholding sex because she believed Colby wanted sex without intimacy – in other words, it wasn't about him wanting to be with her; it was about him wanting to be with her body. However, when Colby *did* attempt intimacy it wouldn't work because of Tyler's conspiracy theory about Colby's true agenda. So, in reality, at this point, she was withholding sex no matter what he did. Because of her unwillingness to question her own logic, she was creating a dilemma that was hurting everybody. The *degree* of her rigidity indicated that there was more going on than what was being presented.

How men and women view sex differently is a very common phenomenon. It wasn't something wrong with Colby – it was simply two different views on what sex meant for each. For men in general, aside from the physical pleasure of it, sex is an affirmation of their partners' love and desire for them. It's how they look to connect. For women, sex is often the *outcome* of feeling emotionally connected, not *how* they connect.

❖　❖　❖

Minimal as it may sound, some marriages do "go critical" even over things as simple as standards of cleanliness. "I am so sick and tired of picking up after him. Yet, he'll still leave things lying around. He knows how much that bothers me." Yes, he may know it bothers her, but that doesn't mean he's leaving things around intentionally trying to upset her.

We pay attention to the things that are important to *us*. A clean house was important to her, not as much to him. That doesn't mean he doesn't work at raising his awareness of mess, but it does mean she needs to also recognize that "mess" is in his blind spot. What gets left "lying around" occurs because the things that are important to him are in a totally different spectrum. Chances are he *is* picking up after himself at times, but what gets noticed, and addressed, is when he doesn't. She concludes that he doesn't care about what's important, that *she's* not important to him, and he concludes that she's overly critical of his oversights.

If she were married to herself, and this other self was ignoring the mess, then she would have a much clearer right to take as much offense as she did. But she needed to grasp that she was filling in the blanks of his motivations by projecting her own, "If it were *me*, the only way I could ignore that mess is if I just didn't care about my partner." He *wasn't* her, and so it was irrational for her to try to attach her meaning to his actions.

So, the two-part solution is that he continues to work on adding "mess" to the things he pays attention to (both partners understanding that it will never be identical to her ideal), and she works on not taking his oversights so personally.

If we give credibility to what Tyler was saying, she thought Colby had a superficial view of sex. For him to be leaving over the sexual issue, confirmed to Tyler that he only wanted her for sex because he was willing to give up the marriage if he didn't get it. But what Colby *was* saying was that the reason it was so important to him was that it was one of the primary ways he felt loved by her. How could he stay in a marriage where he felt consistently unloved?

❖   ❖   ❖

As I said earlier in the book, part of the sorting we need to go through between what's a big thing and what's not-so-big, comes back to being able to make the distinction between preferences and needs. How neat your home is is a preference. While your partner should be respectful of your preferences and try to support them, hopefully you don't lose sight of the fact that it is simply a preference. Many couples find this out for themselves when children come along and there's constant mess, and they simply learn to adjust.

There *are* times when we might need to ask our partners to treat a particular preference like a need because it is a particularly important preference to us. But the greater concern for these types of requests is how *often* they happen. To a "high maintenance" individual the majority of preferences are felt to be needs. These are the people who have a particular way of doing most everything, and they insist that their partner replicate "how I want it done", or how they think it *should* be done.

In terms of forgiveness, it shouldn't be a matter of needing to forgive your partner for not having the same preferences ("I forgive you for not being more like me."), so much as learning to adjust your expectations to fit the reality.

Colby was, in no uncertain terms, saying to Tyler that sex *was* a need for him – in fact, it involved *all three* core needs, so it was triply powerful. It made him feel valued (loved) by her. It made him feel secure in the relationship. And it was one way he chose to have fun with her. For Tyler, while she would say that she thought sex was important, her actions indicated she viewed it as more of a preference, and, therefore, to her, Colby was the superficial one for attaching such importance to it.

Intentional versus Unintentional Harm

"Do you think she's trying to hurt you intentionally by withholding sex?" I asked.

177

"Yes," Colby said.

"Are you, Tyler?" I asked.

"No, I'm not," said Tyler. "I just need this relationship to be about more than what he wants."

"Tyler, do you think Colby's intentionally trying to hurt you?"

"By moving out, yes," said Tyler.

"Are you, Colby?" I asked.

"I'm not trying to hurt her. I'm trying to show her I'm not okay with continuing to live like this," said Colby.

Part of what we need to look at in attaching significance to a wrong has to do with whether or not it was intentional. Like it or not, there is a difference between an accident versus intentional harm - which is why I have much less tolerance for those who intentionally wound their partners than those who do so without intent. It becomes an issue of character. Even the law makes this distinction in passing sentence; attaching a significantly greater penalty if a wrongful act is pre-meditated.

Those who adopt the theme of "an eye for an eye" don't weigh intent as a factor in determining whether or not they hurt back - all that matters is that they've been hurt. Yet it doesn't equalize things to hurt a partner the way you were hurt; it actually puts you *below* them if they hadn't hurt you intentionally. And now there's a whole new level to what the relationship needs to work through because at least one partner has a vindictive style of reacting.

During my daughter's early days I had to wrestle with my own reaction to her mistakes. I would tell her repeatedly to be careful with food and drinks in the living room, but, inevitably, though not often, something would get spilled. My immediate reaction would be one of agitation ("What did I tell you about being careful?"), but I'd have to bite my tongue because she hadn't done it intentionally. She wasn't trying to ignore my warnings or make me upset. Realistically, mistakes were going to happen.

When boundaries fail and couples lose perspective, they often see intent where there is none. Because we supposedly know each other so well, the thinking is, "They know that bothers me; there's no way they could have done that unintentionally." Because our sensitivity about certain things is so visible to us, we assume it has to be just as visible to our partners.

So, does an accident or a mistake even require forgiveness? The answer would be that it really depends on the extent of the damage done. We may find that we are still harboring painful feelings towards someone even though we know what she did wasn't intentional. For the family of the person killed in an accidental car wreck, they may have difficulty not blaming the driver of the car. So they still have to move through forgiveness. For others, because they recognize that the wreck was a mistake, forgiveness isn't necessary; it's simply viewed as a tragic mishap.

In many situations, the person who made the mistake is already experiencing enough self-recrimination that we don't really need to add to it by hanging on to the event. The person who puts her hand on the stove and gets burned really doesn't need any additional judgment for making that mistake. The pain is built in to the experience. So long as they are owning the mistake, the lesson is learned.

For Colby and Tyler, this wasn't about mistakes. They were making *intentional* choices, but the primary motivation *wasn't* to intentionally hurt. That it hurt was more of a side-effect, although I suspect, at this point, the fact that it *did* hurt wasn't necessarily seen as a negative. There *was* an aspect of punishment to what was going on. But what each focused on was how the other was hurting them, rather than paying attention to the *primary* motivators for why the other was choosing to do what they did.

Ownership and Remorse

"So, Tyler, what are you looking for from Colby in order to feel more comfortable with having a physical relationship again?" I asked.

"I need to feel like he cares about me, not just about the sex," she replied.

"Yet, when he's tried to do that, you suspected him of an agenda. How will you know that whatever he does is not about this agenda?" I asked.

"I don't know," said Tyler.

"Colby, what are you looking for from Tyler in order to come back?"

"I want to have a physical relationship with my wife again," he said.

"Which," interrupted Tyler, "only confirms for me that this is all about his agenda just to have sex."

It's much more difficult for us to let something go when there is no ownership taken over what happened. If there's no ownership, we automatically fear that 1) our concern isn't understood or valued, or 2) that it's going to happen again.

Even with ownership, however, the ease of moving through forgiveness still depends on the extent of the wrong. If my partner had an affair, has apologized for it and not had any others, it still doesn't make it a simple task for me to just move on. Because of the severity of the wrong, the wound goes deep.

Sometimes we need to think in terms of a literal wound, "Is this just a scratch, or is it something worse?" If it's a scratch, the band-aid of an apology may be all that's necessary to heal it. If it's a wound, aside from the medicine of intentional positive actions to heal the wound, time plays a big factor. In these terms, unforgiveness is an injury that either goes untreated, or is self-agitated, to the point that the wound becomes infected and starts to spread to the rest of the body.

Forgiveness for the deeper things is a process – just as healing is a process. There will be times when you've moved past the hurt, and other times when events or memories move you back to a place where you'll need to move through forgiveness again – just as there are times when we've agitated old physical injuries.

I mentioned how we can self-agitate a wound. We need to be very careful that, if we're the ones who are trying to forgive, that, in the process, we don't do some very destructive things ourselves that now require *us* to be forgiven. We end up wounding out of our own woundedness.

An understanding partner accepts that forgiveness doesn't always happen overnight. Some things take time. As the offender, because of his own discomfort with his part in causing the harm, he would prefer that his partner moves through her pain as quickly as possible, but he needs to be accepting of the fact that deep hurts don't heal quickly.

Children are often taught that the healthy process is to say "I'm sorry" and then the other person is supposed to say "I forgive you." While, as adults, that's still a healthy process, it often can't occur that quickly if it's going to be truly meaningful. We need to apologize and forgive *when we are sincere*. It's not something that can be forced. ("I demand that you forgive me.") While we don't want to make forgiveness a control struggle by withholding it as a form of punishment, we also shouldn't rush to say that we forgive before we've truly forgiven. (At the same time, we also don't want to hang onto unforgiveness any longer than necessary.)

Discomfort can be a good thing if it motivates change. Rushing through forgiveness, aside from pretending to ourselves we've really worked through it when we haven't really had the time, undercuts the necessary discomfort that the offender, as well, needs to go through in facing the impact of his choices. That time is what makes the extent of the "victim's" hurt real to the offender. By the offender trying to force the victim through quick forgiveness, he's making it about him, when, at this point, it's really about the victim. Attempting to microwave the forgiveness process doesn't work in the long run for either the victim or the offender because it's avoiding legitimate pain. It seems odd to refer to it this way, but taking the time to truly forgive is a form of healthy love.[9]

The offender needs to trust that his partner is working towards forgiveness and allowing her the time to get there.

The "victim" is trying to do several things in the meantime:

---

[9]   This is obviously sensitive territory because this aspect can be abused intentionally by the victim in order to punish – dragging out forgiving menial things and becoming the disciplining parent in the process.

- not using the wrong as a weapon to condemn
- not intentionally withhold being civil while she's working towards forgiveness
- when discussing the wrong, focusing on talking from the heart (which shares the injured love), rather than punishing by advertising only anger
- trying to isolate her pain so it doesn't seep into every other area of the relationship, recognizing that just because one area is under repair doesn't mean that everything is broken

❖   ❖   ❖

So what do we do when our partner will not own her part - will not apologize or change her ways?

Again, it depends on how serious the wrong is.

If this is about preferences, as we've already discussed, you need to learn to accept the differences because it's not really about right or wrong. Why should they apologize for being different? Even in these situations, though, in terms of validation, there is always room to apologize for unintentional hurt. ("I'm sorry, honey, I don't mean to hurt you, or give you that message, by doing that.")

Beyond preferences, if a wrong is need-related or destructive to the relationship, accountability needs to be approached. This assumes we've already approached our partners, educating them about how their behavior is impacting us - more than just a passing complaint, we've had a focused conversation about just how big a deal it is for us. So we've addressed it before, but nothing has changed. Now we're raising the bar to address this fact. "From my perspective, I've approached this already with you and I haven't seen any progress with it. Do you understand how important this particular issue is to me? What I'm asking for from you is...."

If accountability is refused, it brings into question the future of the relationship, because a marriage without accountability is not really a marriage.

❖   ❖   ❖

An example of a dilemma between preferences, needs, and accountability occurs around playful **teasing** – a seemingly benign event. Men, stereotypically, tend to connect with other men through verbal sparring. Women tend to connect with other women through compliments. While some people would label "teasing" as a communication preference, not a need, if it's not correctly understood, and, as a result, taken personally, it can be very destructive to a relationship.

A woman raised with a lot of brothers, or male friends, tends to learn how to handle teasing. She understands that it's not meant as a personal insult. A woman, or even a man, not raised around teasing often takes it very personally because they aren't able to make the distinction between teasing and put-downs. In such mixed relationships where one person teases and the other person doesn't, often the person who doesn't will get to a point where she insists that the partner stop his teasing. Yet, if that's the only way he knows how to playfully "connect", he's now left with no way to verbally have fun with his partner – his primary language has been taken away.

But here, too, there is room for a two-part solution. He needs to build up his language skills in other areas (compliments) while learning to identify what "safe" teasing looks like for her. At the same time, she needs to allow *some* room for being teased, working at not taking it so personally, while identifying for him what is "going overboard" for her.

In addition, since teasing is part of his communication style, she may even want to learn how to tease back. In the intimacy chapter I talked about this – how we need to learn to *incorporate* the positives that each of us brings to a relationship. We become more balanced individuals by being able to speak each other's languages. He learns to better compliment; she learns to better tease.[10]

---

[10]   Let me make a distinction between teasing and sarcasm. Teasing is playful and makes light of flaws and eccentricities; it minimizes them and is not meant to start an argument. Sarcasm has an edge to it that cuts with its humor, often being an indirect way of punishing or bringing up an issue. We have to be careful to recognize the line between the two, because many can't see it.

During times of stress, teasing is much more likely to be taken personally – so you have to be sensitive to time and place. One of the gauges for restored perspective in a relationship is the room for humor and the ability to be teased.

❖   ❖   ❖

In addition to ownership, there needs to be **remorse**. Often, when apologies or ownership are extended, it is still difficult to truly accept the gesture if the emotional sincerity is lacking. ("Yes, she apologized, but she really didn't seem like she was sorry.")

For people who tend to repress their emotions, or those who are thinking-based, this can be problematic because they don't usually convey their emotions in their words. They have to work much harder to emotionally express their regret.

If they can't get the emotions into the words, they need to spend more time verbalizing the extent of the regret so the partner can see they "get it". The quick "I'm sorry," and moving on, for the bigger hurts, just doesn't cut it.

For those that can't express remorse because they don't agree with the seriousness that their partners are attaching to the "wrong", part of the process is getting beyond self, their own opinion, and trying to empathize with their partner - which doesn't require agreement. It goes back to validation. You focus on the partner's perception to the degree that you can feel some of what she feels. If you still care about your partner, you should be able to access some degree of remorse that you've caused her pain.

This is very important since couples caught in pain are each stuck in their own pain. "Yes, that was hurtful for you, but you hurt me over here." But it doesn't matter. One hurt at a time. You have to walk through each, rather than trying to compare. Comparison only creates a stalemate. Your being able to validate (apologize, acknowledge, own) her pain, frees her to validate yours. Who's going to be the model for what needs to happen?

For Colby and Tyler, each was "owning" the choices that were being made. Nobody was denying that sex was being withheld or somebody had moved out, but there was no ownership in terms of wrong – no ownership in terms of "what I'm doing isn't working". And there was no remorse on either side. Both were caught up in the other's wrong. Validation (and, as a result, perspective) was absent.

Forgiveness and Control

"So who's going to be the first to step out of the control struggle?" I asked.

Nobody said anything.

"The problem with a control struggle is that nobody wins," I continued. "The two of you are living proof. Both of you are caught up in controlling the other's choices. Both of you have significant points, but the path you're choosing to take to make your point isn't drawing anybody closer; it's pushing you further apart."

Part of the reason why it's difficult for us to let go, at times, is because we remain over-focused on what's not in our control. We very much want to be able to force a different outcome, or at least have some influence over it, and are struggling with our own helplessness in the situation.

In marriage, we need to accept that there will always be things that are out of our control in terms of our partners. Because they are separate from us, unique individuals, and because healthy relationships are based on freedom and choice, we have to allow for those times when our partners do things that we wouldn't choose for them to do.

The intellectual tight-rope we walk is having to ask ourselves, "Is this an action that requires accountability, or just me fighting with my own desire to control what's going on?" Often, what helps to make that distinction is asking, "Is this about what's best for us, or just what's best for me?"

Frequently, what separated and divorced couples struggle with is managing their own obsessing over the wrongs that were done to them. In a way, they're still trying to resolve past issues in their heads, but they can't get resolution because it requires change from the unwilling and now physically distant partners – who, in turn, are focused on all the wrongs done to them. Each side is looking for some degree of ownership, and not getting it, and so they're unable to "let it go". They're still trying to control each other's choices, even if all they want is some form of understanding from the partner of their perspective in all of it. While letting go of needing to control isn't the same as forgiveness, the acceptance of where things are, and where they're not, is a step closer to it.

The most difficult situations to deal with are where tragic things occur and the "victim" is left feeling like she had no choice in what happened. It's the separation scenario where one partner walks away from the marriage against the other's wishes. It's the person with the lifetime career who is unexpectedly laid off – a significant part of his identity taken away in the process. It's the adult who experienced childhood abuse, helpless to stand up for herself while it happened. It's the victims of natural disasters where the only thing they can do is continue to survive.

Typically, what we want in such situations is justice. We want fairness, or revenge, to have our lives back the way they were before, or to have our own pain validated in some significant way. But because that is unlikely to happen, even though we may try, we continue to remain traumatized, and, sometimes, stuck in our anger or helplessness.

That sense of helplessness, and the need to not continue to feel helpless, becomes a very driving force to make something happen. Security has been taken away and we need to regain some sense of control in order to once again feel secure. **Because letting go, or working towards forgiveness, seems like such passive things to do, they aren't often viewed as choices that restore a sense of control**. But so long as we are caught up in trying to control what is beyond our control, we stay mired in a control struggle we can't really win. Forgiveness and "letting go" restores a sense of personal freedom, rather than remaining in bondage to something or someone else.

The choices in any of these situations always come back to the same thing: separating what's in your control to act on, and letting go of what's beyond your control. So long as we stay hypnotized by all of the things beyond our control, we give up what control we do have to regain our peace.

To effectively take control means that we approach things in healthy ways, though they may still be difficult – ways that bring us closer to a solution, not create more problems. For those difficult scenarios I described, the partner left behind may still choose to let the ex know what she wants from him in order to let go ("What I need from you is ….") but willing to accept that the request may not be granted.[11]

---

[11]   She may even want to make the request easier for him to respond to by first asking him what he needs at that point from her.

The person whose lifetime career is gone puts his energy into finding new options, embracing a new path, with the expanded insight that the job security he'd taken for granted was an illusion.

The adult who went through childhood abuse may choose to confront the offender, but without the expectation that the offender will be able to positively respond to it.

The victim of the disaster focuses on starting a new life, accepting that, while bad things happen, life still goes on – and part of embracing life is remaining open to risk.

What Forgiveness Is Not

Many times couples get stuck in unforgiveness because their perception of forgiveness, what they think it means to forgive, is based on faulty assumptions. Let me itemize some of the most common misperceptions.

"If I forgive her, she'll think that what she did was okay; that it really wasn't that big of a deal for me because I got over it."

While there is always the concern that the offender will view forgiveness as the victim coming to see the wrong really wasn't a big thing, there are much better ways of letting your partner know how big something is for you other than refusing to forgive.

As I discussed in terms of control, in such situations we are often attempting to use unforgiveness as a means to control our partners' choices. But forgiveness, or lack of, is *not* meant to be a tool for compliance or punishment.

Our primary tool is *education* - being clear about the impact certain choices have on us. Couples need to have a clear understanding of the difference between what is a pet peeve, versus what is hurtful, versus what is intolerable for each other.

For those things that are intolerable, while we may be willing to forgive that first time and continue in the relationship so long as change lasts, accountability has us still draw a new line that we need to stand by that, if crossed again, we are willing to follow through on the consequences. For example: the couple who has decided to move past the first affair and stay together. The new line is zero tolerance for any re-occurrence (which it should be). If the prior "offender" knows that that line is real, ideally, the significance of losing his relationship remains his primary motivator to stay committed. If he still crosses it, the relationship ends. In such a case, ending it isn't a lack of forgiveness, it's holding your partner accountable for the choices he made.

"If I forgive, it makes it more likely she'll do it again."

This is often the mentality of the couples who live in chronic unforgiveness. The relationship has this atmosphere of undying condemnation hanging over it. ("You know what you did to me.") Yet, if a relationship is going to continue, it can't expect to stay afloat with an anchor around its neck.

I knew of one couple where the husband had had an affair several years ago, and the wife *had* forgiven him. Yet, since that time, the husband had remained in depression. His pathology was that, if he allowed himself to be happy again, he would be ignoring what he had done. His depression was his personal penance. To forgive, in his own mind, would be letting himself off the hook. He failed to make the distinction that a *healthy* penance would have been to do his best to assume responsibility for healing the damage done to the relationship - correcting his wrongs as much as possible, not living in condemnation of them. Forgiving himself was necessary for the relationship to heal.

We do need to be watchful of negative patterns of behavior in a relationship. But if the same destructive behavior persists, the intervention needed is accountability, not lack of forgiveness.

"If I forgive, she's not experiencing any consequences for what she did."

To forgive does not mean that there is an absence of *natural* consequences. The consequences are built in to the choices. Every serious wound to the relationship leaves a scar. It injures the trust, or the love, or the respect. If the security has been attacked, the reality is that you're going to be less secure. The offender needs to understand that your being less secure is not a lack of forgiveness; it's just a consequence of the wrong that was done. Forgiveness implies that you're *both* invested in healing the insecurity, but that it's going to take time and evidence of change – in other words, there is still accountability for correcting past behavior.

You could rationalize that the anger you show your partner for hurting you is just another natural consequence, but if the anger is shown in a destructive way, it is neither helpful to the relationship, nor healing – it's intentional harm.

The consequences for the serious wrongs that we commit show themselves in deeper ways other than how we, on the surface, attempt to verbally consequent each other. Yet, often, the reason we verbally consequent is because we're trying to get our partner to understand just how deep the hurt goes, especially if they are conveying to us that they don't get it. It's true that many only pay attention when there *are* surface consequences, otherwise they fail to see more deeply how their choices are impacting the marriage.

For such things as affairs and abuse, there are typically separations that occur afterwards in order to get some emotional distance and restore perspective. The separation is a consequence of the negative action, not a punishment. It isn't done to hurt the offender, but to temporarily self-protect.

Ultimately, the distinction between punishment and consequences is the intent behind it – to hurt, to hold accountable, or to heal.

"If I forgive, then I have to forget."

Yet, "He who forgets the past is doomed to repeat it."

Forgiveness isn't about wiping the slate clean. It's not acting like what happened never happened; it's simply choosing to not continue to dwell on it.

There are three negative extremes in regards to time (past, present and future). Looking so rigidly ahead that we aren't able to learn those necessary lessons from our past, and missing out on the moment. Being so stuck in the present moment that we have no long-term perspective and everything is about doing what feels good *now*. Or being so stuck focusing on the past that we continue to fall for lack of watching where we're going - a failure to let go and move on.

The healthy couple incorporates both past, present and future. In order to learn from our past as a couple, we need to remember our past mistakes, using discretion in when, if ever, we choose to bring it up, while staying focused on the present and the path ahead, having learned from those wrong paths taken before.

"If I forgive, I will have to allow that unsafe person back into my life."

I mention this in terms of people *outside* of the marriage relationship, though sometimes it does apply to a marriage if a history of abuse or significantly destructive behavior has existed.

As I said, there *are* consequences for actions, and we should never abandon healthy discretion. If you know someone is not safe for you, while you forgive them for the hurt in order to let go of your own pain, you don't necessarily invite them back into your life. It depends.

We want to avoid being black-and-white (total acceptance or total rejection) because that is an overly simplistic (and not very realistic) way to live. In some situations, we *do* allow friends, or family, who have hurt us back in, but it means we should also have learned *how far* we can trust them and how far we can't. If we know we can only trust them to a certain degree, then that is all that we give them. If we desire to have a deeper relationship than that, at times, we may want to risk a deeper trust in order to test the waters again, but we do so cautiously.

Part of this has to do with adjusting expectations to fit the picture. I have had clients who, whenever they would attend a family reunion, knew they were going to be emotionally hurt by at least one or two family members. It was predictable. So, they'd go, and sure enough, get hurt again. While they were overly-focused on what the family member did or was going to do, they really needed to turn the focus back on why they themselves kept expecting a different outcome from a predictable event. Like the saying, "Fool me once, shame on you. Fool me twice, shame on me."

If you know that a person is, predictably, a certain way, why do you remain vulnerable to that? In other words, if you've decided that they're going to remain in your life, why at some point don't your expectations change to accept what you can predict? If they're being consistent, then you should be able to step around or above that, and not let it ruin things. This is, after all, them being them. ("I know, most likely, they're going to be this way, so my job is staying focused on enjoying my weekend and not letting it get to me.")

I had a couple who would predictably get into a fight the first day of every vacation they took together, and it would take several days into the vacation to recover from it. Usually, as with holidays, these kinds of planned events have a lot of stress attached because we want everything to go well. So, it's *likely* that opinions are going to come into conflict. Once the couple realized that they could predict the fight, when it did happen, they were able to side-step it and not let it get in the way of the rest of the trip.

Sometimes, for those still caught up in being a victim to these predictable events, and just waiting to be hurt, they will even find ways to take offense where none was intended – in the same way that if you're looking for the negative in any situation, you're going to find it. That's not to say that this is always the case. I'm simply saying we need to use predictable information in a positive, pro-active way, rather than to continue to allow ourselves to be re-wounded.[12]

"If I forgive, I'm doing her the favor, when she's the one who hurt me. Why should I forgive her just so she can get past her guilt?"

One of the biggest mistakes people make is thinking that forgiveness exists solely for the sake of the person that needs to be forgiven. We are granting absolution. And, it's true, part of forgiveness positively impacts the person that's being forgiven. So, we are returning a wrong with a kindness.

In a marriage, forgiveness is done not just for the sake of the partner who offended, but also for the sake of "us". Because healthy love is valued, it is recognized that if there's going to be a brighter future, there has to be forgiveness in the present. So forgiveness is also for the sake of the relationship.

Yet, what many don't understand is that **we are also forgiving our partner for our own sake**. If we understand the cost that not forgiving has on us, we value it not just for moving the offender past condemnation, or for the relationship's future, but because we also love ourselves and recognize the need for us to be free of the pain and bitterness that lack of forgiveness creates.

---

12   Cloud & Townsend's book "Safe People" is a great reference for weighing out the qualities that can help you decide who to keep in your life, and to what degree, and who to let go.

There is also the fact that we forgive because there will likely come a time when we will need to be forgiven as well. We are trying to model the same treatment we would want if the roles were reversed.

❖   ❖   ❖

The concept of the **"sins of the fathers"** is that addictions and other dysfunctional problems can be passed down from one generation to another. It's not uncommon to see a family where substance abuse, physical abuse, or sexual abuse is generational – he did it, his father did it, his father's father, and so on. True, for one generation it might have been alcohol and the next cocaine, or one generation spouse abuse and the next affairs, but there is still a *pattern* of dysfunction passed down.

In most of those cases, one of the primary links in the chain that keeps each generation bound to those past "sins" is a lack of forgiveness. Because they remain angry for the injustices done to them as a child, or what they witnessed done to others, that anger poisons them over time. They become so focused on the wrongs done by others, that they are blind to see how the same seeds are taking root in their own lives.

That is the truth of reactive couples. They are so angry at each other that they fail to see how they're adopting the same behavior that they disapprove of in their partners. Their unresolved anger has created a similar issue in them. Left to fester, it will go beyond the marriage into other areas of their lives, gradually making them bitter, critical people.

I had a friend whose family was very critical and negative. She couldn't stand being around them for very long because of how sensitive she was to it. There were a lot of things that had happened to her in that family growing up that she resented them for, and even in the present more hurts were being piled on. The sad thing was that she was also one of the most critical, negative persons I'd ever met. Everything she said about her family was something I could see reflected in her.

By her own perspective, she thought she was a positive person, and maybe in contrast to her family she was, but to someone looking from the outside she was very unhappy. At the end of the day, she would complain about work. If she was driving, she would complain about the other drivers. If she was eating, she would complain about the imperfections of the food.

There were moments of light here and there, but then the clouds would settle back in and she would start the complaint track again. Interestingly, if I would ever strongly complain about something it would actually make her happy - perhaps because misery loves company. It was like she thrived on the negativity. She was too close to it to be able to see it for herself, yet her inability to forgive her family kept her replicating the same issues for herself.

Letting Go

"Tyler, if you were to let go, to step out of this control struggle, what would you be doing?" I asked.

She considered. "Well, I guess I would be giving more room for his advances."

"When you think of your own personal ideal for being a wife, does that include having a healthy sexual relationship with your husband?"

"Yes," she said.

"In the past, was the majority of the time the two of you were together sexually more about having sex than making love? Did it ever feel abusive to you?" I persisted.

"No, there were times it was just sex, but he could also be a good lover," Tyler admitted.

"So what's really going on here?" I asked. "What are you hanging onto that's keeping you from being close again?"

Tyler seemed at an impasse. "I don't know. I just feel like I can't give in."

"And to 'give in' would be to give in to sex?"

Tyler responded. "Not just sex. It's giving in to...well, what Colby wants me to do."

"Do you care about what Colby wants?" I asked.

"Yes," she said.

"So why is that so hard to do?" I continued.

"I don't know," Tyler said.

There are a number of different ways that people learn to let go of past wrongs, some of which don't even require a conscious act of forgiveness. Basically it comes down to three methods: 1) rework the information into something more manageable, 2) step into the role before we actually fit the role, or 3) exercise true forgiveness. I'll explain what I mean by each.

Re-Work the Information

By reframing how we see a wrong, it sometimes allows us to move beyond taking it so personally. Because we have a larger perspective, we're able to move around the issue, rather than, with a limited perspective, the issue being so huge that it's an impassible roadblock to moving forward. We can:

- assess for possible thought distortions
- balance for the positive
- alter our expectations
- humanize the wrong
- re-focus on what's in our control

Sometimes the reason we're hurt is because we've bought into a **thought distortion** (which I'll get into more in Chapter 9). If the thought distortion is discovered, we can let the wrong go because we understand that the actual meaning of the event was different than how we took it.

For instance, one form of **personalization** is taking neutral behaviors or events as intentional personal affronts. A husband is offended because, after they first got married, his wife didn't attempt to cook the meals. Yet, once he discovered that she never cooked for *anybody* prior to him, he is able to let it go.

Certainly the meaning Tyler attached to sex was different than that of Colby. Tyler refusing to adjust her thinking to incorporate Colby's explanation meant that she was now embracing a distortion of the truth, refusing to believe his self-expressed motivations.

❖   ❖   ❖

Sometimes the reason we remain hurt is because we're focused solely on the negative event, but we can learn to "let go" by **balancing for the positive**. In other words, we recognize that while this wrong was done, there are still many more rights than wrongs.

A black-and-white perspective tends to embrace only good and bad. So if we see our partner commit a wrong, we struggle with the reactive perception of seeing them as "bad" for doing so. When we balance this with recognizing all the positive qualities that still exist, restoring a bigger picture perspective, it often allows us to let go of that isolated wrong.

A lot of the limited perspective we bring to a negative event is choosing to focus solely on what didn't work for us. Sometimes balancing for the positive is recognizing that many times in those situations our partners weren't being intentionally hurtful or neglectful, and they may even have been operating with good intentions. They were actually trying to be helpful, but it wasn't what we needed most in that moment. When we take into account their positive motivations, we are able to re-balance our picture.

❖   ❖   ❖

As I mentioned with preferences and the last section in regard to family reunions, another method of letting go is **changing our expectations** about that particular person. If I'm trying to accept that my partner has a particular recurring issue, I can sometimes learn to work around it by recognizing that it may just be their style of communicating, temperament or personality. I'm adjusting my expectations to fit the person, rather than seeing their behavior as something intentionally directed at just me. It's no longer personal, it's just who they are.

Obviously, there are some things that need to change and we can't just ignore or walk around them. But, since we all have our particular areas where we will be repeatedly tested in life, there are some areas that we need more grace to struggle with than others.

❖   ❖   ❖

Humanizing the wrong is when we step back and take into account the background that led the offender to make her choices. "She grew up in an abusive home." "He was never taught good social skills." "He's been under a lot of stress lately." "She's had a lot of men mistreat her in the past." Because we re-connect with the historical and circumstantial influences on the behavior, we can understand it better - though it doesn't mean that we agree with it, or are okay with it.

If Tyler's history involved sexual abuse in the past, Colby might be able to be more forgiving in the present realizing why sex was such an uncomfortable area for her. He would be able to be more understanding because it wasn't completely about him. If there were things he was doing, such as being too physically forceful, that were making Tyler withdraw, it would be useful for him to know the things to avoid.

Humanizing the wrong is a form of better understanding the "why". One of the most common things I hear hurt people say is, "I just want to know why. What made it okay for them to do that?" *If we understand it, it's sometimes easier to move past it.* Because the reasoning is sometimes beyond us, we're stuck until we can have those blanks filled in.

Because many people have very simplistic conversations in terms of the "why", they never get to a point of understanding, because the deeper reasons are never touched on. Yet, it's often the deeper reasons that we can most relate to. If we just stay with "Well, you made me angry", it doesn't begin to address the deeper, "When you do that, it's saying to me that you don't care about how I feel. You know how important an issue that is to me, yet you're just going to do it anyway. It comes across as selfish; that you're willing to put yourself before us. That's why it makes me so angry."

The deepest level for most of us in terms of why we get hurt is because we care and/or because we want to be cared for, but those are often the last things that we bring to the surface, or are willing to admit. And if they *are* brought out it's often in terms of accusations ("You don't care about me.") rather than being vulnerable ("When you do/say those things, it makes me feel like you don't care - which hurts because I very much care about you.").

When it comes to understanding, some people, even when they're given the information as to "why", still can't let it go because the reasoning isn't their own. What they're waiting for is an explanation that would justify *for them* doing what was done. Because the reasons why their partners chose to do what they did wouldn't justify the act for them, they aren't able to accept it. Some will even insist, "That can't be the full reason why. There's got to be more that you're not telling me." Yet, *just because it isn't a good enough reason for us, doesn't mean it wasn't a sufficient reason for them.*

In trying to avoid overly simplistic thinking we need to remind ourselves that rarely are the "why's" any one thing. Because we are complex creatures, we do what we do for any number of reasons that all combine in that moment of choice. Any one thing may have multiple layers of meaning for us, and this is some of what we need to explore in attempting to draw closer and understand each other better – even if it means learning to ask ourselves "why" of our own behavior.

❖   ❖   ❖

By **re-focusing on what's in our control** in the situation, what *we* need to do to heal, what *we* can do to make things better, we start to feel more secure because we're not waiting on our partners to make everything right.

While Tyler was certainly focused on control, it wasn't a positive control. She was controlling things in a way that made her possibly feel safer, but at the cost of the marriage. When she talked in terms of resisting "giving in" to Colby, above and beyond their sex life, it raised the question of how much of this was a greater struggle for control in the relationship, with the sex life just being the arena where it was being played out.

Fake It to Make It

Sometimes the act of forgiving occurs *as* we're moving forward. In other words, it's not always that forgiveness has to happen first. Sometimes the mentality of "**fake it to make it**" applies.

The concept of "fake it to make it" means that we try to step into the role before we really feel the role. "If I were acting like I had already forgiven

197

him, what would that look like?" By actually stepping into those shoes, and playing the part, the feelings will sometimes follow – especially when you take into account that how we feel is often guided by what we do and what we choose to think. If I am acting the part of a forgiving spouse, and thinking thoughts that support my actions, I am opening myself up to the possibility of experiencing forgiving emotions.

It's the same approach taken for couples that have fallen out of love. People look at love as this ephemeral thing that's either there or it's not. But we *create* those feelings in ourselves by how we choose to respond to and interpret the actions of others. Part of what cements our feelings of love for our partner is when we act in loving ways in return, and choose to attach loving motivations to their behavior. We are affirming for ourselves that this is how we feel about this person. Couples who have fallen out of love typically have stopped acting in ways that affirm how they feel. Or, rather, because they are now acting in *unloving* ways, they are affirming that they no longer feel love. So they often have to step back into a loving role *first* in order for the feelings to return.

I would have loved for Colby and Tyler to start practicing forgiveness, to at least be making some small steps to repairing things, but each was rigidly waiting on the other.

Emotional discipline teaches that our feelings are slaves to our actions and thoughts. *Lack* of emotional discipline is the other way around; our feelings dictate our choices. (Because I don't *feel* forgiving, I'm not going to act or think in a forgiving manner.) By playing out what forgiveness looks like, practicing it, sometimes we are able to finally re-embrace it.

True Forgiveness

True forgiveness is for when a wrong is a wrong no matter which way you look at it. For example, an affair can't be justified. There may be *reasons* that led to the affair occurring, but none of those reasons *justifies* having an affair. We can attempt to mentally "rework" an affair in order to minimize its emotional impact on us, in order to begin to see our partners as human again, but there is an aspect of it that can never be excused. We have to make that leap to forgive a wrong that will always remain wrong.

This is why true forgiveness isn't easy. Because we can't completely justify, explain or excuse the wrong, it refuses to be treated so when we try – our brains won't accept it. But if we understand that true forgiveness doesn't really attempt to dismiss that truth, that we forgive because *we* need to, not because it's deserved, we've got a better chance of succeeding at letting it go.

❖   ❖   ❖

"Colby," I said. "If you were to forgive Tyler for pushing you away, what would that look like?"

"I'm not sure," he said. "I've been forgiving her for the past year, but because nothing has changed I've become resentful. How can you keep forgiving somebody that keeps hurting you?"

Because forgiveness is a process, it's not always a matter of "over and done with". We may have forgiven for a while, but then something happens and we need to step back and work through it again – not even necessarily because it happened again, but because something set off that pain or those memories for us.

Obviously, past versus present plays a part. If something has happened in the past, and it's been rectified, the work is mostly on us in the present leaving it in the past. But if what happened in the past keeps re-happening in the present, it's not a matter of leaving it behind since it's still in front of us and we didn't even put it there. We want to get past it, but our partner keeps doing the same kinds of hurtful things. How many times can you keep having your legs knocked out from under you?

Once again, how we're able to deal with it depends on the extent of the damage. Is it an injury to our needs, or just getting over personal preferences?

If this is a need that is being continually re-wounded, we need to see sufficient progress and change from our partner (accountability) in order to have enough time to regain our feet and re-invest. If we repeatedly get knocked down, typically, we get back up more slowly each time.

My concern is for those, like Colby and Tyler, that, on one level, intellectually want to re-invest but become emotionally stuck. They want things to get better but have gone so long with it not, that they've exhausted their emotional reserves. Their practicing this loveless relationship becomes a difficult routine to break.

Even in our hurt, we need to be making *some* steps forward, putting some positive energy into the relationship, in order to keep a positive momentum.

It's still possible to forgive while negative things are going on - often by regaining perspective by getting some emotional distance from what's really happening, rather than being lost in our own pain – being able to see how we are both now contributing to this negative ritual and trying to step beyond it.

❖   ❖   ❖

In the same way that accountability routines exist in a relationship, there needs to be self-checks that we do from time to time to make sure we're not hanging on to old injuries. We need to take the time to think through "Is there anything that I'm starting to resent that needs to be addressed?"

"Needing to be addressed" may mean something you have to work through with your partner, but sometimes it simply means issues you need to address with yourself – things that you need to mentally let go of.

There is often a sense of physical weight with emotional baggage. We literally feel weighted down with the things we carry around with us. This is often the first thing you self-assess. How weighted am I feeling and how much of that has to do with the relationship?

With anger, there is a degree of physical tension. Someone who has anger issues needs to learn to recognize when her own body is telling her she's upset. She may be gritting her teeth, her stomach tightens, she gets a headache, or her fists clench. When we think of bitterness or building resentment, the symptoms are often evident in our body with the sense of tension we retain. So when I think of my partner do I automatically start to feel tension, or am I at peace?

Exercise, relaxation skills, practicing *focus exercises* such as you learn through yoga, are ways of letting go of that tension and emotional weight.

Visual imagery is often used to move through forgiveness. The wrong is given a mental image that we manipulate in our minds. Or, if there is more than one wrong, it can embody all of them. For example, the wrong I'm trying to let go of is given the mental image of an anchor, since it weighs me down. My personal assessment considers if it feels like I've picked up that anchor again, or I've let it lie where I dropped it. If I recognize that I've gone back and picked it up again, I have to walk myself through the process of once again setting it back down.

Whatever image you attach to the wrong is up to you. It needs to be something that personally resonates with what the wrong feels like to you – and something that allows you to sense the difference when you've picked it up and when you've let it go. Sometimes that image isn't just setting that negative object down; sometimes it's about destroying it so there's nothing left to go back to.

In a similar vein, couples will sometimes do a *list exercise* that itemizes all of those past hurts and injustices that each other has done. For those past issues that have been worked through to resolution, but still keep getting brought back up, the burning of that list symbolizes how we're absolving each other of that history. So then it becomes an exercise in the present how to respectfully leave those issues alone. For those issues that have gone unresolved, the present focus becomes on what's needed now to finally move past that baggage. And, once that's accomplished, the issue is added to the list and burnt as well.[13]

◈   ◈   ◈

In most of the major psychologies and theologies there is recognition of the importance of "letting go". For some, forgiveness is leaving things in God's hands ("forgive so you too can be forgiven"), or their Higher Power. For others, it's letting go by changing focus; turning the attention back solely on what is your own responsibility in making the marriage work, and not worrying about everything and everybody else.

---

[13]   A variation of this is when a couple reviews that wrongs list with each other before destroying it. The offending partner takes simple ownership for their part in each item ("I'm sorry for my part in that.") without starting a debate or rehashing the issue if it's already been resolved. Sometimes that short apology *is* the resolution.

◆ ◆ ◆

When I discussed validation (Chapter 6), I mentioned that one of the best questions you need to nurture in a marriage is "What do you need from me right now?" In doing the healing that leads to forgiveness we need to answer that question for our partners. If we need evidence of change, signs of remorse, answers, ownership, apologies, assurances, whatever, we need to be able to identify that for them so they know what will help us heal.

Telling our partners what we need from them in order to heal isn't a one-time thing. When we're closest to the hurt, what we need at that moment is going to be different than what we need three months down the road. Initially, we might need space to regain perspective. Later, we may be more aware of what we need to hear or see from them. But we need to have that dialogue at some point rather than isolate ourselves in our pain.

◆ ◆ ◆

It is said that, "The best revenge is success" - in other words, not allowing ourselves to be taken down by how others have hurt us, but taking back control by re-focusing our energy and time on living our own lives successfully. **For those who use the negative in a positive way, to inspire a renewed effort to improve, they are breaking out of the negative gravity that wrongs done to us naturally create.** For those who become obsessed and over-absorbed with offenses, they feed that negative gravity as it pulls them in; robbing themselves of the strength they need to break free.

For a marriage, we've succeeded if we've taken back control of drawing close again, rather than allowing the offenses themselves to decide how far apart we'll be driven. That doesn't mean a lack of accountability, or ignoring offenses. It means an openness to accept positive conviction, embracing ownership, and righting past wrongs as much as we are able.

Discussion Questions:

1) **Is separating the big things from the little things a problem for your relationship?** In other words, is there often a debate about certain issues being a bigger deal than they should be? Does

time away from directly attacking an issue restore some sense of perspective, or just give time for things to fester? How can the two of you work at attaching priorities to your issues – identifying what's big and what's not so big? And how can you remain open to letting your partner's perspective balance your own?

2) **Do you feel like the hurt in your relationship is sometimes intentional? Is this confirmed by your partner?** If your partner is saying something is unintentional, how do you decide if that's the truth? If intentional harm is not healthy for a relationship, how do you keep from doing it? How do you foster benefit of the doubt in your marriage?

3) **Do you feel like you and your partner are good with ownership? If not, how are either of you going to get better at it?** Why is ownership difficult? When ownership does occur, is there also remorse? What do you look for from each other to feel like remorse is genuine?

4) **Is much time spent exploring the "why's" of what happens when things go wrong in your marriage?** Do you feel like it's easier to forgive when you understand what went into making things go wrong? When things do go wrong, are you more focused on what's not in your control or what is?

5) **Do you buy into any of the following logic when you hesitate to forgive?**

- **If I forgive her, she'll think that what she did was okay; that it really wasn't that big of a deal for me because I got over it.**

- **If I forgive, it makes it more likely she'll do it again.**

- **If I forgive, she's not experiencing any consequences for what she did.**

- **If I forgive, I will have to allow that unsafe person back into my life.**

- **If I forgive, I'm doing her the favor, when she's the one who hurt me.**

If you grasp that forgiveness is just as much for you as for your partner, does it make it easier or more of a priority to do it?

6) **Of the three different methods for "letting go" - 1) reworking the information into something more manageable, 2) stepping into a forgiving role before you actually fit the role, or 3) exercising true forgiveness, which are you most likely to do? Which is the most difficult for you to do?** Is there one of these approaches that you really need to do in the present, but keep avoiding?

7) **Do you do self-checks looking at whether you're hanging on to resentment? Are you able to still positively contribute to the relationship, while you're working through upset?** Are you able to stay focused on the greater goal of healing the relationship, or get too caught up in your personal pain? If you've taken back your control of what you can do to make the relationship work, what does that look like?

Chapter 9
Perception of Reality

One of the most difficult scenarios in a relationship is when, on a regular basis, recall of events is significantly different for each partner. Because one's memory, or interpretation of events, is so far removed from what the other person remembers, it automatically becomes an issue of whose memory, or perception, is accurate.

I have already discussed, in terms of respectful communication, how it's necessary to give room for each other's opinion, even if you don't agree with it. If we continually dismiss our partner's opinion as "wrong" or "inaccurate", then we are dismissing their part in the relationship. Each person needs to have a voice.

Consider a roller-coaster ride. For one person, it's an exciting experience. His heart's pounding; the wind's rushing by. The thrill is exhilarating and he feels alive. For the other person, it's a terrifying experience. Her heart's pounding; the wind's rushing by. The thrill is panic-inducing and she never felt so close to death. It's the same exact physical experience for each person, but completely different emotional experiences solely based on how they are interpreting it. So, in recounting the roller coaster ride, whose perception would be the most accurate?

In relationships, while we share the same experiences, it's vitally important to remember that each other's perception of that experience can be radically different.

We also need to remain open to the fact that *neither* partner's recall is going to be perfect. **We each tend to hang on to the pieces of memory that were most significant or painful for us, missing other bits because of what we stayed focused on.**

If we've accepted that reality is always somewhere in the middle, some combination of his and hers, then it doesn't have to become a battle in terms of whose memory was right and whose was wrong.

But what do you do when your partner's memory of events is consistently, in your opinion, inaccurate or distorted? How do you approach accountability, if they can never see their part? What if they are so insecure, or so wounded, that they are beyond balancing their experience with anyone else's?

Denial

Monica and Brad were attending pre-marital counseling. Both were very involved in their careers and had met through work.

"My concern," started Monica, "is that Brad has an agenda going into this relationship. I know he wants to be married and have kids. While he says he wants to be married to me, I'm not sure if it's about me or if it's about my ability to satisfy his agenda."

"And, for me," said Brad, jumping in quickly, "I'm concerned that work's too much of a priority for her and she's not going to have time to be a mother."

"Are there any other concerns?" I asked.

"Well, I'm concerned about how we resolve things," said Monica. "When we try to re-hash things that have happened, we both have very different accounts of things or ways of looking at things. For instance, we've split up twice now and gotten back together. During one of those times apart, he started seeing other women, yet he totally denies that."

"They were friends," inserted Brad.

"Who you took out on dates!" added Monica.

"They weren't dates," insisted Brad. "They were more like acquaintances I met through work and we were just hanging out."

"Do friends kiss you at the end of an evening?" asked Monica.

"Only one tried to kiss me. I didn't try to kiss her."

"You knew she was interested in you."

"Yes, but I wasn't interested in her, so that doesn't count as a date."

"You admitted you picked up the tab for them."

"As a courtesy. It was my treat."

Sometimes the problem is one of denial. Not that one person keeps denying to the partner that there's a problem, though that may be occurring as well, but moreso that she can't accept that she is part of that problem. So, when it comes to reviewing an event, the focus is totally on the partner's behavior with a blind eye to her own.

If I don't accept that a problem exists, then I don't have to assume responsibility for changing. Yet, you can't move past problems in a marriage if you can't own your part.

If I can't tolerate seeing myself in a negative light, then I can't stand to have any scrutiny of my behavior. I don't want to see what it reveals. And I'll expend great amounts of energy trying to divert that light onto other things.

But, since any individual issue still involves two parts – what *both* sides can be doing to help with whatever the particular problem may be – denial stands in the way of working as a team.

In Brad and Monica's situation, the side-issue that Monica raised was Brad's denial that these brief "friendships" were more than casual. Perhaps he was telling the truth, at least in his own mind, but there was a deeper theme that would come out as the conversation progressed around Brad's difficulty to acknowledge potential negatives.

Poor Recall

"Another dilemma we get into in re-discussing things is that Monica's great with details and I'm not," said Brad, shifting the subject. "She can quote things that I said a month ago, and I can't defend myself because I don't remember what I said and what I didn't. It ends up being potentially unfair, because some of the things she says I said really don't sound like things I would have said."

There are some people who are just bad with recall. It is not about denial or manipulation. For these people, there needs to come a point when they can acknowledge that fact to themselves and their partners rather than overly relying on faulty information.

One of the primary symptoms that go along with adult Attention Deficit is, naturally, attentional difficulties due to the high distractibility. Because their attention in social situations tends to skip in and out, there's a lot of information that they tend to miss. So it's to be expected that their recall is going to be somewhat sketchy when it comes to remembering the specific details of a past event, even one that occurred recently. Yet in relationships, quite often they will still vehemently argue the accuracy of what did or didn't happen. At what point do they learn to question that accuracy, especially if they know they have that condition?

For people with poor recall, when they approach their partners with issues, they need to make an effort *first* to compare notes to see if they're remembering things correctly, and whether or not they still have an issue, rather than take immediate stands on potentially inaccurate recall ("Honey, what do you remember happening last night?"). It's similar to a woman with severe PMS who has to learn not to trust her emotional judgment during those times of the month, or a senior with early dementia who has to accept his increasing mental limitations. That doesn't mean that you just give up what you remember, but you compare it and integrate it.

Often, early in a relationship, you'll see couples be humble enough with each other that they're open to having their perceptions, or memories, corrected. One person recounts an event and the other steps in and adds some forgotten facts to the picture. Memory adjusted, the couple moves on.

If the relationship deteriorates into control struggles, they are no longer as open to accepting each other's perceptions – no longer as open to correction.

In Brad's and Monica's situation, the potential problem was that Brad couldn't defend himself against Monica's recall. I'm sure that some of her recall was tailored by her emotions, but, rather than getting into debates about this, it's usually better to acknowledge the "if" of it.

She says, "You said <comment> during that party last month and I've had a hard time getting past it."

He responds, "I don't remember saying that, but *if* I did, I'm sorry. Is there anything in particular you need from me now in order for us to move on?"

He may want to go a step further and clarify that comment's relevance to the present. "While that may have been what I conveyed then, can I have a chance to correct it – to tell you how I actually feel?"

It's hard for a person to accept that she has a poor memory because, if she can't trust her own mind, what can she trust? Yet, if, over time, she continues to run into circumstances where her memory of events is significantly different from those she's with, she may need to accept that the issue exists. It's not a matter of trusting *none* of her recall; it's just doing the extra foot-work of comparing notes with others before she acts like she has all the facts. As with any couple, it's remaining open to the idea that your memory retains certain pieces - but not necessarily the whole picture.

One of the reasons I ask couples to do *weekly* sitdowns when they are first becoming familiar with accountability routines is that our recall is much better when we are only looking back a week, rather than a month or a year.

Manipulating the Facts

"I agree that's a dilemma for us," said Monica. "But don't shift this just yet. If those women were friends, why didn't you continue to hang out with them?"

"Because I wasn't interested in them," said Brad.

"So, at what point did you decide you weren't interested in them? You were interested enough in them to go out with them."

"Yes," said Brad. "But, at the point we went out, I knew I wasn't interested in going out with them again."

"Which was also the point that you called me and asked me out again," said Monica.

"Well, yes," said Brad.

"But that doesn't sound like dating to you?"

"No, not really" said Brad.

"Do you understand why it sounds like dating to me?" asked Monica.

One of the best classes I took in high school was on journalism – not because of what it taught about writing articles, but because it gave a great education on media manipulation. It showed how advertising and reporting can be used to intentionally shape the emotions and perspective of the consumer, leading the reader towards a particular bias. Later in life I would over and over again run into situations where I saw how the same techniques were used in relationships to distort or manipulate the truth.

There was the *"bandwagon approach"*, where the rationale to buy or endorse something was that "everyone's doing it" – an argument you hear chronically from teens.

There was the *"expert bias"*, where some professional figurehead, an athlete or entertainer, was endorsing a product so therefore it must be good – something that dictates our hairstyles, our designer clothing, our political views and our religious doctrine. There are many church-going couples where one's Biblical knowledge is chronically used out-of-context in order to control or judge the less knowledgeable partner.

Just as important as which facts are used to create a case, are also the facts that are *omitted* because they are inconsistent or counter to the case being made. A particular truth is trying to be presented, but it's not the whole truth and therefore a distortion and a partial deceit.

Deflection is another great manipulator that couples use chronically. Let's not talk about this thing I did, instead, let me throw up all these things about you, hoping it takes the spotlight off of me. Often, we aren't intentionally trying to deflect, we're trying to create balance by getting our partner to recognize that they have done something similar to us in the past, but it doesn't change the fact that they still have an issue that needs addressed regardless.

❖   ❖   ❖

One of Scott Peck's criteria for being mentally and emotionally disciplined is a "**dedication to reality**". It means **being committed to the truth**, especially the truth of what our part is in things. But, to do that, we have to be willing to give up our tendency to manipulate the facts.

Sometimes I'll have a client who has a routine of "telling" on the partner in session, making a dramatic point about how the partner's failed her once again. While part of this can fall under the category of the "blame game", or a mis-guided attempt to apply accountability, there is another aspect to this that becomes problematic.

There is a tendency for people, when making a point, to *embellish* the story – to exaggerate and to "awful-ize". Suddenly it's not about "Tom forgot to call" but how "Tom *never* calls". We may be doing it to make our issue more visible to our partner, but it is coming off as a blatant distortion. Instead of making our point, we are presenting ourselves as unfair, biased and irrational. By using distortions we are coming across as attempting to manipulate the truth.

In such a case, our partner's effort is automatically going to be directed towards clearing up the distortion. The firmer we hang on to the distortion, perhaps seeing it in turn as our partner refusing to validate our point, the more inflexible we appear and the more we give the message to our partner, "She can't be reasoned with".

Monica asked a great question of Brad ("Do you understand why it sounds like dating *to me*?"). If he was refusing to call what he did dating, could he at least understand how it could have that flavor for her? She was stepping around his un-budging perception of what he'd done, and moving him to validate her own.

Many people stubbornly refuse to stop using exaggerations such as "always" and "never", often seeing it as "just words" that the partner is stubbornly refusing to get past. But your partner needs to feel that you see things clearly and, if the message is "You do this *all* of the time," when it's clearly only *some* of the time, the distortion is not going to make her focus on *her* behavior; it will keep her focused on *your* exaggeration.

"All of the time" means *all* of the time – every single chance there is for this behavior to happen, it's happening. If she says "He drinks all of the time", it means that every chance he has to drink, he's drinking. While it may *seem* to us like they're drinking every chance they get, the partner automatically thinks about all of the opportunities he had to drink that he passed up.

Accurate communication requires work, and the exaggerations we use in our communication are often the short-cuts we are taking to make our point while avoiding the tedium of detail. But the more we use generalizations rather than specifics ("You've got no discipline" versus "You sometimes have a problem being disciplined with your money"), the more we are distorting the issue, intentionally or not.

Another aspect of generalizations is that it leaves the tables open to be turned on us. If I'm accusing my partner of being "undisciplined", without specifying what she's being undisciplined about, she can point the finger back to an area where I'm undisciplined, since "discipline" is a very broad category. Or she can point out areas where she *is* disciplined, thus disproving the generalization.

❖   ❖   ❖

When I work with couples there is sometimes one person in the relationship whose recall is less reliable simply because they leave out important details, minimize their own part, or magnify their partner's part. Knowingly or not, they are attempting to create a certain perception, control the information (which is a manipulation), and therefore a potential deception (which is often why the immediate response by the partner to such statements is, "That's not true!"). Some aren't interested in "the Truth" so much as the truth as they want, or need, to see it.

If this happens in couple's work, I can usually take the other partner's complementary information and correct the leaps of logic, or the altered history. And, hopefully, that's an opportunity to lead the person who's editing the facts to see the difference between the edited versus combined pictures.

If this happens repeatedly, at some point, I have to confront the client that this is a problem for her. If this is a pattern for how she processes information, I have to challenge her to either stop trusting her own judgment so much, or help her recognize that her initial take on things isn't balanced. It means continuing to support *sharing* information and memory of events rather than relying completely on self-perception.

Hopefully, **it's the *evidence* of the continuing pattern of distorted recall, whether revealed in counseling or routine sit-downs, that can make the problem visible enough to move whoever has the problem to a place of ownership.**

Addictions, such as substance abuse, involve multiple layers of denial, self-denial and distortions, that require constant confrontation and exposure in order to gradually be corrected – both by those in the abuser's life, as well as the abuser ultimately learning to do it for herself.

One couple I worked with, the woman kept confusing the past with the present. She'd say, "He treats me horribly in front of other people." To which, the husband would step in and say, "Wait a minute! How long has it been since that was an issue?" She'd answer, "For the first ten years of our marriage!" To which, he persisted, "So, how long has it been since the last time?" and she would acknowledge, "Five years ago." Even though this time distinction would be made repeatedly, whenever the wife became upset she would do the very same thing all over again - take those issues from the past and use them as present complaints, even though they were no longer relevant.

While, no doubt, a lot of her rigidity had to do with her own woundedness and being emotionally stuck in the past, to continue to nurse the wound this way, distorting the present and continuing to use the past as a weapon, came off as unfair, unforgiving, and not giving the husband credit for the progress they had made. To let go of those distortions would require her to finally be willing to forgive him for old wounds, and be diligent about separating the past from the present in their current conversations.

❖ ❖ ❖

I tend to separate the people who commit these kinds of distortions into two camps: intentional and unintentional.

For the unintentional, the issue is often one of education (awareness of the problem) and learning new skills to better deal with the problem. They have to be able to catch themselves making the errors, or at least be open to it when their partner points it out to them. They then need to be able to step back and either more accurately re-state, or get help from the partner in order to fill in the missing pieces of their interpretation.

For those who manipulate intentionally, the work is often more difficult because they *know* they're doing it, but they continue to do it anyway. So, either they don't view it as unhealthy, or they don't care if it is.

With Brad and Monica, Brad had a tendency to edit the truth in order to continue to cast himself in a positive light. (Many would have called him a "people pleaser".) The further we went with counseling, the more obvious it became in sessions that he needed me to see him favorably. Whenever any criticism was offered about his behavior by his partner, he immediately defended himself and spent way too much time trying to minimize the criticism. He was extremely uncomfortable with ownership, because, in his eyes, to acknowledge a blemish was more than just saying he was human. It was saying he was flawed and therefore "not worthy" of other people's respect. He thought I would see him as a poor partner for his fiance.

Brad was not doing it on a completely conscious level. It was more of a reflex for him. When this reflex was identified for him in sessions, and we continued to point it out as it occurred, he began to recognize it as an actual problem and started to work at better managing the reflex – not giving in to the need to have to always defend himself, allowing himself room to be less than perfect, not feeding the feeling that I would reject him or see him as not worthy of being a partner if his flaws were revealed.

Often, manipulating information is really about insecurity – which is partly a fear of being vulnerable. Depending on the extent of the insecurity, a person will go to great lengths to over-control events or other people's perceptions. Whether it's to keep from getting too close in a relationship, to stay beyond criticism or consequences, to avoid hurting somebody else, or just to look good to others, that habit of manipulation prevents a relationship from ever becoming truly close.

For some who have made a lifestyle out of it, when a person gets pinned down on one inaccuracy, she'll change the subject or distort something else, so nothing ever really gets resolved – while she progressively loses her partner's respect. It may protect her on one level from having to bear the full weight of being vulnerable or accepting ownership, but it costs her the things that are far more important.

Emotional Logic

"Why is it so important to you that Monica knows these were just friends?" I intervened, asking Brad.

"Well, I don't want her to think I was cheating on her," said Brad.

"But the two of you were split up at the time. You were free to date." I said.

"Yes, but she makes it sound like she wasn't important to me – that I just started running off with other women as soon as she was out of the picture."

"So even though you were well within your rights to date other people, you are thinking that you were going to appear less in Monica's eyes if you had been dating." I continued.

"Well, I think she'd be hurt by it, yes."

"I don't like thinking about you being with other women, Brad, but I don't think your dating people while we were apart has anything to do with your character," inserted Monica.

"Well, you may say that," said Brad, "but I have a difficult time believing that."

What makes the issue of recall and perception more complicated is the presence of **emotional logic**. Different than **rational logic**, which is based on reason, emotional logic is based on feeling. Since it's based on feeling, it changes depending on whatever the feeling of the moment may be. The greater problem is that the person who is caught up in emotional logic often fails to recognize that the logic is no longer rational. She *thinks* she's thinking, but it's the feelings that are actually steering the ship.

Let me distinguish the two.

Emotional logic says: "I can't stay in this relationship any longer. It's unbearable."

Rational logic says: "I know things are currently difficult for us, but it's only been the past few months that we've been struggling, compared to the ten years we've been together. We need to re-group because our relationship is more important than the past two or three months."

Emotional logic tends to be based *in the present moment*, since it's rooted in the feelings of the moment. The problem with this is that it doesn't have the perspective of the big picture and it often distorts the picture of the past.

One of the rules in my books on conflict resolution was "never make a major decision based on strong emotion". The underlying principle was the same – that strong emotion, positive or negative, clouds judgment. While positive passion plays a large part in choosing a fitting career, using positive passion alone as a gauge for choosing a partner can be disastrous, in the same way that ending a relationship based on only negative passion can also be a mistake.

Rational logic keeps the feelings of the moment in perspective because it's more rooted in overall *facts* than feelings. Rational logic is not without feeling; it simply views feelings as one more source of information, but not the *only* one.

❖   ❖   ❖

The neurology of thinking and feeling is significantly different because it involves two different areas of the brain.

Higher reasoning goes through the neo-cortex ("new brain") – which is the last part of the brain to develop.[14] Feelings don't follow the same neural pathways as thinking. They go through the limbic system which is "old brain" - the more primitive part, which is based on instinct – fight or flight.

When we go through extreme emotion, or are reacting, the primary part of the brain that is being stimulated is the limbic system. So when we step back after the emotional wave has passed and say, "What was I thinking?", the fact is that we really weren't. That part of the brain wasn't even involved.

This is why we have to give ourselves enough time, when wrestling with our emotions, to allow our higher brain functions to kick in. We have to give ourselves the time to think, and have some idea as to what line of thought is the most constructive and most firmly rooted in reality.

❖   ❖   ❖

Irrational feelings, left unchecked, can develop into irrational *beliefs*.

Let's say a person starts out with a fear of heights. She has this relatively healthy concern that if she gets too close to the edge of a high place she could fall to her death. So now she starts avoiding high places altogether in order to avoid experiencing this fear. Yet, by doing so, she is *feeding* the fear. *She is treating the fear as a reality and so now it gradually becomes a belief.* She has moved from what started as a potentially healthy fear ("Be cautious in high places.") to an irrational belief ("If I go somewhere high, I'm going to die."), going from "it *might*" to "it *will*".

One primary method for weakening an irrational belief is to live in a way that challenges its truth. The person with the fear of heights would have to risk going to high places again. I wouldn't ask her to go sky-diving, or to take foolish risks in high places, but to not let the fear keep her from doing things that interfere with her normal life. She may never be

---

[14]   It's still maturing even into the late teen years/early twenties.

completely comfortable with heights, but at least she would stop giving away all her power to the fears that were controlling her life.

For someone who believes that abandonment and rejection are going to happen if they trust again, they have to be willing to be vulnerable to that possibility. They have to accept the risk because the only way they're going to feel loved the way they truly want to be loved is to open up. If they open up *with a safe person*, they will deepen the relationship, not threaten it. If they remain closed, they will continue to experience abandonment and rejection but because of their own self-protecting tendency to push people away or keep them at a distance.

The only way Brad was going to get better at his fear of rejection, was to 1) openly acknowledge his imperfections, 2) be willing to risk other's displeasure with his choices, and 3) stop putting so much energy into managing everyone's perception of him. He had to open himself up and be willing to be rejected.

By Brad habitually attempting to cover his tracks, he was *more* likely to be rejected, not less, since he was seen as being untruthful. By him being afraid that his dating would be taken as a mark of poor character, he was actually creating in Monica a concern for his character in terms of honesty and ownership.

❖   ❖   ❖

Usually in a relationship there is at least one person who is **feeling-based**. In other words, her natural tendency is to let feelings lead her decisions. As with other qualities, being feeling-based is only problematic depending on how unbalanced it is. If a person relies *solely* on her feelings to determine her choices, she's going to have a roller-coaster ride of a life because of the potential instability of emotions.

Since the extremes are always the easiest to see, let's start there. An extreme feeling-based person is often described positively as being *passionate,* and negatively as being *overly-sensitive.* The problem for extreme feeling-based people is that they are passionate about *everything* – passionately loving as easily as they are passionately angry. Typically, they are also very much in the moment, caught up in how they are feeling NOW. Because being in the moment can be very short-sighted, they also tend to be very impulsive with their decisions.

The feeling-based individual is the one who can have a great week but one negative event ruins it. For her, looking back on the past week, it all seems like a big failure because the negative emotion is clouding everything else. Aside from being called "irrational" or "overly-sensitive", a more appropriate judgment for extreme feeling-based people is **emotionally undisciplined**. They haven't learned to manage their emotions and so their emotions manage them.

Because feelings shift without warning, an extreme feeling-based individual is often seen as being somewhat chaotic. Her changing mood makes her unpredictable.

The stereotype of such a person usually falls on the woman, but I've met many feeling-based men as well. Women are usually able to access and express themselves better emotionally than men, but men can be just as emotional as women – they just often express it differently.

Let me use depression as another example. The depressed individual thinks depressed thoughts. She is beyond reason since the depressed logic is now making the choices for her. Because she has this depressed filter, everything she looks at is seen through a depressed lens. She doesn't *feel* like she has the energy to go out, so she stays in. She doesn't *feel* like contacting her friends, so she remains isolated. She doesn't *feel* like doing the things she normally enjoys, so she does nothing. The feelings are calling all the shots, and because she is giving them all the power, making depressed choices which simply strengthen her depression, she remains depressed. For her to move out of this she has to begin doing healthy things and embracing positive thoughts, *despite* how she feels.

The extreme **thinking-based** person intellectualizes her feelings to the degree that she appears to have none. She is so over-focused on fact, logic and common sense that she often has difficulty connecting to people on a human level. While she still has emotions, she tends to so over-dissect them intellectually that most feeling is converted into analysis – which results in being removed from the initial feeling. The natural tendency of a thinking-based individual is to gravitate towards structure and order, while a feeling-based person often prefers freedom and a sparsity of rules.

The example of Spock on the original Star Trek would be a good visual for the personification of being overly reason-based.

This is not to say that a feeling-based person is incapable of reason, or that a thinking-based person is incapable of experiencing or expressing strong emotion. It is simply saying that we all tend to lean in one of these two directions.

***Balance* for these two tendencies would be reflected in someone who is able to feel freely but allows reason to moderate the emotions.** Because it's so difficult to examine ourselves this way, we often need to seek out others with a better perspective to help us be sure we aren't just embracing a different kind of emotional logic. In a relationship, it's part of what we depend on our partner for – to help balance our own perceptions.

If you're in a relationship with someone who's strongly feeling-based, and you're feeling-based as well, this can be a problem because *both* of you have the same blind spots. As a result, the relationship will lean towards being chaotic. But I think the majority of people typically choose partners who fall into the opposite camp simply because we're naturally attracted to qualities that help balance our own.

Reactive couples have moved to a position where both partners have become feeling-based, *even if this wasn't the initial tendency.* Now, they are both so lost in the emotion of hurt that neither has a clear perspective. At least one person has to re-embrace reason if perspective is going to be restored.

It's important to understand that *each role serves a purpose.* It's important for the feeling-based person to respect and support the structure that the thinking-based partner brings to her life, just as it's important for the thinking-based person to recognize that a feeling-based partner enhances one's ability to experience and enjoy life.

❖　❖　❖

A feeling-based person typically expects to communicate on an emotional level, so when she is responded to with intellect rather than emotion, she often interprets the absence of visible emotion from her partner as a negative. For instance, the man who says "I love you" without any visible emotion attached is automatically dismissed as not really meaning it.

Sometimes feeling-based people will attempt to do things to *incite* a reaction in their partners, just so they can confirm that there is some degree of emotion, even if it's negative, in order to feel like the other cares. However, inciting a reaction with a thinking-based person usually moves that individual to emotionally retreat or withdraw, not to emotionally express themselves.

Just because a person *manages* his or her feelings, doesn't make them thinking-based. A man who bottles his feelings (emotional repression) may still be very feeling-based; he's just good at bottling them. He might still engage in emotional logic as much as, if not more than, the next person – he just doesn't show the emotion outwardly.

Women are usually shaped when they're children to be emotionally expressive, whereas men are taught to manage their emotions. Men manage their emotions in order to present an image of strength and competence. It tends to go against that learned nature to be emotionally expressive, since it's often viewed as being weak or vulnerable.

Typically, with an "emotionally-repressed" person, the one emotion that's the most easily expressed is anger. What makes it "okay" to express it over the others is that anger isn't viewed as being a vulnerability. Anger is often an attempted show of strength – an effort at taking back control. *It shields the hurt.* (Which is part of why, when it comes to conflict resolution, people need to talk from the hurt and *not* the anger, since the anger only masks the truer feelings.)

I know that no one goes around consciously thinking in these terms – "I'm going to express my anger because it will shield me from expressing my hurt," or, "I'm going to push my partner to cry or explode just so I can see that they feel something." These are the under-workings for why some of us unconsciously do what we do. But if we better understand some of what's going on with us, or our partners, it gives us a better perspective on how to consciously change, adapt or work with those dynamics.

It's unrealistic to expect that a thinking-based individual is going to learn how to automatically shift to talking on an emotional level, but he does need to learn how to express himself on that level when it's necessary - just as a feeling-based individual needs to learn how to discipline her emotions, rather than let them control her.

Thought Distortions

Emotional logic leads to **thought distortions** which are inaccurate ways of thinking that move us further from reality. Cognitive and cognitive-behavioral psychologies have identified several common thought distortions that interfere with having healthy relationships.

All-or-nothing thinking is when thinking is limited to the extremes – "You're either with me or against me". "If I can't go, then nobody's going to go." It is an overly simplified way of looking at things that fails to respect or comprehend the complexity of many situations.

Similarly, a black-and-white thinker tends to view life in overly-simplified ways – rigid "right" and "wrong", "good" and "evil", "his" way or "her" way - without an awareness of compromise or a middle ground. There is often an aspect of immediate judgment that goes along with this kind of perspective towards whoever is in the opposite camp.

Brad bought into a form of all-or-nothing thinking. As with many "people pleasers", he had difficulty seeing a potential criticism as anything other than a character rejection. To be "wrong" in other people's eyes was the same as him being "evil". Even though he really did think the dating was a little thing, his assumption was that to everybody who frowned on it, it would be big. In terms of relationships, he saw himself as either "accepted" or "rejected".

Mental filter is when you only focus on certain pieces of information out of several pieces, disregarding the rest. He says, "You look nice in that dress, but I'm not crazy about the shoes." What she's likely to hang onto is, "He doesn't like my shoes" – hearing only the criticism, not the compliment.

Magical thinking is when you mystify the meaning behind events - interpreting coincidences as fate, a chance meeting as "meant to be", or over-spiritualizing something to the degree that it is now God-directed and above all other information to the contrary.

The dating experience and affairs are both riddled with magical thinking; reading an amazing amount of deeper meaning into the smallest of events, gestures or comments. Suddenly we think we're the exception rather than the rule – the love we share is unique. It doesn't matter that we're both married to other people or that there are kids. This is meant to be; it'll all work out.

In the same vein, thinking "He should know what I need without me having to say anything," is also a form of magical thinking.

Discounting the positive is minimizing the positive when it occurs. When one person actually does something quite thoughtful for the partner, the partner might respond with, "You only did that because you felt guilty".

When conspiracy theories exist, there is a constant disregard for evidence of the positive and an over-focus on the events and words that feed the negative theory.

Mind-reading is the same as defining reality. You automatically assume that you know what someone else is thinking or feeling, despite whatever that source may say about their actual motives or inner world.

Brad was engaged in mind-reading with Monica – assuming how she would take it if he admitted things that he thought would upset her. He also used mind-reading with me, assuming that I would see him as a poor partner choice for Monica if he was revealed as being flawed.

Fortune-telling is when you automatically assume the worst about the future before you've really given it a chance. ("I'm going to fail badly at this." "They're going to leave me.")

The deeper problem with fortune-telling is that once we've decided on a particular outcome, even if we don't really want that outcome to occur, we will often do things that force events toward that outcome – it becomes a self-fulfilling prophecy.

"Should" statements are statements that indicate a right way of doing things and are usually directly attached to feelings of guilt or judgment when they're violated or disregarded.

Some "shoulds" are legitimate and necessary, but many others are simply overly-restrictive and squelch freedom. There is a big difference between, "You *should* not cheat on your partner" versus "This is how you *should* fold the laundry".

Brad had some unspoken "shoulds" going on. "You should never make a mistake." "You shouldn't risk hurting your partner, even if it's with the truth." "You should always maintain an image of success."

Personalization is when you take on too much responsibility for things that aren't really your fault. If we haven't heard from a friend recently, the automatic distortion might be, "I must have done something to upset her." If a partner is unexplainably angry, the assumption is, "I'll never be enough to make her happy." While we do need to sort through things for our part, we need to be careful to not embrace the other extreme.

Blame is the opposite of personalization. Instead of taking on too much, you take on too little responsibility for a problem, displacing the fault on everybody or everything else.

We all tend to participate in thought distortions at one time or another. The problem is with the person who does this *routinely*. The more frequent the distortions, the less the connection with reality, and the greater the potential distance between you and your partner accurately understanding each other. Especially during times of conflict, if we can't rely on our ability to reason things through, or recognize faulty reasoning when it occurs, we remain at risk of either not resolving the conflict, or allowing the faulty reasoning to steer the relationship in unhealthy directions.

Intention versus Result

There are many people out there that operate in the world of good intentions, but ultimately end up doing more harm than good. They will do things that are actually incredibly insensitive, over-controlling or short-sighted but because that's not what they intended, they fail to understand why everyone else seems to be unfairly judging them.

Their perception is that their hearts are pure and that they are only attempting to help, but because they're doing it *their* way, without really considering the person involved, their efforts can wildly miss the mark. They can actually be very egocentric, caught up in only their perspective. And while they expect others to understand *them*, they fail to recognize their own lack of trying to understand others.

On the simplest of levels, it's the person who buys the gifts that *she* likes for others, though if she actually knew anything about the recipient she'd have known the choice was a poor fit. She was trying to be nice, but what comes across is "She really doesn't know me at all", or "She didn't even try".

On a larger scale, it's the wife who chronically gossips about family members, telling things that were shared in secret to everyone that steps into her path. In her mind, it may not even be attention-seeking or trying to create drama, she may truly feel justified because of her over-riding concern for that family member and her need to think it through with others. But when those violations ultimately get back to the owner of the secret, of course the only thing they are going to see is her betrayal.

It's the husband that tries to over-control and over-monitor his wife's behavior because of his overwhelming jealousy and insecurity. In his mind, he's doing it to try to preserve the relationship, which is a positive motive, but *how* he's doing it is actually destroying the relationship.

When it comes to perspective, these people unrealistically expect the world to not take issue with them when confronted. They feel that the accusers are making too big a deal out of it, that everything would be okay if the motives were just understood. They rigidly hang on to their innocence because they are unwilling or unable to broaden their perspective and see the harm that they did, or continue to do. And, further, they are often unwilling to look at how they need to change – it's everyone else that needs to make the adjustments. They continue on a path of relationship destruction because they never step back and change their behavior, but continue to go forward feeling misunderstood and wrongly judged.

Brad might have been displaying good intentions with Monica by avoiding admitting his dating activity was just that. No doubt, in his mind, it was an attempt to avoid being rejected by her, but how he was going about it was accomplishing the opposite. If he had continued with that good-intentioned pattern, with Monica and with me, we couldn't have gotten very far. After all, if you can't be truthful about your issues and your mistakes, there's no real hope for them getting any better.

Understand, we *all* make mistakes at times based on good intentions. Sometimes it does just come down to a potentially good choice but for the wrong person, or made in the wrong moment. Who I am referring to are those individuals who continue to *routinely* do harm in the name of good, who rarely stop to look at the results of their behavior, who rarely take accountability for any of it, and who expect everyone else to do the changing. At some point, they need to start looking at the *results* of their behavior, rather than just their misguided intentions, if their world, and their relationships, are going to improve.

Apples and Oranges

Sometimes the arguments are around "It's the same as when you do that…", and the response is "It's nothing like that". One person is trying to get the other to see the connection in things, and the other is either refusing to see the connection or doesn't believe a connection exists. Different perceptions of the same issue.

Often in these situations the couple is arguing over different *levels* of perspective. For instance, I may have a bowl of fruit that consists of apples, bananas and oranges. On the furthest level out, everything in that bowl is an object, rather than a person, place or idea. Moving further in, becoming more detailed, everything in that bowl is edible, because it's all food. On the next level in, the similarities still hold, since everything in that bowl is also fruit. But going to the next level, the details separate the similarities, since all of the fruit is quite different – an apple looks and tastes nothing like a banana, or an orange. So one person could argue that an apple isn't the same as an orange, while the next person could argue that they are. It depends on which level you're making the argument.

Similarly, a square looks nothing like a circle, but they're still both shapes.

The problems begin when either one person refuses to recognize the similarities that the other person is trying to point out, or is trying to make a comparison with something that has no connection – such as trying to argue that an orange is a square.

I had a couple where each person had had an affair – the difference was that the husband's affair had occurred while they were dating, while the wife's affair occurred several years into the marriage. The husband was arguing that the wife's affair was worse than his because it happened after they'd taken vows of fidelity, so the relationship at that point in time involved a more serious degree of commitment. The wife argued that his having the affair while dating was the same thing as hers since they were both affairs – she was no worse than he.

So who was right in this situation? Well, it depended on what level you were making the argument. It was the same, and it wasn't. Depending on the level you focused on, they were both right.

At the same time, to effectively move past these kinds of impasses, the couple has to realize that *one wrong doesn't neutralize another.* With the blame game, couples are try to stalemate the partner's issue using examples of how the accused has had the same things done to her by the accuser. But moving towards resolution, doesn't involve creating stalemates, it means addressing, validating, explaining and resolving the issue at hand. The wife's affair, being the issue at hand, needed to be addressed and owned, rather than deflected back to the husband's affair from years before. Now, if the husband's affair had never been addressed or resolved, it becomes a relevant issue as well, but it remains a separate discussion.

Usually, finding the point of agreement, looking for the similarities, helps us better relate to what our partner is saying, or to better help them understand our position. If there is no similarity felt to exist, it still doesn't change the fact that there is still an issue on the table that needs to be addressed and resolved, not dismissed. ("Whether it's the same thing or not, I've still got a problem with what happened…")

Strategies

1. If the presence of distortions is up for debate, one option is to track them.

If there is a pattern of distortions, sometimes couples have to start tracking them in order to see how serious or how deep the distortions go. Because we're often too close to the distortions to catch them when they occur, at the start we often have to depend on partners, friends or family to point them out.

The accountability routine of doing sit-downs often can serve as the format for exploring, and correcting, the conspiracy theories that form from the distortions.

For the insecure or those with poor self-esteem, because their fears are often irrational, sometimes there is never enough evidence from the partner to make those worries go away. Hopefully, with tracking, they can come to see that it's their own thinking and not anything the partner is doing that is keeping those issues alive.

Ideally, the person who engages in the distortions (after being assured, re-directed or lovingly corrected), comes to a point where she is able to recognize that they *are* distortions.

At the point that she is trying to manage them for herself, she continues to track them, and balance them, through personal logging and daily self-reflection.

She panics herself by thinking: "He doesn't love me." But then catches it, and starts to self-correct, "Wait a minute. I know he does things at times that aren't loving, but I also know there are other times when he does. I can't expect him to be perfect, or that he's going to be openly loving all the time."[15]

❖   ❖   ❖

The *attitude* behind exploring the presence of distortions is vital. Humility plays a major part - us humbly pointing out to our partners their distortions, and them humbly being open to hearing the observations. Both partners need to be watchful for the distortions because of their regard for the relationship, not out of a competition to point out each other's errors.

---

[15]   David Burns' exercises ("The Feeling Good Workbook") for learning how to track distorted thinking and then re-shape it are excellent.

We foster this regard by *inviting* scrutiny rather than hiding from it. ("Are you hearing anything in what I've been saying that sounds off - that you feel needs corrected, or where I'm not quite hearing/interpreting things right?")

Obviously, there is opportunity for abuse with tracking. You don't want to point out *every* potential distortion that occurs – primarily just the ones that are preventing resolution, or distorting an important truth. Otherwise, you will quickly turn a potential positive intervention into mutual over-monitoring.

If there is evidence of chronic distortions in your marriage, they do need to be explored rather than ignored since they don't typically correct themselves and often sabotage further intimacy. Usually they are most noticeable when we interpret each other's motivations. It's what we read between the lines and behaviors that is often where we start to depart from the reality of the given situation. Often, left to themselves, it's not until we stop editing and verbally react that the distortions finally get expressed. Up until then, they were unvoiced negative fears, beliefs or resentments.

❖   ❖   ❖

When there is a significant discrepancy between you and your partner's perception of the frequency of a problem behavior, tracking the behavior is often the only avenue to establishing the truth.

If he says he's "hardly ever" on the computer, and yet she feels like it's "most of the time", while it's work, the easiest path is to log the time put in on the computer. It still leaves room for debate if she feels the actual amount is too much, and he thinks it's reasonable, but at least then they're debating over the same amount, not a misperception.

2. Be wise with *when* you choose to confront a distortion.

We need to use wisdom in choosing when to address these distortions. When someone is really angry, caught up in emotional logic, it's often better to wait until they calm down before we attempt to reason with them or it can quickly shift into a control struggle.

Relationships have to respect the line of "healthy exits", where either side has the right to shut a conversation down and re-approach it later if things are becoming destructive. The key to this is doing it *respectfully* and then attaching a timeline to returning to the issue.

Extreme emotional logic is beyond reasoning, so we need to be realistic that we're not going to have much success attempting to re-direct it in the heat of the moment.

3. In times of intense upset, when correction isn't being welcomed, we can still be a support.

When emotional logic is dictating our partners' reality, and they're not yet open to hearing anything else, we can still attempt to diffuse it to a degree by simply playing the role of listener. If we give them the room to vent, and not feed into their upset, we're not resisting the emotional wave, we're moving with it, allowing it to possibly pass.

Sometimes just by trying to find the parts of their perception that we *can* validate, or provide assurance for, moves them more quickly to being able to think beyond the emotion of the moment.

4. Distortions don't always have to be directly confronted.

Sometimes we don't necessarily need to confront our partner if we can simply work around it. For many couples a simple, "But remember this…?" is all that is needed to correct an incomplete memory, or an unbalanced perspective – rather than a "Well, that's not true", or "That's a lie." By simply providing additional information we are able to correct our partner's recall without having to directly point out the distortion.

She says, "I know you really don't love me."

Rather than call her out on her attempt at mind-reading, he could possibly counter with, "Honey, I understand that there are things I do that give the wrong impression, and that, if you are only taking those things into account, why you could make that conclusion. But how I try to show you I love you is by <itemize>." He may additionally choose to discuss the ways that he might change those things that give the wrong impression, if that is how she is looking to be loved, since he may be operating in good intentions with bad results.

5. Don't get lost in the petty details of perceptual differences, step back to the point of agreement.

Some of the strategies already mentioned in the chapter on validation come into play. For instance, often debates over perspective come down to debates over *details*.

She says, "You didn't get in last night until 9:30."

He says, "No, it was more like 9:00."

Rather than over-work the discrepancy it would be better to just stay focused on the issue, which, in this case, would be the desire to have the partner home earlier.

So she says, "*Whatever* the specific time, we'd agreed you'd be trying to get home at dinner time, and lately that's been slipping."

She's shifting the conversation back to the original **point of agreement**, which was for him to try to get home in time for dinner.

It is so often a waste of energy getting caught up in petty details rather than staying focused on the relevant content. For the person that is easily distracted, and often reactive, the problem can be that *every* detail seems relevant, when it's not.

6. Avoid judgments with your perceptions.

Couples tend to get led off-track by the judgments they attach to their interpretations rather than staying with the specifics of the issue.

He judgmentally says, "You're such a bitch."

As a better alternative, he could sincerely say, "It's really hurtful to me when you talk like that." Or, "When you do/say that, I can't take it any other way than incredibly disrespectful…"

In terms of the first statement, the two could go back and forth debating the evidence of what constitutes being "a bitch", or the conversation could totally get de-railed by the fact that he used that particular judgmental word. The other statements leave little to debate as there is no direct judgment being made – he is simply identifying the impact those words have for him and the perception that it creates.

In a similar respect, it's being able to direct your partner to what works for the relationship, rather than staying over-focused on what doesn't.

She says, "I can't stand how controlling you are! Stop trying to watch what I eat!"

But it would have been better to say, "I know you're trying to help me with my weight, but let me tell you what works the best if you want to support me with it."

7. Stay focused on solutions when debating perceptions.

He says, "You never give me any freedom! I can't even spend time with the guys without you making me feel guilty."

He's already identifying that his underlying need is freedom (fun), which is legitimate. But, being in a relationship, this needs to be balanced with accountability. So how can she address both?

She could choose to debate his "never" over-generalization, and risk invalidating his point, or argue his unspoken accusation that she doesn't want him to have time with his friends, which isn't true. Both of these are focusing on how what he's saying is wrong – the negative.

If she was focused on solutions, skipping the "that's not true", she could say something like, "I *want* you to feel free in this relationship. I want to feel free too. So, what can I do differently that won't make you feel guilty, but still give me the room to point out when you've made other commitments? I don't have a problem with you spending time with your friends. I just have an issue when it consistently comes before your home."

With this, she has both validated his need for freedom, but underlined the dilemma of the need for accountability. She's *sharing* the problem between the two of them, rather than putting it all on him or her.

He may get defensive and respond with, "I'm a big boy. I can make those decisions for myself."

But it doesn't change the fact that she needs to stay focused on a solution. "So what would you want to change?"

"I want to have time with my buddies."

"That's great. How much time out of an average week do you feel is fair?"

"If I even just had one or two nights a week, I'd be happy. A guy's night out."

"Does that go both ways? Would I have the right to a girl's night out?"

"Sure, I guess."

"So let's try it and see how it goes."

"Okay."

"Are you okay with setting a night? That way we don't have to debate each week when it's going to be, we can just plan on it."

"Alright, Tuesday works for me."

"And I'd like Thursday."

"Okay, Thursday for you."

She moved him to a resolution without having to get into a great debate about the "never" or the implication that she tries to make him feel guilty. The fact that she was willing to work with him on his issue, was enough to take away the power from his distortions. She might choose after the fact to address the distortions themselves if they are a recurring pattern, but he will probably be at a better place to hear this when it's not in the middle of his issue.

Their agreement might initially require some trial and error, and maybe reworking the solutions if the initial solution didn't fit. If he fails to follow through on their agreement, it now becomes an issue of accountability – him not keeping his word – which, as his partner, she has every right to call him out on. If he then refuses to be held accountable, it escalates to ultimatums, since everyone has to realize that a marriage can't exist without mutual accountability.

8. Remember the "if" when it comes to recall.

When there are two different memories of what's been said, after sharing how each remembers it happening, rather than getting into a debate over whose memory is accurate, it's often better to bring "if" into the conversation, allowing for the possibility that either of you might be right.

She says, "To be honest, I'm still not over last month when you called me a bitch."

He may initially reply with, "I wouldn't have ever said that. I may have said you were *acting* like a bitch, but I never called you one."

"You called me a bitch," she insists.

"Well, *if* I did, …," he starts to say.

And at this point, probably what would be most appropriate would be an apology. He's not apologizing for what happened, when he's not sure that it even did; he's apologizing for *if* it happened.

"Then I'm sorry," he concludes.

She could continue to insist that there's no "if" involved, when she's sure that it did happen, but to do so would be being rigid when he's already being flexible enough to allow for her perception. She might also state that, for her, there's no distinction between calling her a bitch, and just saying she's acting like one.

With some incidences, if there is now a false interpretation attached to a past event, after *validating* what you can with their upset (in this circumstance, by apologizing), you'd want to also correct the misinterpretation by *updating the information.*

Continuing with the dialogue, he adds, "I don't want you thinking that that's how I see you. *Whatever* I said back then, I was upset in that moment. I don't see you as being a bitch. I love you! Yes, there are times when we're arguing where I don't like you much in that moment, but we move past it. *Whatever* I felt back in that moment, it's more important that you know how I feel *now.*"

Big Picture/ Little Picture

With couple's counseling, my primary activity as a counselor is to restore some degree of perspective to what's going on in the relationship – to help the couple go from the little picture that they've created for themselves, back to the more balanced perspective of the big picture – to see options and solutions, rather than only the problems with no other choices available.

When a person is depressed, the walls of her world become very closed-in. She isn't taking in the real-world information of the big picture (long-term perspective) anymore; just what she's able to see with her limited vision of the little picture (short-term perspective). The more she concludes that everything in that little picture is all she needs to know (that the little picture is really the big picture), the more restricted her thinking becomes because it's based on limited information and a distorted perspective.

When conspiracy theories form for a couple, and judgments about each other's true intentions start to get thrown around, it's often with the biased vision that the little picture creates. They no longer allow that there may be other reasons for the problems going on in the relationship than that the partner either no longer cares or has a serious character fault. Every action becomes taken very personally, when it's often not initially meant to be.

Reactive couples live in the limited visibility of the little picture. Because they are only able to focus on the partner's behavior, and not their own, they are only taking into account a portion of the necessary information needed to arrive at a balanced perspective.

Staying focused on the big picture, for anyone, is very difficult to maintain for any period of time. For me, the sense is that it's like you've taken a sleeping pill but are trying to stay awake. Every once in awhile an event, a comment, a person, a thought, or a crisis, will jog your perspective and your eyes are open again, but then time, familiarity, or distractions will fog your vision once more.

If we recognize that this is everyone's struggle – keeping our eyes open, staying in touch with reality, trying to stay "awake" – then it becomes a common mission for the relationship to:

- Maintain, compare and restore perspectives
- Gather information outside of ourselves rather than completely relying on our own judgment
- Actively embrace the benefit of the doubt
- Consider other options to explaining each other's behavior than just the ones that are the most convenient, the most over-simplified, or the ones that hurt us the most.

Discussion Questions:

1) **When you think of the conflicts that arise over differences in perception in your relationship, do you feel that it's more about denial, poor recall, manipulating the facts, thought distortions, or good intentions with bad results?** If manipulating the facts, do you feel it's intentional or unintentional? How have you tried to work past any of these when they occur?

2) **Is one person in your relationship more feeling-based and one more thinking-based? If the two of you tend towards being different in this area, how do you attempt to balance each other with your differing orientations?** Have you ever shared what works for you in terms of your partner's attempts to balance you, or vice versa? If the two of you tend to be the same in this area, how do you balance if you share the same perspective?

3) **Are you able to recognize in yourself or your partner any of the thought distortions mentioned?** (All-or-nothing thinking, mental filter, discounting the positive, mind-reading, fortune-telling, "shoulds", personalization, and blame) Do they just occur on occasion, or is there a repeating pattern that has been problematic? If problematic, what specifically needs to be done to help manage it?

4) **Of the different strategies listed at the end of this chapter, which ones work best, or could work best, for your relationship?** Are there any strategies of your own that you've tried that work, or you think would work if you were to use them?

5) **When considering the idea of the "Big Picture/Little Picture", what do you do for yourself to try to stay in the big picture (connected to the real world)?** What do the two of you do as a couple, to avoid the limited perspective of the little picture (only seeing things from your viewpoint, and in the moment)?

Chapter 10
A Healthy, Balanced You

It's only logical that the extent of your marriage's growth is determined by the limits of your own personal growth. The healthier I am *before* I'm married, the more I'm likely to attract and recognize a healthy partner. But it doesn't mean that if I'm not as healthy as I should be, and I'm already married, that I'm stuck. The focus of accountability in a relationship is not just looking at the growth of "us", but also continuing to look at what I'm doing to further my own personal growth.

A healthy you often starts with what you designate as the priorities in your life and how you keep them in balance. Social relationships, healthy hobbies, health and exercise, family, partner, career, and spiritual walk, all need to have a degree of priority attached. The more in balance you are, the more you have to bring to the relationship. Also, the less needy you'll be towards your partner because, aside from your relationship needs, everything else that falls under the category of "taking care of me" is being already satisfied in healthy ways.

It's unfortunate how many couples will overly burden the relationship with all of their needs. The relationship often becomes the target for their individual lives not working out. Yet, when they finally get their ducks in a row, they often see that the relationship was not as much of a problem as they thought it was. It was their life out of balance that was casting a harsher light on the relationship.

Character and Discipline

Chuck was a very likeable guy. He was good-looking, friendly, and in his early thirties - the type of person you'd wonder why he wasn't already "taken".

But Chuck had started counseling over a year ago now because his life really hadn't been going anywhere. He would change jobs frequently. The women he dated he'd either lose interest in, or they'd lose interest in him. Good start-up, but poor follow-through.

When things got difficult, on several occasions he'd even move back in to live with his parents until they finally said enough was enough – essentially, "Get a life!" For the first 6 months of counseling he had floundered, not completing homework assignments consistently, always coming up with reasons why things weren't working out. Attending counseling was really the only thing he seemed to stick with, but my early concern was that, while he enjoyed talking about change, he wasn't really into actually changing.

I knew we were now close to terminating our sessions together because, over the last six months, he was finally taking charge. Chuck was waking up.

"So, what's different for you now?" I asked.

Chuck smiled his winning smile. "Well, the easy answer is that now I'm making things happen, rather than just thinking about them happening."

"And what helped you make that leap?" I persisted.

"Well, part of it was deciding it was time for me to finally grow up. I knew I needed to, but I kept avoiding taking the leap - my tendency to procrastinate, waiting for things to get so uncomfortable that I didn't have a choice.

"Too, I guess I realized that I kept allowing my feelings to make all my decisions – so I was kind of all over the place, depending on whichever way my feelings would push me."

It's easy to be a nice person when everything's going well. Couples will often assess their relationships based on the behavior they display to each other during the good times, when they're each on their best behavior. It's not until crises or struggles occur that we will start to see some ugly things come to the surface.

Part of editing is us managing our baser, more primitive instincts and desires, moving past self to take others into account. Because crises, familiarity and distractions remove our editing filters, what was once managed may now start managing us. What is revealed during such times is the presence or absence of **character**.

Character is about doing the right thing even when nobody else is watching - even when you don't have to, but, especially, even when it's difficult.

Presence of character includes the following qualities:

- **Success at accepting, owning and changing problem behaviors**
- **Consistency in keeping promises made**
- **"Practicing what you preach"**
- **Remaining vulnerable during conflict**
- **The continuing ability to make sacrifices and compromise**
- **The presence of honesty even when it's painful**
- **Consistency in integrity between the public and private faces one wears – a lack of hypocrisy**
- **Being able to act in healthy ways *despite* how you feel**
- **Not resorting to vindictive tactics when you've been hurt**
- **An awareness and consideration of others in your daily decisions**

When it comes to criticisms, it's not uncommon to hear partners defend themselves with, "Well, other people don't think I'm like that." Yes, but other people don't have to live with you. What we see in a daily living-together relationship is what's behind those walls we maintain for the rest of the world. And we need to be continuing to mature in those areas we typically hide from everybody else.

What the women in Chuck's life found out about him as the dating relationship continued was his lack of commitment to anything in his life, including them. He was a person who lived in the moment, with nothing much deeper to bring to a relationship. He had been actively building a narcissistic personality – one where others only existed for him so long as they served a utility. At the point a relationship required more from him than what was comfortable or convenient, he was done with it.

❖   ❖   ❖

There is a direct connection between character and emotional maturity (emotional discipline). If one exists, so does the other.

Let me take a moment and distinguish **behavioral discipline** from **emotional discipline**. The military teaches behavioral discipline. It teaches you to consistently get up at a certain time, dress a certain way; attaches a set structure to doing things. At the same time, it teaches emotional **repression,** not emotional **expression**. Emotional repression *does* require a degree of emotional discipline. It teaches individuals how to *suppress* self in order to put the unit first. But the problem is that if those feelings don't get vented appropriately or processed somehow along the way, they tend to build up to the point of forcing their way out, often inappropriately.

Behavioral discipline in a marriage plays out well in terms of how we fill the roles of the relationship, living up to the behavioral obligations, completing the chores, but, as I've said before, the roles don't equal emotional intimacy, just as behavioral discipline doesn't equal emotional discipline.

Emotional discipline is discipline over our emotions. We still experience emotions, and can express them, but *the feelings don't dictate our behavior.* The emotionally immature individual is ruled by her emotions. (I talked about this last chapter.) We *think* we're thinking, but it's actually our feelings that we're listening to. Emotional discipline says that even though I'm feeling angry right now, I'm going to manage its intensity and stay focused on accurately expressing what's going on with me in a way my partner is going to be able to better understand. I'm not suppressing the emotion; I'm filtering it into something useful.

Emotional maturity is also about having an internal locus of control. I'm able to assume responsibility for my actions because I don't give my control away to the people or events going on around me. Those people, things and situations certainly influence me, but I'm still the one that decides to what degree. I may not *feel* like I have a choice when I'm in the middle of my emotion, and that's usually why it ends up with a negative outcome, because I don't see that I have a choice. But, if I slow the pace of the conversation, think about what I am going to say next for its usefulness, think about what was really going on with my partner other than what she was showing on the surface, suddenly, I am more aware of options because I'm thinking things through, rather than staying stuck with the reduced perspective of my emotion.

Our self-talk needs to move to, "I could lose it here, like I always do, or I could try something different. What if I stepped back a second and thought about what's happening? What do I really want in this situation and what would be the best way to go about doing it? And what is it she's saying she needs from me in this?"

For many people the problem is that what they want in the moment is just to hurt back like they feel they've been hurt – so we're back to character – taking others into account even though we're tempted to become lost in self. "Is my hurting her going to make the situation better or just complicate it? Is hurting her going to draw us closer, or push her further away? If I love her, how can I justify intentionally choosing to hurt her?"

One of the lessons that Chuck had to learn for himself was that, while he was very good at taking care of his own needs, it was still unhealthy love. His emotional immaturity kept him from ever getting closer to any kind of a positive future – it kept him on an unstable roller-coaster, riding one impulse after another.

If we don't know how to love ourselves in healthy ways, we are limited in how much love we can show to our partners since an immature love is a shallow love.

Maturity and Spirituality

"So what does 'making things happen' mean for you?" I continued.

"Well, I'm thinking about more than just what I want to do today. I'm thinking about what I'm doing with my life. If I'm going to commit to

something, it needs to be something that I can completely invest in, not something that's just going to get me by for another year," said Chuck. "Which was why I decided to go back to teaching."

"And what makes teaching work for you?" I asked.

"Well, we've talked about it before," replied Chuck. "I felt like I was educating kids about the important things in life, helping open their eyes. It felt great while I was doing it. But I got distracted over the money. My picture of success at the time was more about how much I made than making a difference. So I stopped because there were more lucrative options. But now, looking back, I realize I was happiest when I was in that role. Apparently, the school thought I was good too or they wouldn't have been willing to give me my old job back."

Maturity means, in part, that we've learned to respect and care about the feelings and rights of others, and not just when it's convenient for us. Because of that sense of other, we should also have a greater awareness of our part in the world around us – that this life isn't just about us.

Spirituality, as I'm defining it here, is our awareness of life beyond what's in front of us, beyond the physical. It's how we struggle with finding meaning and purpose in life.

As I discussed in the intimacy chapters, part of our development on a deeper level, in both our relationships and individually, is valuing and fostering connectedness. If the only thing I have to bring to a relationship is my own selfish ambitions, the relationship is going to be pretty restricted in its depth.

The more I can see that even my small part in this world can make a difference in other people's lives, and that that's really all I have to show for my time here in the end, then my need for significance has a firm foundation.

Our tendency is to be distracted by paths that artificially satisfy our core needs. We may put an incredible amount of effort into immaculately decorating our homes because it gives us a sense of security, of order, or is a reflection of our success. We get lost in careers that allow us to store up wealth – another way to seek security. But, in the process, we get so caught up in these side-paths that we stop looking at the big picture. Because these paths *do* satisfy personal immediate needs, we can often feel content for a time, until things like mortality reconnect us with the deeper levels we overlooked.

For many, it's not until old age that they start looking back on their lives and feel regret for having wasted so much time, energy and money on things that ultimately really didn't matter to anybody else but them.

Chuck was lucky in that he was still young and already being forced to address his life choices. If he found a solid direction for his life now, it would save him a lot of grief and guilt later on. Being able to think in terms of others, and start to truly experience connectedness, had freed him from the black hole of narcissism that had been pulling him in.

The big questions of "Where can I make a difference?", "How do I fit in?", and "What's the point of my life?" can be overwhelming, but they need to be asked and answered to the degree that we have a potential direction to start on. If we can find those answers and live them out, then mortality isn't something to be feared. When it comes to looking at the end of our lives, it's with the satisfaction that we made good use of the time we had.

Part of finding that fit is understanding that we each have skills and gifts. Those are part of what make us unique. **The more we are able to align our vocations and avocations with our own particular talents in ways that positively impact others, the more truthfully we've satisfied our core needs**. Choosing this course both affirms who we are in a meaningfully significant way, and reflects that we are accepting control for our part in this life.

Balanced Qualities

"We've talked about balance many times in the past. How do you feel you're doing with that in the present?" I asked.

Chuck nodded. "Well, I know that I tend to be an idea person, but I had so many ideas that it kept me kind of committed to none, and lost in all the options. Also, I was somewhat impulsive with the next great thing that would come along – both in my work and my relationships.

"Now, while I will still write some of those ideas down when I get them, I'm not leaping in every direction just because I have them. I've slowed myself down now and give time to think things through. Also, I'm kind of funneling most of my thinking into being creative in the current job rather than always looking somewhere else.

"I've been dating the same girl for the past five months, which is a bit of a record for me, and I've actually been committed to seeing where it will go rather than walking away as soon as it becomes work."

Everything in this book is, in part, about balancing the extremes. In addition to balancing priorities in our lives, we also need to examine our strengths and weaknesses for balance.

I'd made the comment before that the positive qualities that we are attracted to in our partner are often the same qualities that push us away later in the relationship - if they're not balanced. For example, a desirably passionate partner is found to have difficulties moderating her passion when it comes to expressing her anger.

In these terms, it's relatively easy to identify our weaknesses by first identifying our strengths.

Chuck was learning to funnel the "creativity" of his impulses into more productive avenues, taking the time to develop them rather than just jumping out on a limb. Also, he was learning how to enjoy his freedom without having to abandon his commitments and relationships.

Once we know our weak areas, and know what balance for them looks like, we need to remain vigilant about not letting them fall back into our blind spots. After all, it's when we are no longer conscious of them that they have the most control over us.

Grace and Forgiveness

"I think part of it, too, is that I'm holding myself accountable more. In the past, I tended to blame everyone else for me not being further along; the jobs where people didn't treat me like I thought I should be treated; the women who couldn't be everything I wanted them to be," said Chuck. "Some of those jobs weren't really bad; I just lost interest. And some of those women would have been great partners. I just wasn't invested."

"Now I'm putting the responsibility back in my lap, but, at the same time, I'm not beating myself up over it. You used the word 'conviction' before, and that's what I'm trying to do – own what's mine to own and do something about it, set it right.

"A lot of the blame I had was towards my parents for not doing more for me when I was younger, but I came to realize they'd actually done a lot for me - probably too much. They bailed me out of a lot of things that were my own fault when I was in college, and I guess I got used to them doing that. I think part of me was waiting for them to make my life okay now, to bail me out again, but I finally accepted the fact that I was the only one who could, and should, do that for myself. They weren't being selfish. It just wasn't their job to make my life work."

While I've mentioned grace in terms of applying loving acceptance for each other's limitations and mistakes, it starts with being able to apply appropriate grace to ourselves. If I can't forgive myself for my own mistakes, when the boundaries fail in a relationship, the tendency will be for that unforgiveness to be applied to my partner.

Also, if I'm going into a relationship with a lot of old grudges, the anger I'm retaining from those resentments can poison my current romantic relationship even though there may be no direct connection. We need to be entering a marriage with as little baggage as possible. If we hang on to anger towards parents, family, friends, or old lovers then we have an anchor attached to us. It keeps us bound to the object of our anger.

Grace allows us, and others, to make mistakes. If we fall, we can get back up again. The most vital aspect being that we *learn* from those mistakes and don't continue on the same path. It may take several tries, and be something that we struggle with off and on throughout our lives, but if we persevere, we can shift that unhealthy course. For those who can't accept their flaws, and refuse to address or own them, there is no true learning because solutions have never been fully explored. So history repeats itself.

It is vital that we are humble enough to be able to own our own imperfections. True intimacy doesn't involve wearing masks in order to be accepted or loved.

Some would say you know you've forgiven when you think back on things and the memory no longer hurts, but I don't think that's completely accurate. Painful memories tend to retain their pain. However, they shouldn't remain *so* painful that if you walk through them from time to time you're automatically overwhelmed. And they shouldn't remain such a pre-occupation that we can't move forward with our lives.

A Personal Accountability System

"So now the big thing for me is to just stay focused – to not let myself get distracted like I used to do. I know what my problems are. I know what to do about them. I just need to keep living the solution," continued Chuck.

Wherever you're at on the maturity scale, you need to have a conscious awareness of what growth looks like for you – the areas you need to improve. Further, you need to develop specific strategies for how you're going to make those improvements. In the same way that the "sit-down" serves as an accountability platform for the relationship, an individual needs to exercise her own personal accountability.

One of the central truths of counseling is that **the only way to sort through chaos is to attach a structure to it. When a relationship is out of control, it's because there are no longer any lines being respected, no rules. For a personal accountability system to work, there has to be a structure to it, or it will remain inconsistent and unproductive**.

The heart of an accountability system is balanced between the positive and the negative – what's working, and what you're still working on. Simple as that.

"What's working" is attended to because there are keys behind what you do that worked. You need to be consciously aware of why things worked if you're going to continue to duplicate your success.

"What you're still working on" needs to have specific strategies attached, and actions acted on, if what you mentally conceive is going to be brought into the real world.

Everything in this book is about putting your marriage on a conscious level. And your personal accountability is about making your own individual life a conscious one that goes through regular reviews.

Lines and Identity

"When I was drifting, I didn't really have any responsibility to anyone, and I liked that feeling of 'no strings'. My sense of self was all about not following the rules that other people would try to set for me – so, in a sense, my identity was all about doing the opposite of whatever I felt pressured to do.

"The payoff for me was the sense of freedom I had – committed to nothing. I felt like I was always keeping my options open, but, I finally realized that by not committing to any path, I was actually going nowhere – like a guy stuck at a cross-roads who won't choose a direction. Giving in to my desire for freedom worked in the moment, but not for the big picture, because it was an extreme.

"I needed to jump in the pool and get wet, rather than just keep thinking about what it would be like to be in that pool, or reacting to the pressure I felt that I should be swimming like everybody else. And maybe a part of me was afraid of drowning, that I couldn't really swim and this was just my way of not having to prove that to be true. I'd waded around before, and I'd tread water, but I never really completely jumped in.

"The things that I wanted to find my own way at - to make a difference, to be successful at something, to have closeness - I was only going to have by learning how to work *with* the world that already existed. The world wasn't going to change for me.

"It didn't mean I had to give up my identity, just the parts that weren't really working for me. I was always so reactive to the choices other people wanted me to make, that I somehow failed to realize that, even if I took their suggestions, it was still *my* choosing. I wasn't giving up my freedom just because I followed someone else's opinion.

"Even if teaching doesn't turn out to be the perfect path for me, it's still a path that I can bring something to - maybe just one more stepping stone to whatever's ahead. But I would never get any closer to 'whatever's ahead' if I wasn't taking these steps." finished Chuck.

When I was in the 3rd or 4th grade I had an epiphany. I was walking out onto the playground at recess. The other kids were already involved with whatever games were going on and I just started to walk around looking at the homes skirting the school property. While the school grounds were fenced in on three sides, on the remaining side there was a driveway (the school's only entrance and exit), that led back to the main street. As I stood there, the thought occurred to me, "What keeps everybody in the playground?" There weren't really any teachers watching. Why didn't some kids just wander off? Why didn't *I* just wander off?

I was suddenly very aware that leaving was an option. The only thing that kept me was a concern for the possible consequences if I did. But it was still very freeing to be aware that it was a choice. I didn't stay because I had to. This one observation shifted my whole world into recognizing the choices that I had in every situation, rather than feeling like I did what I did because there was no other way.

In Orson Scott Card's sci-fi/fantasy book "Wyrms", there is a character called Will who lives as a mute servant to a very difficult woman. At the end of the book you discover he is much more than what he appears, and the other characters are dumb-founded because of his willingness to play such a submissive role to this controlling woman for such a long period of his life. His name, of course, was the key – he stayed because he "willed" to stay. It was his choice. He knew that he was there for a greater purpose, which made it possible for him to put up with being treated as so much less. Now, while that could be a prescription for remaining in an abusive relationship, it better points out the role that freedom and choice play in our lives, particularly in getting through difficult situations.

Part of what defines each of us is the lines that we've drawn for ourselves, or lines that others have drawn for us. Those lines are who we are, and what we believe in. "I don't cheat on my partner" is a personal line, a boundary, a standard. "A father protects his children," is another. "A woman doesn't take out the garbage," is another. "Kids don't leave the playground," was a line for me in grade school. Some lines are moral lines, and others are just ways of doing things - rituals or roles.

There are two problems with personal lines: 1) too many or too little, and 2) too rigid or too flexible. In other words, the extremes.

For the person with too *many* lines, her life is overly ruled by "shoulds". For most everything there is a rule, so she is constantly having to watch every step she takes. For such a person, because there is often a constant sense of pending failure (since there are so many different ways she can fall short), there is usually a strong degree of anxiety under the surface. The person with too many lines may or may not apply those standards to everyone else in her life – it usually depends on how rigid the lines are.

For the person with too *few* lines, her life is typically chaotic. While lines represent order or structure, to a chaotic person they represent a loss of freedom. Obligation, commitment, and responsibility are often viewed as a trap, because they are seen as restricting choice. For the people in her life, while she may be fun to be with in the moment, she is often perceived as being unreliable, impulsive and immature.

For the person with too *rigid* lines, there is often a simplistic black-and-white perspective to the world. Her personal lines aren't just for herself, but everyone else as well, so there is often a strong aspect of judging that she engages in. While those rigid lines serve to make her life seem very secure, they are more binding than freeing. The primary problem with rigidity is that it is closed to new, more accurate information. Such a perspective resists change, because to give up that security would allow for the anxiety of questioning, and the exposure of being vulnerable. Because change does not come easily for such a person, the tendency is for them to harden and draw inwards, rather than soften and grow outwardly.

For the person with too *flexible* lines, she is too easily swayed. She has difficulty taking a firm stand on anything because an alternative viewpoint totally dismantles her own. Everything becomes relative, and so her own identity is often in transition with whatever the current trend may be - the extreme people pleaser would be an example.

The reality is that we all need to have lines in our lives, since those lines are what make up our personalities and give our lives their direction. Without lines we remain without definition, direction or meaningful purpose.

Chuck's lines, in the past, had been both too few and too flexible. He would draw a line, and then not stand by it. Or, somebody else would attempt to draw a line for him, and he would rebel against it. His life had been without direction or identity.

In terms of a "healthy, balanced you", knowing what your lines are and why they exist is vital. It's simple self-awareness. This is who I am. This is what I believe. This is why I believe it. This is why I do what I do. This is why I sometimes fail. This is why I sometimes succeed.

If you turned those statements into questions – "Who am I?", "What do I believe?", "Why do I believe that?", "Why do I do what I do?", "Why do I fail?", "Why do I succeed?" – and your answers to some of those questions are "I don't know", chances are the lines either:

1) don't exist
2) haven't been tested
3) haven't been explored
4) are borrowed

For people who lack that self-awareness, their lives are often like a ship without a captain. Because their lives go unexamined, why they do what they do is often an unknown to them – it's just who they are. Their past is usually unexplored or ignored.

That is not to say that these people are necessarily lazy or unmotivated. Many successful career-track entrepreneurs are handicapped when it comes to self-awareness. They may be very "other" aware in manipulating others to their own ends, and they may be very self-aware in terms of having very clear personal goals, but it's like a train on a track that never looks back. Usually, they are very uncomfortable when it comes to being still and with self-reflection – it's viewed as a waste of time, but often it's really about not knowing what to do with introspection, and, sometimes, even being afraid of what they might have to face if they did.

Whenever I run into people that are "driven", it's a very clear sign that there's somebody else other than them at the wheel – even if it's nothing more than the ghost of a parent that they're still trying to prove themselves to. Sometimes it's an individual hanging intensely on to the one thing she knows she does well. And sometimes it's a distraction from having to do the work of keeping everything else that should be of value in balance.

Let me add that there's a difference between being *motivated* versus being *driven*. Being "motivated" gets the job done, but not at the cost of all the other priorities in life. Being "driven" is a singular focus that consistently comes first – it is without balance.

Chuck was an example of the adult adolescent - the person who's living his life in opposition to everything that comes his way. The only standard he knew was "Draw me a line and I'll cross it." Initially, the closest he could come to the "why" was, "Because nobody's going to tell me what to do." He *thought* he was in charge of his own life, doing only what he pleased, but he was actually living his life in *reaction* to everything and everybody else. He wasn't *in* control; he was *out* of control. He thought he was retaining his own identity this way, but he was really giving up any chance of a true identity because he was at the whim of those perceived outside pressures.

Maturity requires the acceptance and discipline of structure, balanced with freedom and flexibility.

For our own identity, we all need to give up the unhealthy adopted lines that we have for our lives, and embrace those that 1) resonate with who we are, 2) actually work, and 3) move us forward, rather than keep us stuck.

❖   ❖   ❖

One big reason why it's usually recommended that people wait to get married until their late twenties or early thirties is because most people younger than that are still very undefined. Personality only solidifies with age and maturity, so, often, when people talk about having "grown apart" what has actually happened is that, as they've figured out who they are, they've also become more aware of who they no longer are. They've redefined the lines into something that fits them, but may no longer fit the relationship.

It's true that part of the fun of marrying young is the experience of growing together, but it's at the risk of finding that the people you grow into have distinctly different interests and views.

That's not to automatically say that, because you change over time, you should give up on the marriage at the point it becomes inconvenient due to your own personal changes. Some lines, though comfortable for you as an individual, may not be good for a relationship. Just because you discover that, underneath, you're a selfish person, doesn't mean that that should dictate how you act. **Part of the paradox of any relationship is learning how to move past self, while still retaining your own identity.** If you're in a committed marriage, hopefully, the flexibility is on two levels:

1) enough flexibility for the relationship to change as the two of you mature
2) flexibility for you, as an individual, to find new ways to fit into the relationship

❖   ❖   ❖

My daughter's toward the end of her teen years now and it's been a while since we had the peer pressure conversations. I tried to get her to understand the insanity of peer pressure. On the one hand, it says, "Be unique", but, at the same time, it adds "By being like us". If I'm being unique, then I'm automatically *not* going to be trying to be like you.

I understood that in trying to teach her to think for herself I was also supporting her questioning my own rules for her. And that's okay. I didn't particularly need her to agree with the rules (though that would have been nice), but more that she understood the reasons why they exist. It's true for anybody that **the more we understand the reasons for *why* our personal lines exist, the more likely we are to be able to invest in them on a deeper level.**

❖   ❖   ❖

The opposite extreme of living in opposition to the lines is a circumstance called **learned helplessness**. This term initially came from behavioral experiments with animals. One such experiment was where you had an

253

animal that received an electric shock every time it attempted to leave its cage, so it learned to remain inside. At some point, even though the shock was removed, and the cage door remained open, the animal would not pass that point because, in its mind, the threat was still real.

We take our cues of where those invisible lines are from the people around us. We want to be successful in life so we learn from other people what we are supposed to do, and then follow it. But what if those lessons we are given are based on faulty information? Or fit those particular people, but not us? Or were appropriate for us at that point in our lives, but no longer now that we're older?

For many, the problem is they live their lives under the principles of learned helplessness. They don't think "beyond the box". They limit themselves to the degree that they give away their freedom of choice. They do only what they've been programmed to do, and continue to not make any progress. They don't try to expand their options, seeking different approaches to life, but rigidly hang on to doing things they've already proven don't work for them.

In a marriage, we enter it with particular expectations of what the roles look like, realistic or not. And, often, the problem is that when our marriage doesn't fit the lines that everyone else would draw for us, we try to force the marriage into that pre-determined picture versus adjusting the picture to fit the marriage.

There should always be room within a relationship to be creative and explore options for roles that go beyond our own histories. So long as this is done within reason, and things aren't stretched to the point that it becomes destructive, it can breathe new life into a stagnant situation.

In terms of the individual, what I'm suggesting is to be willing to question, test, and re-draw some of the lines that have been drawn because what you bring to your relationship needs to be a unique, balanced, self-aware and other-aware you. The healthier that person is, the less she has to fear about being able to be herself since the healthiness she shows on the surface is just a reflection of the health that is underneath.

Life, by its very structure, refines us or puts pressure on us to improve. The further along we go, the older we get, the more we experience external and internal pressure to find what works and recognize what doesn't. It's up to us whether we embrace that pressure or resist it.

There is a certain security built in to living a borrowed or unexplored life. Ignorance *can* be bliss up to a point, but it's going through life half-asleep rather than wide awake. The natural consequences of the mistakes we make in life exist in order to wake up the sleep-walkers, to get them to pay attention to the course they're choosing.

❖　❖　❖

In summary, working on you is about:

1) establishing and developing character
2) practicing emotional discipline
3) learning to think beyond yourself, attaching a priority to the needs of others
4) understanding and learning to manage your own flaws
5) being able to exercise grace for your shortcomings
6) being able to exercise accountability for the things you need to change
7) having a clear sense of who you are, why you do what you do, and where you're headed
8) living a life that actually continues to progress in a positive, conscious way, rather than one that is lost and adrift

---

Discussion Questions:

1) **When you think in terms of your own character, what positive character qualities do you possess and what needs to be improved?**

2) **How much are you able to put others first?** Do you tend to lean toward the extremes of putting others first too little or too much?

3) **Do you feel like your life has a purpose?** What are your personal goals? Do you feel like you're using your personal skills and talents in meaningful ways?

4) **What are your personal strengths and weaknesses?** What do you do to balance or improve your weaknesses?

5) **Is there anybody in your past that you remain angry at? Is there anything you haven't been able to forgive yourself for?** If so, what would forgiveness look like – what would you have to do to let that go?

6) **Do you have a personal accountability system that works?** If it doesn't, or you don't have one, what would a working one look like?

7) **Do you feel like your life is your own, or that it's living out what other people want for you? If you were living your own life, how would that look any different?** In your marriage, are you able to balance your own beliefs and desires with that of your partner, or does one have to give hers up for the other? If both of you retained your identity in the relationship, while still meeting the needs of the relationship, what would that look like?

Afterword

For those who have read this book only to conclude that they have a long road ahead of them if they're going to get their marriage back in shape, the work can appear to be overwhelming. And why should a relationship be so much work? After all, aren't there couples out there that are happy with doing a whole lot less?

It is true that if all you know is the life you've led and you've led it the way that you feel you were "supposed" to, you're typically going to feel a degree of contentment on your part because you're living up to your own expectations. So, finding out that there can be more can be a mixed blessing. It's nice to know that you can improve the quality of your relationship, but a pain that it's going to require some more work from you to get there.

I'm not trying to promote perfection, just *progression*. Ideals may not often be reached, but it doesn't change the fact that we still need to have them to strive towards. The fact of the matter is that when we get close to consistently living those ideals, we also experience the most satisfaction.

The "rules" and "essentials" I've pointed out aren't theories or hypotheses, they're simply methods that make things work better. When they're ignored or forgotten, the relationship starts to suffer. In the same way that if you don't drink you're going to get thirsty. It's a natural consequence.

For the very "out-of-shape" couple, the nice thing is that any small change is noticeable because it's become so out of place.

What's important to keep in mind is that 1) you're not trying to do it all at once, and 2) you don't have to do *everything* for the relationship to work. You're taking small steps towards change in any number of different ways. The fact that I've itemized a lot of different areas to explore is not to say that you have to do it all; it's simply giving you as many different avenues as possible. When things start to go wrong, we are often lost in terms of where to begin exploring for cracks, but, if you know what the essentials are, you now have some short-cuts to making some important fixes.

❖   ❖   ❖

The marriage relationship isn't a sprint, it's a marathon. The key to getting through a marathon is to set a realistic pace - not so fast that you're going to wear yourself out, and not so slow that there's no significant progress.

Your partner isn't a competitor in this race. She's your team-mate helping you along the way. **The goal of the race isn't to "win", or even just get to the finish line –** *the goal is to run the race well*. If you're turning it all into work, making it about immediate demands and just another "to do" list, then you're going to be undermining each other's motivation. Keep it about choice and restoring physical, mental, emotional and spiritual intimacy - finding what works for "us".

The bottom line is that you work on the relationship because you care about it, not because you have to. The underlying motivation to remain disciplined with necessary change is always healthy love - for your partner, for you, and for your family. The strategies for creating a conscious marriage exist to give you a full life together that works for the long-term, not just for today.